W9-AEQ-866

The Challenge and practice
of academic accreditation

DATE DUE

ILL			
3 # 95			
ILL RSD			
9107094			
3-29-99			

DEMCO 38-297

THE CHALLENGE AND PRACTICE OF ACADEMIC ACCREDITATION

Recent Titles in
The Greenwood Library Management Collection

The Challenge and Practice of Academic Accreditation

A SOURCEBOOK FOR LIBRARY ADMINISTRATORS

EDITED BY

Edward D. Garten

THE GREENWOOD LIBRARY MANAGEMENT COLLECTION
Gerard B. McCabe, Series Adviser

GREENWOOD PRESS
Westport, Connecticut • London

Library of Congress Cataloging-in-Publication Data

The Challenge and practice of academic accreditation : a sourcebook
   for library administrators / edited by Edward D. Garten.
        p.   cm.—(The Greenwood library management collection, ISSN
   0894–2986)
     Includes bibliographical references and index.
     ISBN 0–313–28897–6 (alk. paper)
     1. Academic libraries—United States—Accreditation.
   2. Universities and colleges—United States—Accreditation.
   I. Garten, Edward.   II. Series.
   Z675.U5C42   1994
   027.7'0973—dc20   94–2190

British Library Cataloguing in Publication Data is available.

Library of Congress Catalog Card Number: 94–2190
ISBN: 0–313–28897–6
ISSN: 0894–2986

First published in 1994

Greenwood Press, 88 Post Road West, Westport, CT 06881
An imprint of Greenwood Publishing Group, Inc.

Printed in the United States of America

∞™

The paper used in this book complies with the
Permanent Paper Standard issued by the National
Information Standards Organization (Z39.48–1984).

10 9 8 7 6 5 4 3 2 1

To the Memory of

John H. Russel
Professor Emeritus, Higher Education Administration
The University of Toledo

Contents

Tables

Introduction

This book was developed as a means of providing librarians and other campus information professionals with insight into some of the contemporary challenges being posed to and by regional and professional accreditation as a result of the rapid changes that are now occurring in academic libraries, academic computing services, and other academic support units. When I began my administrative career in 1977, my experience with and knowledge of higher education accreditation had been limited to readings and lectures during doctoral study. At that time, I held the belief that accreditation was something good and wholesome for higher education, a means of self-regulation of sorts for what some loosely and humorously called an organized anarchy. I still hold to that belief, although it is well known that accreditation has come under severe criticism within the last few years. As an administrator I had my initial practical engagement with self-study and accreditation during my first library directorship when asked to participate in both the institutional self-study and several disciplinary and professional self-studies. In subsequent positions, I was privileged to serve on several self-study steering committees and assisted in the writing of scores of professional and disciplinary reviews. In 1981 I began service as a consultant–evaluator, first with the Southern Association of Colleges and Schools and, since 1985, with the North Central Association of Colleges and Schools. Issues related to accreditation have continued to occupy a central place in my professional thinking since that time. When I surfaced the idea for this book among colleagues several years ago, I learned that there was a need for a professional reference work for library and information professionals currently involved with accreditation-related issues.

I have been on both sides of accreditation. I have chaired visiting teams that have worked long into the night, and I have served on local self-study committees, members of which have devoted hundreds of hours to the task of gaining a better understanding of a local academic environment. I have witnessed the benefits and value to universities of an accreditation review and have been encouraged, even in the face of what are often disappointing and discouraging changes taking place in American higher education, to believe that accreditation continues to serve a vital purpose. It seems the academy has an abiding desire to evaluate what it does, remains open to outside criticism, and has the courage in most instances to make improvements and changes resulting from the accreditation process. Collectively my experiences do not make me an expert in accreditation; rather, they have simply made me aware of the complexities associated with effective and successful institutional and programmatic evaluation.

Accreditation today is plagued with uncertainties and pressures. Among the pressures, we must certainly note the increased emphasis on institutional accountability and integrity, demands for the improvement of teaching and learning, and the emerging technologies that are transforming classrooms and academic libraries. Other pressures that cannot be escaped include heightened state and national expectations for assessment and documentation of the achievement of students; demographic shifts that are affecting the numbers, ages, and ethnic makeup of students who come to our institutions; and the many threats to institutional autonomy, peer review, and self-regulation that come from increased federal and state oversight.

The intent, through Part I of this book, is to provide several chapters that will set the context for the challenges currently being faced by libraries and information technologies within the process of accreditation. These challenges are being experienced by both sides, as the accreditation associations themselves are quite often in the position of trying to remain ahead of the rapid changes affecting libraries, information technologies, and academic computing services. I am especially grateful for the contributions to this section made by Kenneth L. Perrin, former president of the Council on Postsecondary Education; Ralph A. Wolff and Mimi Harris Steadman of the Western Association of Colleges and Schools; and Delmus E. Williams of the University of Akron.

In Part II, I offer several chapters based on my own experiences in self-study and accreditation. It is my hope that these chapters prove useful to campus information professionals getting started in self-study. I am assisted in this section of the book by practical contributions by librarian colleagues Susanne O. Frankie and Joan H. Worley, both experienced individuals in the area of academic accreditation.

In Part III, I have brought together five chapters that discuss a few of the especially challenging issues facing libraries and information technologies and the accreditation process. The issue of off-campus library services and distance education and their relationship to accreditation is ably discussed by Thomas E.

Abbott of the University of Maine at Augusta, while the prevailing concern with information literacy within accreditation is brought to the foreground by Howard L. Simmons, executive director of the Middle States Association of Colleges and Schools. Several years ago while serving on a North Central Association Commission on Institutions of Higher Education visitation team to the University of Phoenix I met Robert W. Tucker and Cynthia Hartwell. Dr. Tucker offers a provocative set of assumptions that question traditional accreditation and licensure and challenge information professionals with respect to their own assumptions about client-centered information delivery. Ms. Hartwell and I coauthored the chapter on the challenges posed to library administrators and accreditors by the nontraditional and adult-centered university. Finally in this section, Ralph Wolff again offers his insight—this time noting some important challenges to both accreditation teams, librarians, and other campus information professionals relative to the manner in which self-studies and on-site visits are conducted.

In Part IV, I present the current criteria and standards for academic libraries, information technologies, learning resources, and academic computing as found in the accreditation handbooks of the six regional associations. Subsequently, I present the standards and guidelines related to the above areas for forty-one professional and disciplinary accreditation associations. I would like to express my appreciation to the approximately fifty accreditation agency executive directors who took time to respond to my surveys and request for information. While the reader can find many ways to analyze or criticize the information presented within the standards sections, I have offered only a minimal set of observations about those collective criteria. While I have attempted to ensure that the most recent standards and guidelines are represented, I take full responsibility for any errors related to currency that may occur. While many of the accreditation associations do not anticipate revising their library and information technology standards over the next few years, a few of the associations may well have made slight or even major changes in their requirements by the time this book is in print. Consequently, individuals involved with either regional or disciplinary self-study will want to obtain the most current handbook or manual for accreditation from those associations with which he or she is involved.

Part V of the book, an extensive bibliographic essay on libraries and accreditation, was written by colleagues Delmus E. Williams and Phyllis O'Connor of the University of Akron Libraries. This contribution is an updating of a portion of Del's earlier doctoral dissertation and contributes in substantial fashion to the overall book. While I have only known Del for a few years, I have come to appreciate his warmth, sense of humor, and intelligence. Likewise, I have been impressed with Phyllis's considerable insight and leadership, especially with the Ohio Library Information Network (OhioLINK) project.

I conclude the book with a short glossary of commonly used accreditation terms that may be of value to readers.

As with several of my earlier ventures in print, this work would not have been possible without the able assistance provided by Teresa Davidson of the University of Dayton Libraries. Her ability to cheerfully take on "one more thing" on top of an already big workload always makes me shake my head in amazement. And while as an administrator I generally maintain an open-door policy, my administrative assistant Zenobia Charity would at times allow me to close my door to focus, between meetings and crises, on the final preparation of the manuscript. To my many colleagues associated with the North Central Association of Colleges and Schools, Commission on Institutions of Higher Education, who have taught me much about accreditation and higher education, I express my gratitude.

PART I

The Challenges of Accreditation

1

Challenges for Accreditation in a Rapidly Changing Environment

Kenneth L. Perrin

Accreditation is a uniquely American process of self-regulation that is almost a century old. Through this continually evolving process, postsecondary education has been improved, and the public has been assured that at least minimal standards have been met by either an institution or program of study.

While the accreditation process itself is little understood by the public, most Americans know almost instinctively that it is far preferable to attend an educational institution or to graduate from a program that is accredited. The variation in standards for colleges and universities by geographic region has been largely ignored.

The importance of accreditation was reinforced by the federal government in 1952 when it was determined that federal financial aid only would be provided to students who attend accredited institutions. Although a rare exception could be made to this rule, this decision literally changed forever the relationship between the accrediting commissions and the institutions they accredited. Accreditation moved from being a totally voluntary process to one that was essentially mandatory in nature. To lose accreditation was, in some instances, literally a death sentence for an institution, as financial aid would no longer be available.

Until most recently, accrediting commissions carried out their activities in relative obscurity. This situation has now changed with more attention being directed at accreditation than at any other time in the 100-year history of the process. Unfortunately, the attention has not been focused on the many positive contributions accreditation has made over the years but on what some perceive as serious shortcomings.

Accreditation is not alone in this negative climate. Concerns ranging from practices related to indirect cost recovery, campus crime, and intercollegiate athletic scandals have all contributed to a perception that there is a general problem with American postsecondary education. Since accreditation has been the primary way the public has been assured of an institution's or program's educational quality, it is not surprising that some of the blame for the "failings" in postsecondary education have been justifiably as well as unjustifiably directed at accreditation.

Many of the negative perceptions relative to accreditation stem from the 1990 public hearings that U.S. Senator Samuel Nunn conducted relative to the national scandal associated with student loan defaults. Then Secretary of Education Lauro Cavazos stated in part at one of these sessions: "[I]t is becoming increasingly clear that accrediting agencies are not doing the job we have entrusted to them" (Senate 1991, 2). With this one statement the government shifted the blame for the student loan default to the accrediting community.

While these criticisms were primarily directed at the proprietary sector, they quickly generalized to the entire community. This negative climate was further exacerbated by Secretary of Education Lamar Alexander's public criticism of the Middle States Association of Colleges and Schools for utilizing a diversity standard in evaluating institutions. Secretary Alexander contended that such a standard was irrelevant to academic quality.

As a result of the attacks on accreditation, a few members of the U.S. Congress determined that accreditation could no longer be relied on. They proposed severing the link between federal aid eligibility and accreditation in the 1991 reauthorization of the Higher Education Act. These members suggested that the states be given total responsibility for institutional oversight. Because of the good efforts principally of college and university presidents, who opposed increased state oversight, the law was revised and accreditation was retained.

While the U.S. government will for the foreseeable future continue to rely on accreditation in terms of student aid eligibility, Congress's negative attitude toward the process was not fundamentally changed. The perception that accreditation is a monopoly and "an old boys' network" in which trade associations protect the membership, not the public, is pervasive. Generally, these are erroneous assumptions but are the accrediting community's current reality.

Unless, over the next several years, the accrediting community moves to take charge of the future, both on and off campus, it is very possible that the process of self-regulation will be replaced by state oversight and national assessment. Accreditation must be seen as being responsive to changing societal expectations as well as changing needs on campus.

To reclaim the public trust, the accrediting community must involve an increased number of the public in the process and conduct more of the commissions' business in the sunshine. In this age of accountability, accreditors must provide the public with more relevant information about the institutions and programs they accredit. In so doing, however, accreditors must never lose sight of their other responsibility, which is to stimulate educational improvement. If accreditation is to remain a viable force on campuses nationwide, accreditors must critically assess the relevance of their standards. For example, the concept of geographically derived standards must be acknowledged as a historical artifact.

Most institutions and programs are already inundated with some form of externally mandated assessment; therefore, the "value-added" aspect of accreditation must be seen as truly relevant, especially in times of severe economic downturn. As institutions operate with continuously shrinking budgets, it is time for accreditors at both institutional and programmatic levels to cooperate maximally with each other to ease the economic burden that multiple accrediting visits and processes may place on a campus.

Finally, the possibility of returning to a truly voluntary system of self-regulation by volitionally severing the tie between accreditation and student financial aid must be carefully considered. The separation of financial aid eligibility from the process of assessing educational quality might give both accreditors and institutions greater flexibility to initiate educational reform and establish improved standards.

Accreditation is at a very critical time in its evolution. If the accrediting community uses the next several years to truly engage in thoughtful introspection, accreditation could become the cornerstone of educational reform in our nation.

REFERENCE

U.S. Senate. Permanent Subcommittee on Investigations of Committee on Government Affairs. 1991. *Abuses in Federal Student Aid Programs.* 102d Cong. 1st sess. S. Rept. 102-58.

2

Accreditation Expectations in the Age of New Technology

Ralph A. Wolff and Mimi Harris Steadman

INTRODUCTION

Technology has far-reaching implications not only for libraries but for accrediting bodies attempting to define and evaluate libraries and their relationship to institutional quality. All regional accrediting associations consider libraries to be an essential part of *institutional* quality. Standards of each of the regional associations address holdings, services, staffing, and facilities. Should new technologies be incorporated into existing accrediting approaches, or does the advent of new technology suggest the need for changes in accrediting standards and processes?

Over the past two years, we have been studying the impact of technology on libraries in relation to the accrediting process. We have talked with librarians, faculty, and presidents, circulated a paper for institutional comment throughout the Western Association region, and worked with a task group on this issue. What is clear is that new technology is expensive, and the full range of its impact has yet to be developed. Nonetheless, the push for libraries to invest in new hardware, software, and training is occurring right at the time library budgets are becoming increasingly constrained.

At the present time, regional accrediting associations are more neutral than proactive with respect to technology. But decisions of accrediting agencies to be neutral or proactive in relation to technology can have significant implications for library priorities and budgets. Accrediting agencies, in turn, need to be careful that their standards reflect more than traditional practices and address the needs of students entering careers in the twenty-first century. We have learned that accrediting agencies can play a valuable role by creating guidelines to assist institutions in addressing the many implications of new technologies.

To begin our research, we asked three questions:

- How is new technology changing traditional library service delivery and definitions of the library?
- How should new technology affect expectations for quality in the provision of library services at both off-campus and traditional degree programs?
- Even with new technology, is it appropriate to continue to expect library collections and usage in all disciplines?

As we have gathered information to respond to these questions, we have also explored implications for accrediting agencies.

HOW IS NEW TECHNOLOGY CHANGING TRADITIONAL LIBRARY SERVICE DELIVERY AND DEFINITION OF THE LIBRARY?

The information technology affecting traditional library usage and services delivery can be categorized into three major areas: on-line catalogs, bibliographic databases, and telecommunications. A fourth new category that has not yet had widespread impact on most library users includes nonbibliographic full-text and numeric databases.

On-Line Catalogs

First, on-line catalogs, which provide instant access to a listing of library holdings in a computer database, are replacing the traditional card catalog consisting of heavy oak drawers containing three-by-five cards. Faculty, staff, and student users can access library holdings through terminals on-site in the library and, at some institutions, through dial-up access by modem from their home or office computers (Weiskel 1989). In addition, On-Line Public Access Catalogs (OPACs) expand access to multiple on-line catalogs and to statewide, nationwide, or even international users. Internet is an example of an umbrella network that enables users to dial up hundreds of on-line catalogs, and systems such as the Online Computer Library Center (OCLC) provide "patrons information about 22 million items and the locations of libraries that own them" (Gherman 1991, A36). To provide patrons with greater access to materials they discover through an on-line catalog search, most libraries have interlibrary loan arrangements that enable their users to borrow materials from other institutions.

At the present time, none of the regional associations require on-line catalogs, yet the time will soon come when they are considered an essential component of library quality. On-line catalogs provide access to a range of information and data collection typically not available with card catalog systems. Increasingly, evaluation teams are recommending that institutions move in this direction, and there is considerable peer pressure as more institutions are doing so. Accrediting standards also suggest, but do not require, that library collections be supplemented by agreements with other institutions or services for interlibrary loan. The ready availability of computer networks and OPACs has already made this a reality for most institutions.

Bibliographic Databases

A second category of electronic research tools includes the frequently updated, easy-to-use bibliographic databases. These databases are essentially periodical indexes that provide citations and often abstracts to articles and research reports. Some databases are on-line and can be accessed from home or office computers (Rice 1989). Others such as the CD-ROM (compact disk read-only memory) systems are databases contained on small laser disks that are generally used by one person at a time on-site in the library (Rice 1989). Networking of CD-ROM workstations is a possible means of addressing the one-station, one-person limitations of the CD-ROM databases. Common databases on CD-ROM include ERIC (Educational Resources Information Center), PsychLit (psychology abstracts), and DAI (Dissertation Abstracts International) (Lyman 1991).

At present, most electronic databases are still "bibliographic," that is, they simply list a citation for text that must be obtained elsewhere in print form. Recently developed commercial database systems enable users to order by credit card a hard copy of a cited document to be delivered by fax or by mail. According to Peter Lyman, university librarian at the University of Southern California, the development of on-line collections has both advantages and disadvantages: "On the good side, it will provide access to journals that many libraries cannot afford. On the bad side, it shifts the cost from the institution to the user, information access will not be subsidized, and unequal wealth will lead to unequal access" (personal communication, November 8, 1991).

Improved bibliographic systems enable libraries to save money on some print materials, but not necessarily patrons' time, by switching from extensive and expensive local periodical collections to "on-demand" service. Lyman describes a shift from the "just-in-case" philosophy of collection development to the present trend toward "just-in-time" collection of resources (personal communication, November 8, 1991). Students and faculty can gather citations from a database, then libraries will order, either at their own or the user's expense, individual copies of articles from other libraries or commercial library services (Gherman 1991). Thus, libraries pay for periodicals on a per-use basis, rather than sustaining enormous budget allocations for periodical subscriptions that sit on a shelf awaiting possible usage.

As institutional accrediting bodies, regional associations do not mandate specific holdings for each discipline. It would seem a reasonable expectation, however, for disciplines where certain reference materials are available only through electronic delivery that students should be provided with access to them and training in their use. We also seem close to a point where students in certain disciplines need access to bibliographic databases as an essential element of their disciplinary training. For example, is PsychLit essential for programs in psychology, Lexus in law, or ABI/Inform for business? To many the answer is yes and evaluation teams may find quality suffering when such bibliographic services are not available.

Telecommunications

The third category of information technology impacting libraries and scholarship is in the area of telecommunications, including computer conferencing, electronic mail (E-mail), and electronic journals. These "conversational technologies" enable scholars to use E-mail and electronic bulletin boards to communicate instantly, even share drafts of papers, with colleagues around the world. In addition, new refereed electronic journals, in disciplines from communications to theology, are appearing across the country (Lyman 1991). These on-line journals, which may eventually expand our notions of acceptable scholarship, provide an immediate exchange of information in an era when research findings may become outdated before they are ever published in a traditional journal.

Accrediting agencies have not placed as much attention to this issue of campus connectivity. Rather, linkages to E-mail and use of electronic communication have been viewed more as a matter of individual preference than institutional requirement.

Full-Text Services

A fourth category not yet widely available but that is predicted to be in the future includes the nonbibliographic, "full-text" electronic text or numeric databases that provide entire articles, books, or other data on-line. Nonbibliographic sources already exist in many disciplines but at present are only available at a few institutions. Some reference materials, such as the vast data from the government census, are moving completely away from print formats into a nonbibliographic electronic format.

This area will likely be the last for accrediting agencies to address. Not only do technology and cost issues remain unresolved, but the accrediting tradition of respecting institutional autonomy will likely prevail in providing institutions the freedom to choose between hard-copy and electronic collections.

In summary, technological innovations including on-line catalogs, bibliographic databases, electronic mail, and in the near future, nonbibliographic databases enable library users to "renew their loans from the comfort of their offices or dorm rooms, ask reference questions via e-mail at times convenient to them, and browse the library's shelves electronically in the middle of the night" (Molholt 1990, 21). Accreditation has yet to require institutions to adopt technological innovations, but it is likely that within the next five to ten years such requirements will be implemented by modifications in accrediting standards and in the recommendations of accrediting evaluation teams.

Additional Issues

Several questions accompany these innovations in information technology. First, where will the financial resources come from to provide new services? One consensus among librarians and others is that a major impact of new technology is on library budgets, in addition to the costs of institutionwide computer and telecommunications networks. Libraries need both electronic and print resources; thus, new technology supplements but does not replace traditional materials, resulting in a cost increase for library budgets. Even after libraries have invested in the necessary computer hardware and software systems, updating databases presently costs thousands of dollars each year. And it is suggested that even when an institution can offer the full text of books and articles on-line, most of the information will still be printed out, as paper remains the most "user-friendly" medium for reading (Molholt 1990). A second concern is that although the futuristic "library without walls" (or shelves) provides the technology to browse electronically through diverse databases, it takes away the opportunity to make serendipitous discoveries while browsing through actual books in the stacks. Another danger expressed by one graduate dean is that students and faculty may become "prisoners of the electronic bibliographer," who, when unable to find a source through a database search, may assume that the information does not exist. Others we spoke to, however, did not share this concern, noting that all research is limited by the chosen search strategies, whether they be print or electronic. Third, just a few of the many anticipated challenges of delivering documents on-line include free speech issues, publisher cooperation, pricing, licensing, and copyright concerns (Lyman 1991).

A final concern is organizational: Who is in charge of library and information technology? Is it a librarian with information services and some computer expertise, or is it a computer and telecommunications specialist with some knowledge of academic libraries? Are librarians included in educational and technology planning decisions, and are faculty and technology experts included in library planning? Our experience is that on many campuses there exists a serious lack of coordination in the development and planning for campus computing and library services. Often, directors of the library and computer services report to different vice presidents, thereby exacerbating communication problems. Furthermore, on many campuses budgets for computers and telecommunications are expanding, while budgets for libraries have become more restricted, without much coordination between the two. These are significant issues that institutions rarely address in their self-studies or that evaluation teams comment on.

Technology and the Idea of the Library

Although technological innovations have significantly streamlined the library cataloging and research process, they have not revolutionized library services.

Two frames of reference about the impact of technology on libraries have emerged during the course of our reading and conversations. The first frame of reference is that new technology is enhancing the existing mission of the library. The conclusion of several librarians interviewed, as well as a number of recent articles, is that technology is presently being used to do what was already done in the past more efficiently, and it is significantly expanding patrons' access to already existing collections.

A second frame of reference is that new technology has the potential to fundamentally change our conceptions of the library beyond what we can presently imagine. In this second frame of reference, there is a shifting notion from the library as a *place* to the library as an *idea,* a concept put forth by James Govan, university librarian at the University of North Carolina at Chapel Hill (Molholt 1990). Molholt describes the idea of the library as embodying ''the attributes of organized information, easy or mediated access to knowledge, and availability of information resources, regardless of location'' (1990, 42). The library, rather than being considered a structure on campus, is ''a concept not bound by physical dimensions: The library is a medium through which we gain access to information from all sources and a variety of format.'' Furthermore, the ''definition, location, and function of libraries in today's university cannot be divorced from the information networks and telecommunications infrastructure which extend far beyond their physical boundaries'' (T. West, personal communication, March 11, 1992).

Charles Martell (1991), dean and university librarian at California State University at Sacramento, puts forth a parallel notion of the evolving library paradigm in which there is a change from the library as a product, such as a building, books, and journals, to the library as a process, including access to a variety of traditional and technological resources. Martell explains that changes in the culture of human communication have resulted in changing perspectives on the role of libraries. Human communication has evolved over time from a primarily oral culture to a scribal culture with the advent of writing, and to a print culture with the development of printing. More recently, with advancing computer technology, we are entering an era of an electronic culture. Previously, in a period of a print culture, libraries were thought of in terms of their physical *holdings* of information resources. In an electronic culture, the library paradigm has shifted to one of *access* and will continue to evolve toward a paradigm of *use* that will emphasize the dynamic interactions between users and new forms of library media.

Today patrons can interact with the library from almost any location. The place of the library has evolved from a physical, local one—the building that patrons visit—to a universal place unlimited by physical boundaries, with technology enabling patrons to access materials from other libraries across the country and around the world. In the future, the place of the library will be personal, with users at any location being able to access virtually all libraries and collect for their personal use increasingly diverse forms of information. Previously, the user's interaction with the library was primarily passive, relying on the expertise of highly trained reference librarians to assist in information searches and retrieval. At present, more user-friendly electronic catalogs allow patrons to actively search for materials on their own. Later, we can expect an interactive relationship between users and the library in which patrons not only can access documents through technology but can create, organize, and modify information for their own purposes.

This interactive relationship is tied to the changing nature of information, which has evolved from the static printed book of the past to present alterable on-line information, to future dynamic information products that we cannot as of yet imagine. This movement toward new ways of defining the thinking about the library is reflected in Martell's (1991) summary table below:

Time	Paradigm	Place	User/Library Interaction	Nature of Information
To 1980	Holdings	Local	Passive	Static
1980	Access	Universal	Active	Static/dynamic
2010	Use	Personal	Interactive	Dynamic

Changing notions of the library require intelligent library planning and development that recognizes practical constraints and considers an appropriate balance of resources devoted to print and electronic sources of information. Martell suggests that implications for evaluation include flexibility on the part of accreditation agencies to provide institutions the time to adapt to swiftly changing technology and the opportunity to experiment with different approaches to providing information resources.

In these emerging views of libraries, the emphasis shifts away from the physical facility and holdings to the quality and diversity of services provided. The library would become not only a place to conduct research, study, and socialize but a comprehensive learning center to be accessed both physically on campus and from afar through technology. In this model for the future, the roles of the library, the learning resource center, the classroom, and the computer and communications network would be thoughtfully integrated by faculty, library, and learning resource staff to apply research findings in cognitive development and teaching and learning. Libraries and learning resource centers are envisioned not just as support for classroom activities but as key players in providing learning experiences within and beyond the classroom.

Scholars and librarians, whatever their expectations for the library of the future, agree that advancements in library technology, as well as traditional library resources, are only valuable to the extent that students and faculty take advantage of them. One mission of higher education is to promote students' development as lifelong learners with an ingrained "library habit" and the ability to use technology to access current information in their fields. "Technology is only a means to an end," according to Peter Lyman: "The degree to which technology is used appropriately and effectively to provide resources depends on the skill of library staff and information professional to help students make connections to books, catalogs and resources at other sites, and equally as important, to educate them for information literacy" (personal communication, November 8, 1991).

The American Library Association Presidential Committee's report on information literacy provides a definition for *information literacy*: "[T]o be information literate, a person must be able to recognize when information is needed and have the ability to locate, evaluate, and use effectively the needed information" (1989, 1). Additionally, "information literate people are those who have learned how to learn. They know how to learn because they know how knowledge is organized, how to find information, and how to use information in such a way that others can learn from them. They are people prepared for lifelong learning, because they can always find the information needed for any task or decision at hand" (American Library Association 1989, 1). To promote information literacy on the part of the academic community, faculty and library staff must work together to convey the power of technology in retrieving information and to encourage library use as an integral part of the academic experience.

While an accrediting agency should not mandate that institutions adopt one frame of reference over another, it should evaluate an institution on the basis of the stated role it ascribes to technology in the provision of library services. Moreover, as all institutions identify lifelong learning skills as part of their educational mission, it will be important to learn how information literacy is considered to be part of this educational goal.

HOW SHOULD NEW TECHNOLOGY AFFECT EXPECTATIONS FOR QUALITY IN THE PROVISION OF LIBRARY SERVICES AT BOTH OFF-CAMPUS AND TRADITIONAL DEGREE PROGRAMS?

The previous section suggested that new technology holds great promise for making library services accessible to students at remote locations, but concern for the equality of educational experiences remains. Aguilar and Kascus pose the question: "How does an academic institution ensure that the education delivered to students at remote sites is equivalent to the education delivered on the main campus?" (1991, 368). This section will consider what resources are required, given new technology, to provide off-campus students with sufficient and equivalent access to library services.

Cases of actual institutions in the process of evaluation elicited concern about the interpretation of accreditation standards for off-campus programs. How should accreditation standards be applied in light of new library technology and in light of the unique circumstances of certain institutions? For example, a new doctoral degree granting institution in a large urban area asserted that it did not need, and that it would be inappropriate for it to invest in, a complete library to support its programs when a wealth of major research libraries existed within a fifty-mile radius. This institution argued that rather than working to build collections, its commitment should be toward supporting students' access to other libraries by developing consortial relations and interlibrary loan arrangements with other libraries in the region.

Second, an institution with external degree programs, also granting the doctorate, asserted that because its students were dispersed geographically, no purpose would be served by developing a library collection. In a third case, a medium-sized institution with a large number of off-campus and adult programs was serving students' library needs through innovative arrangements with the main campus library. Even as the institution began to take responsibility for providing library services to off-campus students, the question arose as to what should be the balance between the services the institution itself provides and what the institution does to support students' access to other libraries.

Off-campus and external degree programs share several common elements: They are usually removed from campus, they offer a majority of programs in professional fields, their faculty often teach part-time, and their students are predominantly adult learners. Many such programs are operated on an accelerated basis as well, with academic terms compressed to as few as three to six weeks, in some cases. Experience from site visits shows that faculty in off-campus programs, frequently part-time instructors drawn from practitioners in the field, are often not engaged in research or intensive library use. Moreover, students typically work full-time and carry family responsibilities. Both part-time and full-time faculty in off-campus programs are often reluctant to assign library research under these circumstances. This situation is magnified when no library collections or reference support is readily available as part of the program. We have found in such circumstances that the library is "out of sight, out of mind." This often leads to an altered curriculum for many off-campus programs, where textbooks and duplicated materials become the sole foundation for courses and entire programs.

In terms of the student population, some adult learners may not have stepped foot in a library in the fifteen years or more since they completed high school or college and may be quite surprised by how the library has changed. Others may be comfortable and familiar with their local public libraries or libraries where they work but not with a full-range academic library. Adult learners in general are more interested in gaining practical and applied knowledge, rather than developing a conceptual and historical grounding in their fields. Without ready access to a library and librarian assistance, adult students are less likely to explore theoretical issues in their fields beyond what is presented in class, especially when library use is not required by their instructors. Whether they are adult learners or traditional-age students, students at off-campus sites who pay comparable tuition and earn identical degrees are entitled to access to library

resources and exposure to the library research process. Will the new technological advances mentioned earlier improve institutions' ability to provide library
services to off-campus sites?

As reviewed in the previous section, new technology can reduce the problem
of distance by providing students with access to information about holdings at
other locations that can then be acquired through interlibrary loan. Also, telecommunications such as E-mail, and in the future, interactive video, will be
increasingly utilized to enable students to ask reference questions of librarians
at other locations. Currently, a number of institutions rely on toll-free telephone
lines to provide reference support to students off campus.

The major limitation to providing off-campus services, however, is that access
to information about materials in no way guarantees their availability. Remote
access to the main campus library through a document delivery service does not
prevent materials from being borrowed by students at the home campus, nor
does it ensure timely delivery of resources. This poses particular problems for
courses with accelerated formats, for programs serving working students, and
for undergraduates who complete assignments in a relatively short time frame
(often the night before an assignment is due) and who use common reference
materials that are in high demand.

To compensate for the document delivery time lag, faculty at some off-
campus programs transport selected materials directly to the class site (Kascus
and Aguilar 1988). While this speeds up availability, students do not gain hands-
on research experience or access to a wide variety of materials through browsing. At other off-campus programs, students may be encouraged to use local
public or institutional libraries. Local public libraries may be limited in their
ability to provide materials to support college-level work (Kascus and Aguilar
1988). Even university libraries may not have the special collections needed to
support the highly specialized or state-of-the-art courses offered in many off-
campus programs, which, by their nature, often have different areas of emphasis
than campus-based programs.

Sending students to libraries at local college campuses is a common means
of addressing library services for off-campus and external degree programs. In
some cases, institutions enter contractual agreements in which they provide compensation to other libraries that provide services to off-campus students. Even
if students have access to such resources, institutions that do not take primary
responsibility for providing library services may not give library issues adequate,
if any, attention in the curriculum planning and budgeting process. In other
cases, institutions with off-campus programs rely on the resources of other institution in a parasitic relationship with no collaboration or compensation. In
these instances, there is a shift in cost from one institution to another. The shift
in costs may also be transferred from the institution to the student who is forced
to pay for access to other libraries.

In California, for example, many off-campus programs have relied on public access for their students to the University of California (UC) libraries, but budget and resource limitations may soon change the reality of open access. At Berkeley, for example, a "Library Service Priority Program" was instituted due to budget cuts and heavy use of resources to try to preserve library services for the library's "primary clientele" of UC faculty, staff, and students. When a line forms for services or materials, library staff may request that patrons show UC identification, then encourage any non-UC users to try their local public libraries before using campus facilities. Although this type of policy is contrary to librarians' professional philosophy of open access, other UC campuses are expected to follow suit as budget cuts force them to reduce costs in areas that do not involve serving their own UC constituents. Gloria Werner, university librarian at UCLA (UC at Los Angeles), explained that research on library usage at the UCLA library determined that 40 percent of people seeking reference assistance were not UC affiliated and that between one fifth and one third of all books were checked out by non-UC patrons (personal communication, October 1991). At present, non-UC student library users pay a lower rate for library card privileges than the general public. Werner projects that in the near future the cost of library cards will go up to $100 per year for non-UC users, with reduced rates for students in public community colleges and the California State University system but not for students at private or proprietary institutions. Increased rates and other policies can be expected to limit the availability of UC library resources to students enrolled in off-campus and external degree programs.

According to Aguilar and Kascus, the "principle that library services and resources are an integral component of higher education is one that is rarely challenged; however, it is often circumvented" (1991, 369). Until technology takes another leap and until all institutions can afford existing technology, what are reasonable expectations for the provision of library services, an "integral component of higher education," for off-campus programs? Regional accreditation agencies vary in their requirements for institutions providing actual library collections as compared with merely providing access to other libraries. Accreditation standards in some regions require only that institutions provide students with access to public libraries or the libraries of other institutions. In our view, however, it is essential that institutions take a more active role to provide library services.

Our interviews with librarians suggest four key elements in the provision of library services for off-campus programs. First, institutions should take responsibility for developing library support for off-campus students, rather than transferring such responsibility, often unknowingly, to other institutions' libraries. Second, all institutions should develop a basic collection at each site where degree programs are offered or provide immediate access to such collections through on-line services under the institution's control. Third, institutions should provide research support to students directly, rather than assigning this to the staffs of other libraries. Fourth, institutions need to engage in periodic reviews not only of library collections and services but of the expectations of library usage for each discipline and course and how those expectations are being realized.

The Association of College and Research Libraries (ACRL) has recently addressed these issues in their *"Guidelines for Extended Campus Library Services"* (1990). The *"ACRL Guidelines"* expectations for responsibility for library services in off-campus programs are as follows:

The parent institution is responsible for providing support which addresses the information needs of its extended campus programs. This support should provide library service to the extended campus community equitable with that provided to the on-campus library.

The Library has primary responsibility for identifying, developing, coordinating, and providing library resources and services which address the information needs of the extended campus community." (1990, 354)

We support the philosophy behind the *"ACRL Guidelines,"* which emphasize the primary role of the institution in providing library services to all students in regular and extended campus programs.

IS IT APPROPRIATE TO CONTINUE TO EXPECT LIBRARY COLLECTIONS AND USAGE IN ALL DISCIPLINES?

Accreditation agencies generally consider the provision of library services a critical element in educational quality at the undergraduate as well as the graduate level. Some critics, however, have argued that the requirements that collections exist to support *all* degree programs comes from a humanities and social science frame of reference. In some fields, such as certain programs in engineering or accounting, it is argued, what students need to learn can be effectively presented with textbooks and duplicated supplemental material. Library research is not considered an important dimension to such programs. Why should collections be developed in these fields? These issues remain largely overlooked and unexplored in the accreditation process.

According to Beverly Lynch, dean, UCLA Graduate School of Library and Information Science, every discipline requires library resources, but requirements for usage vary across fields of study (1991). While students majoring in engineering, for example, may use the library considerably less than their counterparts in English or history, librarians and faculty members surveyed agreed that basic library literacy is or should be an expected outcome of undergraduate education. Ideally, all students, regardless of academic major, should gain proficiency in library use through their general education course requirements, as well as through courses in their major field. Although we often associate heavy library use with students in the humanities, Susan Perry, director of the Departmental Systems Group at Stanford University, maintains that students in the sciences need the library as much, if not more, than students in the humanities, since science scholarship is updated so swiftly (personal communication, October 1991).

The three following examples illustrate how students and faculty in diverse departments require and use library resources. First, although nursing and physical therapy students have a heavy lab and clinical component to their course work, students and faculty rely heavily on current periodicals since the technology in their fields changes so rapidly. Also research-oriented health science programs require significant library resources.

As a second example, students in the design fields, such as architecture, graphic arts, fashion design, and interior design, spend far more time in their design studios than they spend in the library. Nevertheless, the disciplinary accreditation agencies for these fields have stringent requirements for library resources such as slides and projection equipment and books on the history of design. Fashion design, for instance, requires expensive and quickly outdated books and journals, and architecture and interior design and multidisciplinary fields in which students and faculty require resources from related areas such as engineering, fine arts, psychology, and sociology.

Students in engineering also devote much of their time to laboratory rather than library work. In engineering courses, much of the quantitative and practical curriculum is conveyed through a textbook and an instructor who reviews course material and works through equations on the board. Depending on the requirements and level of the course, and on the initiative of the students, engineering majors will ideally use library resources to seek novel and alternative approaches to problem solving. According to Steve Gass, head of the Engineering Library at Stanford, the Accrediting Board for Engineering and Technology is calling for library skills to be an outcome of all undergraduate degree programs (personal communication, October 1991). At the graduate level, library research is essential to engineering programs requiring a thesis, although our conversations indicated a trend in master's programs away from a thesis requirement and toward additional course work.

The examples of health sciences, design, and engineering indicate that each discipline requires library resources but in different ways. In the same way that scholarship and research methods differ across disciplines, requirements for library materials to support those disciplines differ as well. At a minimum, students in all disciplines need access to periodicals, appropriate bibliographic sources, and new nontext databases in their field of study. Additionally, it is an appropriate goal of all undergraduate and graduate programs that students develop skills in library technology to encourage lifelong learning and the ability to stay current in their professional fields. Accreditation agencies need to work with faculty and librarians to reflect on what constitutes appropriate resources by discipline. Most important, accrediting agencies can place emphasis on the collection and analysis of data on actual library usage by students in various disciplines. Program review procedures as well should address how, and under what circumstances, library usage is a part of each course of study at the institution.

THE THREE "I's"

From this initial research, we conclude that at present new technology is not radically altering the nature of traditional library use, but it is substantially improving the efficiency of existing library services, significantly increasing the potential for providing library services to remote locations, and setting the foundation for changing our overall definition of the library.

As libraries continue to approach technology and its implications, we propose the application of a three-pronged approach we call *the three i's—intelligence, investment,* and *integration.* The significant costs of new technology require careful planning and a long-term vision of the role technology is to have within the overall mission and design of the library. We characterize the need for conceptualizing these issues as the need for intelligence. What library services are needed most? and at what locations? Who uses the library the most and for what purposes? What collections, resources, and technologies are most in demand? Are data on circulation by discipline and by type of user collected and analyzed? The librarians with whom we worked concluded that careful thought and planning around these issues must take place *before* new technology is acquired.

The second *i*—investment—comes from working through a set of tough questions that need to be addressed. The costs of new technology are substantial. They include the capital costs of acquiring new hardware and software, the expense of service and upgrades, and the time for training of personnel and users. New technology becomes an investment when it is wisely planned. We believe that all sites where degree programs are offered should be supported by at least a basic library collection, supplemented by access first to the institution's main library and reference services, and only secondly to local library resources.

The third element is integration, the extent to which the library is integrated into the life of students and faculty. This requires a conscious effort to assess the effectiveness of library services and support, moving beyond resource data on holdings, size of physical facility, and number of professional staff.

CONCLUSION

Accreditation agencies can work cooperatively with institutions to explore how new library technology can enhance student learning. A proactive stance should be taken so that issues of ease of access, shifting of costs, delivery time for interlibrary loan materials, requirements for bibliographic instruction, and provision of services for off-campus students can become part of the dialogue of the accrediting process. At this point in time, accreditation may not have the answers, but it can provide a useful process for asking and answering a wide range of questions.

REFERENCES

Aguilar, W., and M. Kascus. 1991. "Introduction." *Library Trends* 39(4): 367–74.

American Library Association Presidential Committee on Information Literacy. 1989. *Information Literacy, Final Report.* Chicago: American Library Association.

Association of College and Research Libraries (ACRL). 1990. *"ACRL Guidelines for Extended Campus Library Services."* *C&RL News*, April, 353–54.

Gherman, P. M. 1991. "Setting Budgets for Libraries in Electronic Era." *Chronicle of Higher Education,* August 14, A36.

Kascus, M., and W. Aguilar. 1988. "Providing Library Support to Off-Campus Programs." *College and Research Libraries* 49 (1): 29–37.

Lyman, P. 1991. "The Library of the (Not-So-Distant) Future." *Change* 23 (1): 34–41.

Lynch, B. 1991. Presentation at the Western Association of Schools and Colleges Presidents Forum, San Francisco, Calif., November 6.

Martell, C. 1991. Presentation at the Western Association of Schools and Colleges Presidents Forum, San Francisco, Calif., November 6.

Molholt, P. 1990. "Libraries and Campus Information: Redrawing the Boundaries." *Academic Computing* 4(5): 20–23.

Rice, J. 1989. "Managing Bibliographic Information with Personal Desktop Technology." *Academe* 75(4): 18–21.

Weiskel, T. 1989. "The Electronic Library and the Challenge of Information Planning." *Academe* 75(4): 8–12.

3

Challenges to Accreditation from the New Academic Library Environment

Delmus E. Williams

Accreditation is a time-honored institution that has contributed much to making American universities the best in the world. It is not a perfect evaluation tool, and many have found it convenient to focus on its shortcomings. The reality is that the process used in accreditation has evolved as a unique evaluative structure that has done much to ensure quality control and continuous improvement in the diverse community that is American higher education.

Over the years, libraries have gained much from the visit of accreditors. The existence and enforcement of standards that require institutions to have appropriate information resources to support research and teaching have led to a continual upgrading of library collections and services and a constant updating of library technology. Forcing libraries to constantly look at themselves critically has clearly been to their benefit.

Times are changing, and the evaluative processes that have served universities and their libraries well in the past are finding themselves to be less useful in the current environment. The students who are coming to the university to be taught do not fit the traditional picture of white, eighteen-year-old men and women who enroll in college full-time and expect to graduate in four years. The classrooms to which they come might be on campus, a hundred miles away, or somewhere in between. Research is no longer based on the efforts of a resident community of scholars and scientists working in a single institution. Higher education has been moving for some time to create an environment in which society can use the full capacity of every scholar, in every field, on every campus. Colleges and universities are working hard to overcome the uneven distribution of resources available to these scholars by developing virtual communities that connect faculty with students, colleagues, and resources using a variety of technologies, old and new. Bitnet, Internet, and a variety of state networks using microwaves, fiber optics, satellites, or telephone lines quickly offer the opportunity for scholars to communicate easily. Supercomputer networks are making these resources widely available to everyone, from the faculty of Harvard to high school teachers. Statewide library networks, such as Illinois's Illnet Online, the Colorado Alliance of Research Libraries, and Ohio Library Information Network (OhioLINK), are developing service programs designed to make the same resources available to faculty on small campuses that are available to those on large ones.

Developing an evaluative procedure that can encourage these developments and that can help all institutions move to open the world to their students and faculty and at the same time maintain their unique character is a major challenge. To be successful, accrediting agencies must come to understand (1) the new models being developed for the various services offered by colleges and universities that utilize the increasingly sophisticated tools becoming available to educators and (2) the complexity that these tools are introducing into academic life. Accreditors have just begun to focus on this challenge, and new approaches to evaluation that can cope with it are just beginning to develop.

ACCREDITATION AND THE LIBRARY

Service agencies, such as the library, present accreditors with some of their more complex problems. It is difficult enough to come to grips with what teaching is and does, but at least universities have a base of information in front of them as to what good teaching is and how it affects the students within the university. But libraries have too often been referred to as what Michael Harris (1973) once called "requisite goods" providing benefit simply because they existed. At the same time, assessments of their quality have too often consisted of an inventory of holdings, space, and services offered in the library, with little attempt made to connect that inventory to the mission of the institution.

But this is changing. Accreditors are now beginning to look at libraries differently, and this challenge consists of two primary elements. To be effective, accrediting standards must first redefine what the library is, does, and should be in the new world of information resources now available to faculty and students. Second, accrediting agencies must develop new measures of effectiveness for library services that tie together the capabilities of the library to deliver information to patrons and the mission of the university.

CHANGES IN UNIVERSITIES

First, accreditors must come to grips with the fact that the expectations on campus for libraries and other information resources are changing. Twenty years ago, it was relatively easy to find consensus as to what a library was and what place it held in the university community. Libraries had changed little in almost half a century, and it was widely believed (at least ideologically) that they occupied a central place in the intellectual life of the campus. Good libraries were defined as libraries with large, well-selected collections, and even as the library profession began to shift its view away from collections to a facility where students and faculty could use those collections, the idea remained that campus libraries were free-standing agencies designed to support students working on a single campus. Libraries consisted of books and journals, or at least things that could be equated to books and journals, and the expectation was that everyone who went to college was familiar with how one obtained information from books.

Times have changed and are continuing to change as both the clients served by the library and the structure of delivery systems for information change. The complexion of the college campus is not what it was in the 1970s. More and more of those enrolled in classes are not white, are well past eighteen, and employed full-time, are not as well acculturated to reading and critical thinking as earlier generations of college students, and have families or other responsibilities that divert their attention from their studies. Many commute to and from campus, often at night or on weekends, and many are enrolled in programs offered at some distance from the campus and, even at times, some distance from the instructor. It is one thing to talk of opening the library a sufficient number of hours to serve dormitory students; it is perhaps a bit more difficult to make sure that this kind of captive population learns to use library resources, especially if the population comes from a variety of ethnic and cultural backgrounds. But it is quite another thing to talk about providing library resources for a student taking courses from the University of South Carolina that are broadcast via satellite to a site in West Virginia or that is delivered via videotape to a student in Ohio.

CHANGES IN THE MANNER IN WHICH INFORMATION IS DELIVERED

The complexion of the research community is also changing. In the 1960s, research projects were place-bound, with research teams being formed on a single campus. The primary means of scholarly communication was the journal article, and while informal communities of scholars developed, the crudeness of written communication limited the capacity of those communities to respond to research problems in a timely fashion. That has changed as E-mail has made it possible for colleagues to work almost anywhere and still communicate with one another quickly and easily.

But the information community has also changed in the last twenty-five years. The development of improved methods of electronic communication and the spiraling cost of print media are changing the way we look at and deliver information. As noted earlier, library collections that were once based on books and other printed materials have been enriched with information that is now delivered in a wide variety of formats. This makes it possible for students and faculty to have access within the library to more information than was ever before possible. While this has greatly enriched their educational opportunities, the fact is that each format that is introduced is perfect for delivering some kinds of information but is limited in some respects. As a result, microfilm supplements books without replacing them; on-line databases add new capabilities without eliminating the need for other media; and CD-ROM (compact disk read-only memory) provides inexpensive opportunities to provide some electronic data without replacing completely the need for on-line files.

To further complicate matters, libraries have taken upon themselves added responsibilities to get whatever users need from wherever it is housed. As a result, researchers are increasingly coming to rely on a wide array of information resources that can be critical to support teaching, research, and learning but that will never appear in the libraries of their home institutions. These resources may be held in nearby public libraries; may be retrievable from other libraries with access provided through networks; or may be available through commercial services, provided via the Internet, or from other sources. But no matter where they originate, local access to them and a capacity to use them effectively are becoming increasingly important. In some disciplines, we have already reached a point where books and journals have been found too slow to materially assist researchers and are viewed merely as places where scholars can document and archive their accomplishments. In those disciplines, the primary tools for exchanging information about ongoing research projects are electronic mail, listservs, and journals that are developing on the Internet that may never see print. With the emergence of the National Information Infrastructure, reliance on these resources may be increasingly important.

The upside to all of this is that the new array of information resource materials gets more information to more people more quickly than was ever before possible. The downside is that the array of formats for the delivery of information is becoming increasingly complex. Library managers must make trade-offs that can be expensive in monetary and political terms to fit the mix of media available in the library and the support services that must be provided to support those media to the mission of the university.

CHANGES IN THE UNIVERSITY COMMUNITY

The challenge for accreditors is further complicated by the fact that institutions are becoming increasingly different as time passes. This diversity within the higher education community is not new. In fact, it has been one of the defining characteristics of that community since the Civil War. But in recent years, the emphasis on research in large universities, the emergence of the regional universities, the development of new disciplines and interdisciplinary programs of study, and the growth of single-purpose universities have created more differences in that community than ever before. As universities become more dependent on technology and equipment for their research, it is likely that more specialization will occur and that the differences between institutions will be accentuated. Developing a single set of standards that can serve technical universities specializing in ceramics, colleges basing their curriculum on the "Great Books," the U.S. Army's field artillery school, schools offering programs throughout the United States and abroad, and classic liberal arts colleges has never been an easy task, and it is likely to get even harder.

ACCREDITATION AND THE ACADEMIC LIBRARY

In short, accreditors are being challenged to find a way to evaluate whether or not an institution can provide the proper array of collections and information services to its students and faculty using resources available on campus or retrievable when students are working off campus. While it is unlikely that accreditation standards and criteria will ever completely disregard the need for resources on campus, it is no longer enough for them to consist of only printed materials or of only those materials housed in the library's collections. In fact, we may well be approaching a time when that may not even be the primary focus for evaluations of libraries. Libraries have now begun to substitute access for ownership as the primary measure of what constitutes a "good" library program. If the Western Association of Schools and Colleges (1991) is to be believed, then the next step is to develop criteria for evaluation that substitute "use" for "access," and that is likely to require another shift in the way libraries engage in the business of relating to accreditation agencies.

Accreditation has always had some difficulty determining what a good library contributed to a university. In times when print was the only real technology available capable of conveying information to scholars, it was often considered enough to accept the idea that universities were built around collections of printed information housed at the center of the campus as a point of faith. By so doing, accreditors could limit the evaluation to the quality of the collection and the services available to connect users to those collections. After all, John Harvard got his name on a university by giving his books to it.

As we move into an age in which there is no "best" source for all information, accreditors are faced with determining whether institutions are getting information to users in the best possible way while at the same time outfitting students to function in a world that is information rich. Educational assumptions relating to libraries that have been in place for a hundred years are losing their validity, and those who would evaluate the library are expected to cope with situations that combine a legacy of large library collections with a dynamic environment in which new methods for delivering information are constantly coming on-line.

EVALUATING ACADEMIC LIBRARIES

The problem that confronts accrediting agencies is the need for developing both a set of standards or criteria for academic libraries and a process to apply those standards or criteria in a way that makes sense to the library and its parent institution. It is critical that a process be developed that can conform to the specific needs of individual institutions rather than one that tries to develop a model library that is just the same as the library on every other campus. The development of information technology has allowed us to customize the library to meet the individual needs of the campus and individual students and faculty on those campuses, and it is important that evaluative tools be developed that encourage this kind of tailoring. It is equally important that we ensure that the institutions are not allowed to use speculation about what they might eventually be able to do technologically to avoid paying the price for adequate support for their users. And at the same time, it is critical that evaluation make sure that reliance on new information services is supported by an appropriate array of services and that all of the potential costs of utilizing these technologies are addressed by the institution.

At the same time, a new challenge confronts librarians and other information professionals. While libraries have always seen themselves as teachers who assist classroom instructors by helping their students use information, there has always been an assumption in the academic community that most students at least understood how information in a print format was organized and delivered in society and could use that information with minimal assistance. That certainty is no longer possible. As the array of information broadens and the number of front ends increase, there is an increasing need to make sure that students and other users are acquainted with the possibilities that are available to them and that they are encouraged to accept and use new technologies as they emerge. If, as noted above, libraries are to move from measuring "access" to information to measuring its "use," educational objectives will have to change, and the way libraries evaluate their services will have to change with them.

DEVELOPING MEASURES FOR THE ACADEMIC LIBRARY

The introduction of criteria into the accreditation process that emphasize outcomes assessment and performance measures shows promise in addressing this need. While this approach provides a good framework for assessing libraries, using it has proven to be complicated. Russell Linke (1992) says that there are at least three characteristics required to provide a valid and effective guide to institutional performance—namely, relevance to the central functions of teaching and research, reliability of measurement, and a recognition of the intrinsic merit or worth of the task being performed. In principle, this is clear, but as Pierre Lucier (1992) noted, our performance to date in developing performance indicators for higher education has consisted of efforts to develop quantitative measures that do not tell us what we need to know. As institutions seek aggregates that will ensure statistical accuracy, they seem to lose sight of the subtleties that influence decision making.

Areas like the library present particular problems in this area. Everyone instinctively knows how important it is to the campus, but none has spent the energy required as to why it is important. As Williams Troutt noted in a 1979 survey of the literature regarding outcome assessment, the only documented correlation between library services and the outcomes of universities was a direct relationship between the size of the collection and the prestige of the institution. Little has changed, and much needs to be done to explain in a meaningful way what the library does for students. While it might be important to have sets of outcomes like those developed by Nancy Van House and others (1990), those outcomes relate only to products of the library and do not speak to the contribution that the library and its services make to undergraduate and graduate education. Until that issue is addressed, it is unlikely that meaningful performance measures can be developed for libraries.

Work to define the kind of preferred outcomes or performance measures that best fit library operations has begun. As might be expected, different regional associations have taken different approaches. The Southern Association of Colleges and Schools has developed a set of criteria that is largely tied to the traditional measures of library quality expanded to accommodate the need for user instruction and regional cooperatives. The Middle States Association has taken bolder steps to try to encourage a more direct kind of assessment of educational outcomes, urging evaluators to look at syllabi for dated materials or materials not held in the library and checking circulation records for materials on reserve or on reading lists. Antoinette Kania (1988) recently proposed a model set of outcomes-based standards that relied on existing standards, but much review needs to be done.

The literature of library instruction has long advocated a proactive role for librarians in developing students who are information literate and purveyors of a wide array of information resources. But it is not clear that campuses have taken that concept to heart and even less clear that they have developed an operational definition of the concept. Library use instruction is ever present through often badly done. If improvement is to be made, how can libraries be encouraged to evaluate their programs and to vary the content and methods used in their service programs to help them address the needs of diverse clientele more effectively?

Efforts to improve user performance with electronic media are often nonexistent. User instruction for Internet and other electronic resources tends to fall between a computer center that is equipment driven and a library that focuses on its holdings, and this kind of assistance is often not being addressed by anyone. Who is to say whether the university should be expected to prepare information-literate students, and if it is, how do accreditation standards that tend to divide these resources into discrete standards for the library and the computer center address the issue? For the student studying off campus, how does the campus connect a student who lives, works, and studies a hundred miles away to Internet resources, and how does it make sure that the student knows how to use them?

What about services to remote populations and support for curriculum provided by libraries and other information sources not controlled by the university? It is easy enough to say that a small college located across town from a larger one should not be able to blindly point to the larger campus as its library support without agreement from that institution. What happens in the case of a small art college in Atlanta that is located within easy walking distance of the outstanding art collections of the main Atlanta Public Library, a library that is readily available to all of its students? Or the case of doctoral students at a university in Huntsville, Alabama, who have a major scientific library available for use provided by the National Aeronautics and Space Administration (NASA)? At what point does the mere fact that these resources are nearby and available to students make the requirement to develop a library on campus beyond that needed for direct support of instruction an unneeded expense? And, of course, how does one deal with distance learning? Is a phone line with an 800 number and a librarian on the other end sufficient to support instruction or at least to supplement resources held at the place where instruction is delivered? And what responsibilities does the institution offering instruction have to make sure that students are connected to the information resources that are available in the community?

THE NEXT STEP

While most of the accrediting associations have backed off from developing true performance measures for libraries, opting instead for the broader concept of outcomes assessment, libraries must face up to the fact that they must be able to say what they contribute to the university. The challenge is to move beyond the sort of "home, mother, and apple pie" statements that so often find their way into library literature and into on-campus justifications for the library without trying to quantify what they do to the point that they tease out consideration of everything that is important to the operation. The line is a difficult one to walk, but the health of the library as a part of the campus and its ability to fend off raids on its coffers depends on the capacity of library managers to meet this challenge.

REFERENCES

Harris, M. H. 1973. "Purpose of the American Public Library: A Revisionist Interpretation of History." *Library Journal* 98: 2509–14.

Kania, A. M. 1988. "Academic Standards and Performance Measures." *College and Research Libraries* 49: 16–24.

Linke, R. D. 1992. "Some Factors for Application of Performance Indicators in Higher Education." *Higher Education Management* 4: 194–208.

Lucier, P. 1992. "Performance Indicators in Higher Education: Lowering the Debate." *Higher Education Management* 4: 204–14.

Troutt, W. E. 1979. "Regional Accreditation Evaluative Criteria and Quality Assurance." *Journal of Higher Education* 50: 199–210.

Van House, N. A. Beth T. Weil, and C. R. McClure. 1990. *Measuring Academic Library Performance: A Practical Approach.* Chicago: American Library Association.

Western Association of Schools and Colleges. 1991. *Summary of the WASC Presidents' Forum Panel Presentation: Evaluating Library Quality in the Accreditation Process: What Changes Do the New Technologies Bring?* San Francisco: Western Association of Schools and Colleges.

PART II
The Practice of Accreditation

4

Reflective Self-Study as Cornerstone of Accreditation: Part I

Edward D. Garten

Academic librarians and information specialists are increasingly familiar with the obligation to periodically review their organizational and operational processes. Most academic libraries conduct a yearly review as part of their budget cycle, and many conduct program reviews every three to five years. Many academic librarians and information specialists, however, have had little involvement in a broad sense with either institutional or disciplinary and professional self-studies. On occasion, the chief library or information officer will serve on an institutional self-study steering committee or a self-study subcommittee, or a librarian or two will be asked to serve on a self-study subcommittee. Even less frequent is the opportunity for a campus information professional to serve on a departmental accreditation study. More likely in the latter instance, the department chair of the department undergoing self-study will consult, as needed, with the appropriate information staff to obtain information for the self-study.

The purpose of this chapter will be (1) to define self-study, (2) to discuss the relationship of self-study to the academic process and suggest a model self-study process, and (3) to raise a set of questions that must be addressed within a typical self-study. Chapter 5 will (1) define the critical role of the self-study coordinator, (2) offer some observations relative to the final self-study report that is produced, and (3) offer recommendations relative to follow-up after the self-study is completed. Taken together, these facets of self-study should be of value in familiarizing the academic librarian and information professional with this historically important area of academic life.

WHAT IS SELF-STUDY?

At its best, the process of self-study involves both process and product. The process, at its best, is one that can lead to important new insights about the college or university. The process can lead to new affirmations about what is really important and valued within the institution. And the process can lead to new opportunities for innovation and change in a climate of new-found consensus among many campus constituencies.

Self-study is, again, at its best, a process through which a college, university, or academic program consciously describes, evaluates, and in follow-up steps, improves the overall quality of its efforts. Through self-study many campus individuals associated with campus units identify institutional and programmatic strengths and weaknesses. Fundamentally, the attitude toward self-study must involve a commitment to progressive and responsive change. Once an institution has completed a successful self-study, the process of reflection and programmatic refinement must continue into the future. Active, ongoing commitment to self-study reflects a conscious commitment to the notion of providing students and other constituencies with a quality educational experience. The benefits of quality institutional reflection will be proportional to the incisiveness of the initial inquiry. The aim of all self-study must be to understand, evaluate, and finally improve the institution. Describing what the institution is doing is simply not sufficient.

When done correctly the self-study becomes the most important part of the overall accreditation process. It offers the college or university opportunities for careful and critical self-analysis. Well-done self-study provides for objective feedback that will allow for the implementation of constructive change both during the accreditation review by the regional or disciplinary commission and in the period immediately following the formal site visit.

While the criteria and standards set forth by both the regional commissions and the many disciplinary and professional accrediting agencies are fundamental as reference points in self-study, it must always be kept in mind that self-study, as a process, is always local and unique in nature. Perhaps the Middle States Association has stated this best:

Because institutions are different, situations change over time, and external influences and internal conditions vary on every campus, several approaches to self-study and evaluation are available. No matter which approach is chosen, however, every institution should remember that the teaching and learning process is at the center of its endeavors and must, therefore, be a compelling concern in any self-study. Further, institutions should bear in mind that the assessment of student outcomes, by appropriate qualitative and quantitative means, is essential to judging institutional effectiveness. Finally, because national needs and priorities inevitably change, it is necessary to take stock of the extent to which graduating students will emerge prepared to deal with the future. (Middle States Association of Colleges and Schools 1991, 7)

The essence of excellent self-study is the systematic examination of the environment in which the institution operates. The twin objectives of the accrediting process—that of quality assessment and quality enhancement—depend on a reflective and thorough self-study.

A Unifying Vision of Quality in Self-Study

E. Grady Bogue in his 1992 book exploring the evidence for quality in American higher education has offered a unique and progressive way to look at quality, especially in the context of the reflective institutional or disciplinary self-study. Bogue talks about a unifying vision of quality, with such a vision opening "with the realization that there is no policy, no behavior, no practice, no value that does not have a direct impact on the condition of quality on a college or university campus" (258). In such a vision, he notes that the following perspectives will be honored:

- A philosophical perspective: The qualitative concerns of a campus constitute a philosophical window into its commitments and values.
- A definitional perspective: The definition of quality embraces both technical and ethical performance questions.
- A commitment perspective: The commitment to quality is one in which there is an awareness of and allegiance to quality that penetrates to the heart of the institution, constituting a premier call on administrative and faculty values.
- A client perspective: The judgments of quality attend first to the interests and developmental needs of our students and then to the interests of civic accountability.
- A time perspective: The time frame for evaluating quality is both short term and long term.
- A funding perspective: The linkage of quality to funding does not assume that quality always associates with funding in a linear relationship.
- A systems perspective: There is a coherent and logical system of interactions among the various institutional approaches to quality assurance, and this system is clearly linked to institutional purpose and decision needs.
- A proactive perspective: There is no waiting for the stimulus of agencies external to the campus—boards, legislatures, accrediting agencies, and so on. The campus demonstrates an aggressive and offensive initiative. (259)

The self-study is a mechanism for change within the institution. It is also a mechanism to help identify benchmarks for the administration and delivery of quality instruction. While a major focus of any self-study is the extent to which the organizational unit or institution complies with accreditation standards, it is also a period in which many campus leaders envision a higher-quality and more responsive future for the academic enterprise.

Types of Self-Study

There are typically four types of self-study in which an institution may be engaged. The most common institutional self-study is the comprehensive one in which virtually every aspect of the institution, including its governing and supporting structures, is reviewed. With established institutions a comprehensive self-study and visit is scheduled every ten years; however, previous commission actions may have stipulated a comprehensive review in five or seven years, or some other time frame. With some developing institutions, one often finds a comprehensive self-study performed every five years.

A second type of self-study might be termed the comprehensive self-study that at the same time emphasizes certain institutional programs or services. This type of self-study is becoming more common as institutions seek broad legitimacy and acceptance for one, two, or more relatively new initiatives. Conducting a specialized and focused review of these new programs (or older, more established programs, in some instances) at the same time that a comprehensive self-study is being undertaken can be quite valuable.

A third type of self-study gaining favor today might be termed the comprehensive self-study with strategic planning emphasis. This model is often chosen by those colleges or universities that have no strategic planning process in place or have chosen to retire an older and perhaps antiquated model of planning and move toward a newer and more refined model of planning.

Finally, some institutions choose to follow the focused review model of self-study whereby a particular academic or academic-support unit is intensively studied. Normally, following a focused self-study, a regional commission sends a small team to campus to conduct a focused visit. The process laying the groundwork for a focused visit in the case of a university library is discussed in Chapter 7 of this book. In some instances, a focused self-study and its subsequent site visit may be the outgrowth of a recommendation that issued from the prior comprehensive site team's visit.

Individuals experienced in self-study recognize that whatever model is chosen, self-study and long-range planning are closely related. Indeed, the distinction between the two may be only a matter of perspective. Self-study tends, by and large, to be more descriptive and evaluative, while long-range planning tends, in practice, to end with a document that is more prescriptive in nature. Institutional long-range planning can be strengthened when in-depth self-study becomes an integral component of the process. Daniel Brobst (1988) visualizes this assertion in Table 4.1.

RELATIONSHIP OF SELF-STUDY TO THE ACADEMIC PROCESS

All successful self-study is grounded in institutional commitment. It is critical that the college, university, or academic unit undergoing self-study perceive the

Table 4.1
Strengthening Long-Range Planning Through In-Depth Self-Study

Commitment		Institutional Research
Assessment of strengths and limitations	Institutional effectiveness	Factual and Assessment Information
Public Forum I (mission/ philosophy)	Mission and purpose	
Public Forum II (institutional goals)		
Identify planning objectives and action plans	Organization of resources	(Demographics, trends, forecasts, performance)
Prioritization of objectives	Future Commitment	
Implementation of plan		
Continual review of plan		

Source: Brobst 1988, 114.

centrality and importance of the self-study process. Institutional commitment can be found in one of several ways. First, there must be genuine leadership from senior administration. Appropriate senior administrators, indeed the president of the institution, must be involved with the development of the self-study plan from the beginning of the process. Senior administrators must be willing to offer advice and information at every stage of the self-study and demonstrate through their openness to the process that all institutional questions can and will be fairly addressed.

An important element in the relationship of self-study to the academic process can be found in the question posed by Mason (1988): "How does an institution use an on-going self-study process to monitor its changing character and status—and also to assess any warning signs that may threaten fulfillment of its vision?" (118).

In connecting any self-study plan to the academic process, faculty will play an essential role. Self-study steering committees need to obtain their support, in particular. Glenn (1992) has noted that the self-study coordinator "should let faculty know that they can assist by making available examples of the teaching/learning process and by agreeing to have their credentials reviewed by the evaluation team." He suggests, as well, that faculty "should be urged to respond to any institutional climate surveys that may be distributed as part of the self-study" (36).

A MODEL SELF-STUDY PROCESS

With regional accreditation self-studies, it is typical to see a commission staff person visit the campus undergoing self-study six months to a year before the self-study process commences. This visit will orient many campus leaders to the purposes and procedures of regional accreditation and familiarize those leaders with the current criteria and expectations of the commission. Typically, new commission emphases are highlighted during this visit. The visit will provide opportunities for campus leaders to have a face-to-face discussion with a commission representative. Normally, the commission representative will be either the commission's executive director or one of the associate directors. At times, another commission official or staff person may accompany this person to the campus undergoing self-study. Finally, a major function of the pre-self-study visit is to establish, in mutual fashion, the basis for determining the nature and scope of the soon-to-be-initiated self-study. During this visit the tentative date of the on-site visit normally is established. The commission representative likely will meet the self-study coordinator if he or she has been appointed, meet with the chief administrative and academic officers, and perhaps meet with a few individuals being considered for appointment to the self-study steering committee.

During the preplanning for self-study it is important to address, with as many individuals as possible, at least these questions:

1. What are the institution's mission, goals, and objectives and what educational obligations does it have?
2. Are these appropriate in its present time and place and for its present constituencies?
3. Are all of the institution's activities consistent with its mission and goals?
4. Are the goals and objectives of each program congruent with activities designed to achieve them?
5. Is there solid evidence that they are being achieved?

6. Are the human, physical, and fiscal resources needed to achieve institutional aims available now? Are they likely to be available for the foreseeable future? (Middle States Association of Colleges and Schools 1991, 19)

At this stage in the self-study process, it is typical to find the self-study coordinator submitting a self-study design to the regional commission. In many instances, disciplinary and professional accrediting agencies require also a draft outline of the model to be employed in self-study. Such plans might be expected to include:

1. A rationale for the self-study as well as a statement of the scope of the intended self-study. What type of self-study will it be, for example, comprehensive, comprehensive with emphases, comprehensive with strategic planning attached, or a focused self-study?
2. A statement describing the anticipated organizational structure of each subcommittee under the self-study steering committee.
3. A brief description of the methodology to be employed in gathering data that will be used in the self-study, including the type of questionnaires, surveys, or other instruments to be employed.
4. A brief discussion of departmental or programmatic self-studies that might have been conducted in the last three to five years and that may be relevant to the present proposed self-study.
5. A fairly detailed time line for the self-study.
6. A proposed outline of the final self-study report.

Data Collection

Self-study leaders will need to gather data in at least four areas: data on students, data on institutional financial resources, data on faculty, and data on instructional programs (Hooper 1991, 49). With respect to faculty, biographical information needs to be collected as well as educational and professional attainments. Information about faculty compensation, how faculty members are evaluated, and the faculty's role in the governance of the institution should be collected. In addition, it is useful to gather information relative to the faculty's role in determining course and degree requirements (Hooper 1991, 49).

Useful student information that may be gathered includes data about enrollment trends, retention rates, and graduation rates by school, division, and department. This information normally is obtained for a five-year period. Other student data that will be collected include information about how student achievement is measured and information that might suggest to what extent students are satisfied with their academic programs and campus life (Hooper 1991, 49).

When collecting data on institutional financial resources, a self-study steering committee will desire to obtain current information on fees and tuition and to

Table 4.2
Major Steps in the Process of Self-Study

Initiate self-study program.

Develop statement of program objectives.

Assign responsibilities for data collection to describe the program's status.

Collect data from the administration, instructional staff, student body, governing board, graduates of programs, employers of graduates, and other appropriate constituencies.

Evaluate data in light of stated objectives.

Assess program attainment of stated objectives.

Determine program strengths and limitations.

Develop plans for strengthening programs.

Ensure continuation of self-study in the future.

gain a sense of how dependent the institution is on grants and contractual research overhead. Information on fund-raising efforts and the cost per dollar raised is essential for inclusion in the self-study as is information on how budget decisions are made on the campus (Hooper 1991, 49–50). Information about the instructional program as well as the full range of instructional support programs needs to be obtained early in the self-study data-gathering process. Information about requirements for various degree programs needs to be obtained as well as information with respect to how decisions are made on courses, majors, and degrees to be offered. Critical as well is information on retention and graduation rates for all majors (Hooper 1991, 50). Hooper has noted that since a college or university's self-study ''requires an evaluation of how well the institution is achieving its mission now and how well it can achieve its mission in the future, data collection should provide information that can be used in this evaluation. In using data in the self-study, balance must be maintained between written descriptions of data on the one hand, and visual charts, graphs, and exhibits of data on the other'' (52). There is no question that an organized effort to collect and analyze information about the college or university can contribute substantially to a quality self-study effort.

A Flow Chart for Self-Study

While there are certainly a number of approaches that can be taken to the process of self-study, I have suggested a model in Table 4.2 that notes the key elements in a self-study process.

QUESTIONS THAT MUST BE ADDRESSED IN SELF-STUDY

At the outset of self-study, certain key questions need to be addressed if success is to be achieved. Field and McDonald (1991) have suggested at least four of the more important questions that need to be addressed early in the process:

- Is the self-study viewed as an opportunity or as a threat?
- Based on past performance, are there widely respected individuals whose active participation will promote thoughtful analysis while reducing institutional anxiety?
- Have institutional reviews in the past frequently encountered recurrent difficulties that might be avoided?
- How can fundamental institutional values be enlisted and validated as part of the self-study process? (40)

In an effective self-study, any institution will want to address a number of environmental questions. The Middle States Association of Colleges and Schools (1991) has suggested a number of such factors:

- Do you have a functioning strategic plan? Is it working? What forces, either internal or external, have affected the success of the planning?
- During the self-study period, will existing institutional research be plentiful and readily available? Moderately so? Not at all? What other accreditation bodies have or will require reviews in the next several years?
- Have the past five (or ten) years seen large changes in the institution's mission, goals and objectives? Its administration, faculty and staff? Its academic programs? What do the new people know about the institution?
- Is morale high and current participatory behavior productive? Since the self-study report is collaborative, which of the various approaches will best suit present levels of need, interest and involvement?
- Are the challenges and problems you face institution-wide? Program, system, or area related? Is the best way to tackle these issues to look at the whole picture in a relatively even-handed way or to single out areas of concern?
- All self-studies work over a minimum of 18 months. Would an approach spread over a longer period of time be more appropriate to your needs? (9)

In most self-study processes, leaders will want to review all college, division, or department self-studies or unit reviews that have been completed within the last five years. These often provide leads for areas that the present self-study will need to explore further. Some of the questions that should be asked of previous studies include the following suggested by Mary Jo Clark (1988):

- To what extent have institutional research and program review activities been focused on issues of importance to the institution as opposed to simply being exercises in number-crunching?

- Is there any evidence that results from these earlier self-studies or unit reviews have been used by and contributed to good planning and decision-making at the institution?
- What changes have resulted from the earlier studies and reviews which have been done?
- What is the coordination of earlier self-studies and unit reviews with the institution's planning and budgeting cycles?(106)

REFERENCES

Bogue, E. Grady. 1992. *The Evidence for Quality: Strengthening the Tests of Academic and Administrative Effectiveness.* San Francisco: Jossey-Bass.

Brobst, Daniel. 1988. "Self-Study and Long Range Planning: A Complementing Process." In *A Collection of Papers on Self-Study and Institutional Improvement.* Chicago: North Central Association of Colleges and Schools.

Clark, Mary Jo. 1988. "Strategies for Assessing the Quality of Systematic Institutional Evaluation and Research Efforts." In *A Collection of Papers on Self-Study and Institutional Improvement.* Chicago: North Central Association of Colleges and Schools.

Field, Michael, and Judy McDonald. 1991. "Overcoming Institutional Barriers to a Successful Self-Study." In *A Collection of Papers on Self-Study and Institutional Improvement.* Chicago: North Central Association of Colleges and Schools.

Glenn, Terrence J. 1992. "The Communication Challenge of the Self-Study Coordinator." In *A Collection of Papers on Self-Study and Institutional Improvement.* Chicago: North Central Association of Colleges and Schools.

Hooper, William L. 1991. "Data Collection for the Self-Study." In *A Collection of Papers on Self-Study and Institutional Improvement.* Chicago: North Central Association of Colleges and Schools.

Mason, David J. 1988. "Self-Study: Key to Successful Institutional Renewal and Change." In *A Collection of Papers on Self-Study and Institutional Improvement.* Chicago: North Central Association of Colleges and Schools.

Middle States Association of Colleges and Schools. 1991. *Designs for Excellence.* Philadelphia, Pa.: Middle States Association of Colleges and Schools.

5

Reflective Self-Study as Cornerstone of Accreditation: Part II

Edward D. Garten

This chapter, a continuation of the discussion started in Chapter 4, will (1) define the critical role of the self-study coordinator in the accreditation process; (2) offer insights into the development of the typical self-study report; and (3) offer some observations with respect to the work that needs to occur after a self-study cycle is completed. As with Part I, this chapter is meant to be of value to librarians and information specialists who have had little involvement with the institutional and disciplinary or professional accreditation and self-study processes as well as those individuals who are beginning to be involved in these processes.

THE CRITICAL ROLE OF THE SELF-STUDY COORDINATOR

All successful self-study begins from common reference points as well as confidence in the process. This is why the appointment of a recognized campus leader as self-study coordinator is so important. A good coordinator will be one who can help bring consensus to common institutional reference points but will also inspire confidence within many campus constituencies with respect to the integrity of the process to be employed.

Although one can imagine faculty members serving in the capacity of self-study coordinator, there are compelling advantages for the selection of an administrator for this role. Indeed, as Peters (1992) has suggested, a coordinator at the dean's level or above normally has more resources at his or her disposal to bring to bear on the self-study. Such an administrator can arrange for adequate secretarial assistance, computer support, hospitality considerations such as refreshments for committees, and so on. Assigning the role of coordinator to a higher-level administrator, so argues Peters, reflects the importance that the college or university attaches to the self-study process (30). My own experience would suggest, however, that good self-studies can be led quite ably by a senior faculty member who has had some significant campuswide leadership experience.

More important than position within the organization is the prospective coordinator's ability to answer some of the following questions suggested by Peters (1992):

1. Can I do this job and my regular job? If not, what provisions can be made to cover my regular assignments during my tenure as coordinator?
2. Will the institution set aside adequate funds for the task at hand?
3. Can I get help in the person of a professional secretary dedicated to the project?
4. Can I hire a writer or will I be expected to prepare the final self-study report personally?
5. Can I be assured that necessary equipment, such as computers, printers, telephones will be made available when they are so that the work can be kept separate from more routine College business?
6. Is the self-study to be a "global" one extending over all aspects of the institution or is it to address "special emphases"? (20)

Among the more important functions that the self-study coordinator will perform are those noted by Eric Gould (1992):

1. He or she will effectively manage the vast flow of information which is part of self-study. The coordinator will maintain the consistency of information flow, will assess the timelines of the materials which are passed to him or her, and will synthesize and interpret data as it becomes available.
2. He or she will provide reasonable schedules for obtaining information from the academic community and for preparing drafts of the self-study narrative.
3. The coordinator will maintain an effective ongoing dialogue in the academic community to allow for a shared and growing understanding of the self-study process.
4. The coordinator will allow for creative responses to attitudes which impede the self-study process. (45)

Gould has suggested that the self-study coordinator's role is one of "orchestrator of a community process of self-discovery" (47). Indeed, the self-study coordinator must take an active role in the design and implementation of the entire self-study process. It is critical, in the case of regional accreditation, for the self-study coordinator to make early contact with regional association's institutional liaison. Most likely, this contact will occur during the regional association's annual meeting and be followed up with letters and telephone conversations.

In taking an active role in the design of the self-study, the coordinator early will face the critical task of appointing self-study subcommittees. My own experience suggests that this is best done by forming functional committees headed by chairs who are recognized as efficient and effective group leaders. Committees that are formed along functional lines will often have individuals who have worked with each other on other projects. In addition, they will know who to call for specialized assistance. To bring balance to a committee, however, my own experience also suggests that the addition of one or two strong leaders from other, less related areas is useful to committee functioning. All subcommittees of the steering committee must, however, be kept involved, kept focused, and given sustained communication.

The responsibilities associated with being named self-study coordinator can be both daunting and overwhelming. These responsibilities can be rewarding as well. Perhaps the challenges of the coordinator's task are best summed up by Gould when he observes that these challenges are

not simply matters of timing and efficiency in producing the self-study document. They are not summed up by simple anxiety over the rate of responses, different writing styles from various contributors, or by having to tell the wood from the trees and some trees from others that look curiously alike. They do not even lie in deep fears on non-accreditation. They are, in the end, a matter of defining one's role not as a chronicler but as a lively facilitator and interpreter of the communal process of self-discovery and self-evaluation—which is a very subtle narrative indeed. (49)

THE WRITTEN SELF-STUDY REPORT

A final goal of all self-study is the creation of a report that will document the ability of the institution, or an academic program within the institution in the instance of disciplinary self-study, to comply with the standards set forth by the accrediting commission.

Timing is always important in the development of the written and final self-study report. As Zingg (1992) has observed, the first rule of timing is to "set each timeline for early completion. Rule two is to have a backup timeline (not published) that is still early. Rule three is to have a third timeline that still gets the work done on time. Expect that some work will be done by the first timeline, some by the second timeline, and some by the third timeline. Plan your resources, reviews, and final completion accordingly" (33).

Perhaps one of the places that has bogged down or substantially delayed many written self-study reports can be found in the area of surveys. Nearly all institutional self-studies use surveys to provide important data for analysis, and one must be aware that they often take longer to prepare and to complete than is typically thought going into the self-study process. Analysis of survey data can also delay the written report for several reasons. Zingg has noted that first "the data must be appropriate in order to derive the desired perspective of the outcome. Make sure that the gathered data are appropriate to provide the needed result" (34). Second, Zingg observes that "analysis can get bogged down in detail and wind up answering the wrong questions. Maintain a high level of focus and keep the report perspective in mind during all reviews" (24). Finally, he notes that "analysis can place the outcome into a perspective that is not appropriate for the question being asked" (34).

Statistical and demographic summaries, in graphic and tabular form, should be appropriately included in the final written document. Conciseness in the report is suggested, and supportive data and appendices documenting the body of the report should be included, often as a separate volume of the self-study.

During each stage aiming toward the final written report, one must not assume that the work that must be done will be carried out in a timely fashion. Every self-study represents an increase in workload for many people on campus—and in some instances, a hefty increase in workload. A self-study coordinator can expect to spend much time in helping campus leaders and contributors to the self-study maintain focus and perspective.

A strong editor is essential in producing a readable and ultimately useful self-study. As is often the case, the editor may be a member of the English Department. The editor may also be appointed a member of the self-study steering committee as a way of familiarizing him or her with the process. In the end, the self-study report should reflect the various reports from the subcommittees as faithfully as possible and yet should read as a common document. Most self-study coordinators will allow a month prior to the due date for final editing and printing. Copies are then mailed to the individuals who have been appointed to serve on the visitation team.

RESPONDING TO THE TEAM REPORT

Once finished with a self-study, some institutions file the accreditation report and take it out only a year or so before the next self-study cycle is to begin. Smart institutions, though, realize that today self-studies are part of a continuing institutional planning process, and the recommendations resulting from self-studies and on-site visits must be acted on early.

It is highly desirable, almost immediately following the exit interview, for the institution to commence to address those areas that have been identified for correction or remediation. Ideally, the process of institutional self-study should culminate with a goal-setting process that incorporates an explicit set of activities that are deemed appropriate to accomplish these goals. Institutions typically assign this duty and accompanying authority to one individual. While the self-study coordinator might be viewed as the ideal person for this job, he or she may desire to exit the process at this point. In many instances, follow-up coordination is assigned to a member in the institutional planning office or a campus opinion leader who has served on the self-study steering committee.

Ruth M. Roberts (1988), in working with self-study at the University of Arkansas at Pine Bluff, has suggested that, indeed, the steering committee can, if willing, be used to address issues or problems identified by the visitation team. She suggests the following four-stage model that might be employed:

1. Making the Commitment to Resolving the Issues
   a. When should the commitment be made?
   b. Who should be involved?
   c. Whose support is needed?
   d. What are the advantages and the pitfalls?
2. Establishing the Process to Resolve the Issues
   a. What is the focus?
   b. What is the charge?
   c. How is it to be implemented?
3. The Follow-Up
   a. Which concerns have been adequately addressed?
   b. Which concerns are ongoing?
   c. What, if any, new concerns have arisen?
4. Summary Report
   a. Response to institutional concerns.
   b. Recommendations. (162)

Institutions successfully completing the self-study cycle often display the same emotion among staff, faculty, and administrators: emotions of relief and joy that the job has been completed. But as Cook, Avant, and Nutter (1991) have noted: "the primary interest of most campus personnel, a good bottom line, that last line in the Team Report, is not what will propel the institution to higher levels of accomplishment. In fact, it is the many words proceeding this bottom line, particularly the sections titled concerns, strengths, and advice and suggestions, and can be the catalysts for continued institutional improvement. . . . Regardless of what the bottom line recommendation is," they point out, "the team recommendations and suggestions are truly the silver lining of the report if studied, discussed, and acted upon by the institution" (94–95).

LEVERAGING SUCCESS

As Susan Carroll (1991) has pointed out, there is "no penalty for articulating the desired future within the self-study, when such statements address the ways by which students may be better served through, for example, a more comprehensive library, better laboratory equipment, or more modern facilities" (92). She points out that the self-study report can be leveraged quite effectively with many constituencies. She also notes that "institutions should consider the publication and wide distribution of a special announcement that highlights strengths cited by the evaluation team. Such good news accentuates the positive image of the institution within the community'' (92). And, she notes, ''a favorable accreditation report, like all awards, honors, and recognition, should be viewed as part of the institution's 'resume' '' (92).

The events that occur immediately after the institutional self-study are critical to the future of the institution. As Lila Seaman (1990) has observed, in effective self-study ''the relationship of self-study to planning has been strengthened; new links have been made between research, planning, and allocation of resources'' (92). In effective self-study and in effective follow-up, the purposes of the self-study will ''have been effected through the courageous leadership of the administration, judicious allocation of resources, strategic planning, and dedicated contribution of personnel'' (92).

CONCLUDING OBSERVATIONS

In the end, what are some of the benchmarks of successful institutional or disciplinary self-study? My own experience in working with three self-study steering committees and in observing the work of many more would suggest the following benchmarks.

1. Successful self-study begins and ends with the support of key people on campus. All successful self-study has the early and consistent support of the institution's president, opinion leaders within the faculty, and the heads of major academic support units.

2. The most successful self-studies are, from the outset, very clear about their goals and objectives. There is careful early attention, as well, to the methodologies to be employed and the kind of data to be collected during the course of the self-study.

3. Successful self-studies start with a plan that is carefully written and discussed with a range of campus constituencies and the executive officers of the regional or disciplinary accreditation association.

4. The formulation of adequate and appropriate committees reporting to the steering committee is critical to the task of self-study. Each committee must have a chair who is respected campuswide. Informed and focused committees are essential to data gathering and interpretation.

5. The time line for the entire self-study process is absolutely critical. More than a few self-studies have faltered due to inadequate and short time frames for various parts of the self-study.

6. Remember that while carving out adequate time in many individuals' schedules to actually do self-study is critical, self-study itself is experience. Those involved in self-study leadership are typically those involved in other day-to-day aspects of campus leadership. Deploy their talents and time in self-study in a targeted fashion.

7. Employ the use of surveys with great care. Using too many surveys and in untargeted fashion can become an impediment to producing a timely report. The best institutional

self-studies employ no more that two campuswide surveys in addition to a few more targeted and focused area surveys.

8. Do not assume that all campus groups and individuals are onboard the self-study process or even are aware of their need to be involved in the self-study. Self-study leaders must expect to spend much time in communicating, focusing, and maintaining an awareness level among many constituencies during all stages of the self-study process.

Self-study is a deliberate and substantive activity that requires a fundamental resolve on the part of many campus constituencies to comply with both the spirit and requirements of external accreditation commissions. As such, it requires extensive preplanning as well as active coordination during its life to be successful. Because it is a voluntary activity, self-study requires positive and supportive leadership that moves the process toward a final written report that embodies the recognized strengths and limitations of the institution. By way of its institutional reflections, made real through a written and widely disseminated report, the college or university says to both internal and external stakeholders: "This report clearly and candidly describes and reflects on who we are and what we intend to be." In the final analysis the quality of the self-study will say much about the nature and quality of the institution. Those who guide the process of self-study are obligated to explore both institutional data and the collective memories of the institution. No self-study process can be guided by a set, formulaic checklist. As Gould (1992) has noted, it is "the essential personality of an institution that the self-study seeks to describe, and this, in a sense, is the telling afresh of one's story to oneself and others, as if for the first time" (46).

REFERENCES

Carroll, Susan C. 1991. "Making Good on Your Promises: Planning for Future Effectiveness." In *A Collection of Papers on Self-Study and Institutional Improvement.* Chicago: North Central Association of Colleges and Schools.

Cook, Jim, Linda Avant, and Larry Nutter. 1991. "After the Visit: Ongoing Self-Study and Institutional Improvement." In *A Collection of Papers on Self-Study and Institutional Improvement.* Chicago: North Central Association of Colleges and Schools.

Gould, Eric. 1992. "Enlivening the Self-Study Process: The Coordinator's Role." In *A Collection of Papers on Self-Study and Institutional Improvement.* Chicago: North Central Association of Colleges and Schools.

Peters, Till J. N. 1992. "Finding the Handle: Getting the Self-Study Process Off the Ground." In *A Collection of Papers on Self-Study and Institutional Improvement.* Chicago: North Central Association of Colleges and Schools.

Roberts, Ruth M. 1988. "After the Visit: Ongoing Self-Study and Institutional Improvement." In *A Collection of Papers on Self-Study and Institutional Improvement.* Chicago: North Central Association of Colleges and Schools.

Seaman, Lila. 1990. "Beyond Self-Study: Responding to the Findings of a Self-Study

Report.'' In *A Collection of Papers on Self-Study and Institutional Improvement.*
Chicago: North Central Association of Colleges and Schools.

Zingg, John A. 1992. ''Ten Suggestions for Successful Self-Study.'' In *A Collection of Papers on Self-Study and Institutional Improvement.* Chicago: North Central Association of Colleges and Schools.

6

Understanding the Purpose and Nature of the Site Visit

Edward D. Garten

The on-site visit to the institution is one of the more critical, if not the most critical, stages of the overall self-study and accreditation process. The weeks that lead up to the visit by a group of academic peers are always hectic with loose ends and logistical arrangements being resolved. It is typical to find some level of anxiety present on both sides of the on-site visit process. First, various self-study leaders on the local campus may feel some sense of insecurity at this stage. Have all the bases been covered? Have we disclosed ourselves, as an institution, in as fair of a fashion as we can within the written self-study? Will this outside team put us on the spot and reflect our weaknesses back to us in a highly critical fashion? Self-study teams, themselves, even though they have read through much material about the institution and its programs can evidence some anxiety just prior to the visit as well. Will there be surprises during the visit for which we as a team have not prepared? Is the institution experiencing some level of conflict or internal friction, and will these tensions be reflected on the team in negative and unproductive ways?

The on-site visit is critical to the total accreditation process and cannot be taken lightly. The purpose of this chapter is to illuminate the on-site visit in both its theoretical and practical dimensions. While the chapter focuses largely on the on-site process associated with the regional accreditation commission visit, many of the observations hold as well for visits by representatives of professional and disciplinary associations.

ASSUMPTIONS BEHIND THE SITE VISIT

Accreditation in American higher education has always been seen as a process of peer review. Peers holding expertise in academic and administrative areas work with peers from other institutions in a continual process of self-improvement and refinement. The on-site visit is at once consultative and evaluative.

Regional commissions and disciplinary/professional accreditation associations select members for appointment to visitation teams from their evaluator or consultant registries. Commission or association staff match the experiences and credentials of each potential committee member with the needs of the institution to be visited. Faculty and administrators are placed on evaluator registries after having been recommended by their presidents or other senior administrators and after having been reviewed by members of the commission. Once selected for a consultant-evaluator registry, a future team member will be asked to participate in a new consultant-evaluator training program. Individuals selected to serve on professional or disciplinary accreditation teams must have a broad understanding of the profession or discipline and an appreciation for the purposes of accreditation. All individuals selected for service on visitation teams need to have strong communication skills, strong interview skills, and skills in maintaining appropriate interpersonal relationships. They should have the ability to critically analyze, verbalize, and record pertinent objective data during a visit. And finally, individuals selected to serve on teams should have the professional commitment to give the extensive time that site visits require in terms of reading and study.

SELECTION OF VISITING TEAMS

It is typical for the staff of each of the regional commissions to identify in the spring or summer of each year the team chairs for those institutions to be visited in the following academic year. Team chairs are seasoned consultant-evaluators who have had experience working with institutions of the type to be visited. Normally, institutions are provided an opportunity to review the team chair nominations. Moreover, institutions to be visited normally are given a list of commission-suggested team members. On occasion, an institution will wish a name struck from the list and replaced with another suggestion; however, the final team composition always rests with the accreditation commission.

In offering observations to the commission or accrediting agency, the institution also has an opportunity to identify particular academic areas that ought to be represented on the team in order that the institution might take advantage of a team member's consultative expertise. Often, an institution is concerned with making certain that at least a few of the team members are familiar with its kind of institution, for example, public or private, independent or strongly church related, traditional or nontraditional (Forbes 1988, 24). Commissions often will accommodate these team composition requests if possible.

Avoiding Conflict of Interest

Conflicts of interest can arise when conditions preclude or interfere with a team member's capacity to make the detached and objective decisions and judgments that the accreditation process requires. Some of the conditions that may create a conflict of interest include the following: (1) A potential team member has a personal or professional relationship to the institution to be visited; (2) a potential team member has a financial interest in the institution to be visited; (3) the potential team member has been a recent consultant to the institution or has a commitment to serve as a consultant to the institution near the time of the proposed team visit; (4) the potential team member works in close proximity to the institution to be visited or is employed as a faculty member or administrator in an institution in the same system; (5) the potential team member is a graduate of a degree program at the institution to be visited; or (6) the potential site visitor, within the last few years, has sought employment with the institution to be visited. These factors are often considered as primary conflicts of interest with respect to the appointment of team members to regional commission teams. However, professional or disciplinary associations may have other factors that they consider conflicts of interest, to include (1) having been a former student with an academic program up for review; (2) having a family connection with a particular academic program—example, one's spouse may be a graduate of the program; (3) having close friends who are associated with the academic program in faculty or administrative roles; (4) having trained with key personnel in the program being reviewed; and (5) having a close professional acquaintance with the academic leadership of the program.

PREPARATION FOR THE VISIT

Self-study coordinators and many self-study steering committee members, and perhaps others, will want to be involved in helping the accrediting commission or association design the on-site visit. The coordinator most likely will have several lengthy conversations with the person who has been designated as team chair. These conversations will help establish the overall tone of the visit, further refine the process itself, and assure both sides that logistical arrangements are in order. Self-study coordinators will want to meet with various campus opinion leaders to make certain that these individuals know that visiting team members are to be viewed both as evaluators and as consultants. Indeed, individuals on campus should make as much use of team members in their consultative role as time will allow.

All of those who have been involved in the self-study process will want to review the self-study a few weeks before the visit. The self-study coordinator will want to make an announcement of the visit in various campus news publications. He or she will want to make certain that the entire academic community is aware of the purposes of the visit. It may also be wise to identify university trustee or board members who may desire to talk with members of the team. The academic deans will want to urge their department chairs and program directors to be on campus during the visit. These people should be asked to clear their calendars, as much as possible, during the visit. However, team members realize that an institution cannot come to a grinding halt for the three or four days of a team visit. Team members realize that the normal operation of the university must continue and typically show some scheduling flexibility themselves. Board members, faculty, and staff also should be briefed on the expectations for a team visit. Typically, this is done through the release of a campuswide memorandum that lists the names of team members and the institutions with which they are affiliated and their responsibilities there. If there are open meetings, for instance, for faculty or support staff, then this information normally will be included in the campus memorandum.

THE RESOURCE ROOM

At an early point in the preparation for the visit, the self-study coordinator will want to make certain that a comfortable resource room is prepared. The resource or exhibit room should include a broad range of institution documents including brochures, viewbooks, catalogs, departmental or area self-studies, or reviews, curricular white papers and planning documents, statistical analyses of various aspects of the institution, and copies of audited budgets. Several team members likely will be interested in an examination of the institution's financial affairs. Financial data given to the institution's board of trustees should be provided for the current and immediate past years. If available, the projected budget for the next fiscal year is valuable as well. Financial experts who may be part of a team are interested in documents that show institutional revenues, expenses, assets, liabilities, and fund balances.

It is also helpful for the self-study coordinator to make available in the resource room various college or university organizational charts, schedules of classes (since some team members may like to visit a few classes in session), and building and room numbers of key contacts on campus. All of the documents in the exhibit room should be clearly marked, corresponding to a specific category of the standards or criteria. Finally, it is always a gesture of hospitality to have coffee, other drinks, and fruit available in the resource room.

In order for the team to get the most from its evaluation visit, it needs as much information about the institution as that institution can provide. In an information-rich environment, the team can more rapidly gain a clear and comprehensive picture of the institution.

Final preparation for the visit will include preparation of clear campus maps, directions to off-campus locations, and details on arrangements to escort team members from meeting location to meeting location. The latter arrangements are particularly appropriate and important at an especially large institution or at an institution where there will be team visits to many off-site instructional locations. Team members are very busy in their three or four days. Making them more comfortable with the physical environment in which they will be working is not an insignificant detail.

TYPICAL VISIT SCENARIO

Regional accreditation teams normally begin their work on a Sunday afternoon. This is often the case, as well, for many of the disciplinary and professional accrediting agencies where three-day on-site visits are commonly employed. Team members get acquainted in the hotel conference room that has been provided for them and often, later in the afternoon or evening, are invited to a welcoming reception hosted by the president and other officers of the college or university. Following the opening reception, the team returns to their workroom where the chair will set forth a tentative work agenda, raise issues or concerns that only he or she may be aware of, and generally set the context for a cooperative and productive team information-gathering and analysis effort.

From its earlier reading of the self-study report as well as other materials that the institution has provided, the team will begin to develop questions to explore during the site visit. It is not uncommon to find team members noting additional information that they would like to secure early the first workday. Self-study coordinators can be helpful to a team by calling the chair late Sunday evening to inquire if there are materials that he or she might secure early the next day.

On Monday morning the team will have a meeting with the president and selected other administrators, the self-study coordinator, and perhaps a few members of the self-study steering committee. Following this brief meeting, many team members will desire to set up appointments and interview sessions with selected administrators and program directors. The president's office typically supplies secretarial support to assist in this logistical coordination. Often the president's office will provide team members with microcomputers or laptop computers as a way of facilitating their work. At this point, team members fan out across campus, visiting with many people during the day. If off-campus instructional sites are to be visited, they are normally visited the first day if arrangements can be made.

Each evening, team members will compare notes and discuss observations that have been made during the day. Typically, on a three-day visit beginning on Sunday, Monday evening is the time when team members will have many initial observations to share. Often, some of these initial impressions deserve additional investigation on Tuesday, and a chair will often assign one or two team members the responsibility to follow up on these impressions, ask additional questions, and seek out additional data that may shed light on a situation that might be suspected. By the Tuesday evening meeting, a consensus will have developed with respect to the institution's strengths and weaknesses. Indeed, by late Tuesday evening the team's recommendations are being drafted. While it is fairly uncommon to serve on teams where discussions last well into the night, it can happen if consensus cannot be reached. An astute chair and aggressive team members, however, can normally move toward consensus with most institutional visits by nine or ten o'clock. An exit interview is then scheduled with the president for Wednesday morning if the team is involved with a three-day visit. Four- or five-day visits are sometimes called for with institutions having numerous off-campus instructional locations that might include team member travel to other states and to military installations. On occasion, a team member may be asked to review an institution's international instructional site.

TEAM PROTOCOL

Team members must always remember that the institution being visited is measured against its own objectives and not the objectives of the team members' institutions. While it is rare for a team member to bring his or her own institutional prejudices or bias along on a visit, it is wise to continually guard against the possibility of showing any bias. In addition, it is wise to avoid such suggestions as, "This is the way I think you should do it," or "This is the way we do this where I am employed." The site visitor must always remember that he or she has the role to verify information in the self-study; that role *does not* include sharing a "right" way of doing things with the institution.

Earlier it was noted that team members need to have good skills in interviewing. This is true simply because much of a team member's day is spent in interview contexts. As team members appear in various offices, initiating discussions, they will attempt to start the interview on a general topic and place the interviewee at ease. They will state their position on the team and attempt to create an atmosphere of openness. Following an interview, they may indicate that they may find a need to return later in the visit for additional conversation and information.

Site visitors must always maintain a posture of flexibility. They must demonstrate consistency in judgment and action and yet recognize that desirable change and accommodation may also be necessary. Most of all, they must recognize that accreditation is the application of professional judgment in the absence of absolute standards. And they must be judicious since the integrity of accreditation depends on its quality of judgment.

There are always a number of written and unwritten protocols that visitors are expected to observe. In its site visitor's manual, the American Speech-Language-Hearing Association (1992) has delineated some of the more obvious behavioral expectations for its site visitors. Listed below is a sampling of these expectations:

- Site visitors should allow sufficient time to satisfy comfortably all commitments of the visit; late arrivals and early departures should be avoided.
- Site visitors should exercise tact and care in everything they say and do, both when soliciting information and when answering questions. The site visitors are invited guests

of the institution and are expected to render a professional service for which the facility has paid.

- Site visitors should exhibit an attitude of encouragement. Words with negative connotations should be avoided, as should reprimands and lectures.

- Site visitors must maintain confidentiality. All information gathered by the site visitors is confidential. Problems in the specific facility must never be discussed with others.

- Site visitors should appear calm and confident, although it is normal to feel some apprehension the first time one serves as a site visitor. A site visitor should not inform people at the site that he/she is inexperienced and that he/she hopes that they will make allowances for it.

- Site visitors should be sensitive to feelings of anxiety or apprehension evidenced by others during the site visit review.

- Site visitors should use extreme caution to avoid any situation that might be construed as affecting their integrity or objectivity in the site visit process.

- Site visitors should not indicate whether they believe the program being visited will be awarded accreditation or not. (9)

Other protocols have been suggested in more humorous yet still meaningful fashion by Hector Lee (1976) in his much-quoted "ten commandments" for on-site visitors:

- Don't Snitch: Site visitors often learn private matters about an institution that an outsider has no business knowing. Don't "tell tales" or talk about the weaknesses of an institution.

- Don't Steal Apples: Site visitors often discover promising personnel. Don't take advantage of the opportunity afforded by your position on the team to recruit good faculty members.

- Don't Be on the Take: Site visitors may be invited to accept small favors, services, or gifts from the institution. Don't accept, or even suggest, that you would like to have a sample of the wares of an institution—a book it publishes, a product it produces, or a service it performs.

- Don't Be a Candidate: Site visitors might see an opportunity to suggest themselves for a consultantship, temporary job, or a permanent position with the institution. Don't apply or suggest your availability until after your site visit report has been officially acted on.

- Don't Be a Nit Picker: Site visitors often see small problems that can be solved by attention to minor details. Don't use the accreditation report, which should deal with major or serious policy-level matters, as the means of effecting minor mechanical reforms.

- Don't Shoot Small Game with a Big Gun: The accreditation process is developmental, not punitive. Don't use accreditation to deal heavily with small programs that may feel that they are completely at the mercy of the site visitors.

- Don't Be a Bleeding Heart: Site visitors with "do good" impulses may be blinded by good intentions and try to play the role of savior. Don't compound weakness by sentimental generosity in the hope that a school's problems will go away if ignored or treated with unwarranted optimism.

- Don't Push Dope: Site visitors often see an opportunity to recommend their personal theories, philosophies, or techniques as the solution to a program's problems. Don't suggest that an institution adopt measures that may be altered or reversed by the review committee or by subsequent site visit teams.

- Don't Shoot Poison Darts: A committee may be tempted to "tip off" the administration suspected treachery or warn one faction on campus of hidden enemies. Don't poison the minds of the staff or reveal suspicious to the administration; there are more wholesome ways to alert an administration to hidden tensions.

- Don't Worship Sacred Cows: Don't be so in awe of a large and powerful institution that you are reluctant to criticize an obvious problem in some department. (3–4)

THE EXIT INTERVIEW

With regional commission visits, exit interviews are typically held in late morning of the last day of the visit, normally Wednesday if the visit began on Sunday. Most likely, the chief administrative officer will invite those individuals to the exit interview who were present at the initial entrance interview, although some presidents choose to invite only their president's council or other smaller leadership body. Team chairs always explain that the exit interview is not a time to debate the report that is to follow; rather, the exit interview is simply the formal time for the team to verbally report the strengths, concerns, and recommendations that it has found. It is important that the verbal report not differ substantially from the subsequent written report that comes back to the institution.

While exit interviews are normally quite pleasant, cordial, straightforward, and above all, brief, there can be the occasional exit interview that is stiff, awkward, and even exceedingly uncomfortable due to the critical nature of the news that must be conveyed. If very unpleasant news is to be voiced by the team, it is wise for the team chair to confer privately with the chief administrative officer an hour or so before the exit interview. By doing this, some of the tension may be avoided and a more cordial foundation laid for the exit interview. Following the verbal report (which typically does not include all of the suggestions and certainly very little of the narrative of the final report), the team will depart from the campus. Hands are shook, best wishes are extended, and the team is on its way.

THE TEAM REPORT

Typically, a draft report is ready to be sent to the institution about four weeks after the on-site visit. The chair sends the report to the chief administrative officer of the institution with the instruction that he or she is to read the report and correct errors of fact only. It is rare that the leadership of an institution will argue with the content of the report and demand changes of substance, but this can occur. Team chairs will very rarely offer to make substantive changes in draft reports, preferring to allow the institution to go to an appeals process established by the regional commission or the disciplinary or professional accreditation association. After the institution receives the draft report, it is invited to make a formal and written response to the report.

Experience reflects a number of guidelines that visiting teams need to follow in leading up to the final report. Perhaps the American Psychological Association (1991) has best summarized some of these guidelines:

- Visitors should not leave the site visit until an outline of the report has been established and agreed upon.
- Before leaving, the site visitors should agree upon the recommendation regarding accreditation status and the reasons for the recommendation.
- The site visitors should be certain as to specific assignments in regard to writing assignments.
- The site visitors should agree upon a date for first draft and revisions.
- The report should be of reasonable length. Short, declarative, simple reports that convey the integrations, impressions, evaluations, and recommendations of the site visit team are preferred.
- The report should avoid superlatives, hyperboles, and pejorative speculation.
- In the report, the site visit team can refer to the self-study supplied by the program for factual information and statistical data that, if they seem to be accurate to the site visitors, need not be repeated in the report.

CONCLUSION

Maestas (1988) has observed that "the more open and receptive the institution is to the on-site visit, the more productive and beneficial the experience can be" (151). He goes on to note:

Having completed the rigorous process of self-study required before the site visit, the institution has bared its soul and identified all aspects of its strengths, weaknesses, opportunities, and aspirations. This process enables the institution to take a critical, inward view of itself and to review its mission and purposes, its resources, plans and needs. The awareness of the institution's status, coupled with the participative spirit permeating the faculty, staff, students, and all entities involved in the self-study process, charges the atmosphere with positive vibrations which are advantageous in making the on-site visit success full. The atmosphere created within the institution during the self-study process and the preparedness for the visit have a direct correlation to the success of the on-site visit. (151)

Individuals experienced with both institutional and disciplinary/professional on-site visits realize that the success of the visit depends heavily on the preparations that are made prior to the visit. A positive and reflective frame of reference on the part of many campus constituencies is critical as well. Most important, after the visit the institution's ability to view the site-visit report as a framework for institutional self-improvement is essential.

REFERENCES

American Psychological Association. 1991. *Handbook on Accreditation.* Washington, D.C.: American Psychological Association.

American Speech-Language-Hearing Association. 1992. *Site-Visitor's Manual.* Rockville, Md.: American Speech-Language-Hearing Association.

Forbes, Malcolm H. 1988. "Making the Most of the On-Site Visit." In *A Collection of Papers on Self-Study and Institutional Improvement.* Chicago: North Central Association of Colleges and Schools.

Lee, Hector. 1976. "A Decalogue for the Accreditation Team." In *Council on Postsecondary Education (COPE) Agenda*, Washington, D.C., February 5, 1976.

Maestas, Sigfredo. 1988. "Making the Most of the On-Site Visit." In *A Collection of Papers on Self-Study and Institutional Improvement.* Chicago: North Central Association of Colleges and Schools.

7

The Focused Visit: A Special Type of Library Assessment

Susanne O. Frankie

In addition to institutional and program accreditation, accrediting agencies also conduct focused visits. Such visits, which occur between comprehensive visits, are used to evaluate specific areas or issues within an institution or to review proposed institutional changes. This chapter will discuss focused visits mandated by the accrediting body to evaluate a specific area within an institution—the academic library.

In most respects, the policies and procedures governing focused evaluations are similar to those governing comprehensive evaluations; however, there are some differences among regional accrediting bodies. The policies and procedures described here reflect those of the North Central Association of Colleges and Schools. Instead of an institutional self-study, an institution undergoing a focused visit prepares a report that addresses the areas to be evaluated. Such reports will vary considerably in concept, structure, and length, and an institution has wide latitude in preparing the report. However, such reports should include notation of accrediting agency action or policy that prompted the visit, explanations of actions taken in the areas to be examined, an evaluation of the progress made since the last evaluation, and indication of any further actions that may be planned (North Central Association of Colleges and Schools 1990).

The focused evaluation team is not charged with evaluating whether an institution fulfills the criteria for accreditation; nor is it empowered to recommend that candidacy or accreditation be granted, continued, or denied. In special circumstances, the team can recommend that sanction or probation be applied, or that a program, site, or other operation be restricted or even discontinued.

Typically, for a focused visit, a two- or three-person team is sent to campus for a two-day visit to determine if the institution has addressed the areas of concern, to assess the impact of significant changes related to the areas, and to provide the accrediting agency with a progress report on developments at the institution since the last evaluation. Preparations for activities during the visit may be similar (if on a smaller scale) to those needed for an institutional evaluation, for example, meetings with administrators, interviews with faculty and staff, and review of documentation on-site.

The evaluation of an academic library poses special problems for accrediting agencies for several reasons. Because of the rapid and dramatic changes occurring in the scholarly communication infrastructure and processes, the role of the academic library is changing in fundamental ways. The economics of academic libraries and the new capabilities available through computers dictate that academic libraries today must move beyond the traditional concept of serving as repositories for printed information that is purchased and made available on-site to patrons. Rather, academic libraries are evolving into information utilities, which provide access to information wherever it is located. Thus, new mechanisms that provide for sharing resources, for reciprocal borrowing agreements, and for alternative delivery mechanisms for information located elsewhere are becoming the central organizing components for the way academic libraries design and offer services.

However, as noted by Ronald Leach (1992), the changes occurring in academic libraries, generally speaking, have not been acknowledged by accrediting bodies in their evaluations, and it may be some time before evaluation guidelines and team members are fully cognizant of the changing role of academic libraries and of how the impact of technology is changing the definition of what constitutes quality in library services.

The criteria used by these agencies continues to focus on input measures, and too often, team members still think in terms of information ownership. They may still count books on the shelves and seek figures for dollars spent on collection building rather that on dollars spent on information access including activities relating to resource sharing, networking and expedited document delivery. Because of this, caution must be exercised to avoid simply throwing money at the problem as defined by the accrediting agency, particularly if there is some question as to the validity of their definition of the problem. If the defined problem is that the book collection is too small, a knee-jerk solution is to buy and shelve more books in the library. But if the real problem is the need for ready access to information needed by faculty and students, allocating funds to obtain borrowing privileges from other institutions, to purchase articles on demand, to access electronic data bases, and to provide networking capabilities may be more effective and efficient ways of addressing the need for more and better access to information.

In time, accrediting agencies (and university administrators, faculty, and students also) will come to accept these options. For a time, an institution preparing for a focused library visit needs to test access concepts with the accrediting agency and needs to be prepared to educate the team members who may arrive with collection standards and statistics in hand, seeking evidence of significant collection growth and budget increases.

As a framework for preparing for a focused visit to the library, there are three critical components to be considered: (1) the institution's role, mission, and vision for the future; (2) the university administration's view of the visit; and (3) the accrediting agency's criteria for evaluating academic libraries. Of these three, by far the most critical for the campus visit coordinator is the administration's view of the seriousness of the "library problem" and the importance of the focused visit in the larger scheme of things. There may be a complex set of political dynamics operating as an institution undergoes a focused library visit. Administrators in the institution may regard the library problem on the campus as considerably less important and less pressing than many other problems confronting them. Particularly, they may look on the visit as an unwelcome and costly interference by an outside agency. Their irritation may be exacerbated by the fact that library staff, faculty, and students may be required to address some long-standing library problems.

Suffice it to say that the occasion of a focused visit should unite, not divide, the campus. Therefore, political skills are needed to ensure that there is a common campus agenda for the conduct and outcomes of the visit, including a proper tone employed in the preparation of the reports and documentation prior to the visit and in interviews and meetings during the visit. Beyond this, however, there is no one right way to prepare for a focused visit. The preparation for such a visit can involve the use of outside consultants, dozens of people on campus, hundreds of clock hours, and thousands of dollars. Or it can involve considerably less than these. Sometimes, less is more, or perhaps more accurately, sometimes less is *sufficient*. It is easy to become distracted with all of the information that could be used to describe the resources and services of an academic library, or even to raise issues and concerns not identified in the previous evaluation that prompted the focused visit. This should be avoided. For a focused visit, it is important to *focus* on specific concerns expressed by the accrediting team. The important thing, at the outset, is to determine the amount of time and effort the visit warrants, based on institutional values and administrative priorities.

At a minimum, administrative approval is needed of an outline of the report to be sent to the accrediting agency, of a schedule of activities planned to prepare for the visit, and a proposed budget. A listing of the kinds of documentation and data needed and materials to be assembled for the team inspection on-site also should be compiled.

Returning to the other two critical components to be considered to preparing for a visit, it is important to be able to articulate the relationship of the library to the institution's mission and vision. In addition, it is also important that the institution is in contact with the accrediting agency prior to the visit, particularly if fundamental concepts relating to the changing role of the library are at issue, for example, the extent to which the agency views information access as a viable option to information ownership in fulfilling the role of the library in supporting academic programs. If the agency is willing to accept your premises, an institution can proceed with some confidence with its planning and preparation for the visit. If the accreditation agency is unable to accept these premises, an institution may have a serious problem on its hands, and the institution's administration must decide how to proceed.

Certainly, in the case of the academic library that serves the entire academic institution, the accreditation visit can be an important vehicle for education:

• Accreditation is an important vehicle for educating our campus administration and campus community: to our role, our policies, our costs, and choices we are making, and the reason for making the choices we do.

• Accreditation may be a useful mechanism to educate the library administration and library staff, who are forced to look critically at what they are doing and why they are doing it, and to formulate a vision of where the library is headed in the next five to ten years.

• Accreditation is an important vehicle for educating the accrediting teams. The institution has the opportunity to be involved in the selection of the site visitors, most of whom come from institutions that are in some ways comparable with the one being visited. Understanding their backgrounds, knowing some key information about the libraries on their campuses, and being aware of the missions of their parent institutions can be of critical importance in understanding their frame of reference and perspective on the role of the academic library.

There are a variety of data-gathering techniques described in the professional literature that are useful in evaluating library services and resources (e.g., user surveys, focus group discussions, statistical analyses). These techniques will not be reviewed here. However, it should be noted that the increased emphasis on assessment and outcomes poses special challenges to libraries that, like other academic units, have relied in the past on counting inputs (e.g., number of staff, size of collection, hours of service) rather than on measuring how successful we were in serving our patrons and contributing to the achievement of the institution's goals relating to teaching and research.

Particularly since the academic library serves the entire institution, the use of representatives from the major academic units on campus to advise the library may be an important part of an institution's strategy in preparing for the visit. In addition, an internal library committee will be needed, not only for developing documentation and strategies for evaluating library resources and services but, equally important, for ensuring that the library faculty and staff develop an appreciation of the importance of their accountability in the conduct and outcomes of the visit. A focused visit may stimulate action on important projects, such as a comprehensive analysis of collections, that have been long deferred owing to the press of more immediate concerns. A focused visit also is an effective stimulus to reviewing library goals and objectives statements, policy manuals, and other official documentation that represents a philosophical framework for understanding and evaluating whatever library services and/or resources are the focus of concern.

An institution should anticipate that site visitors will want to confer with the users of the library as well as with university and library administrators and library staff. Thus, it will be desirable to disseminate statements regarding library goals and objectives, current activities, and the vision and future plans to elicit campus reaction and prepare key constituencies for the visit.

Following from the comments here, a few additional guidelines in preparing for a focused library visit are offered:

- Check first with your chief administrator to ensure that you do no more, nor no less, than he or she feels is needed for an accreditation review.
- Be politically astute in preparing for a visit. Involve key players and prepare your community for the visit. There is no telling whom those team visitors may want to talk to on your campus.
- Understand the campus agenda for the visit. The tone of the visit can be upbeat, defensive, apologetic, or something else. Looking good, looking bad, being cautious, or being totally candid are all decisions that can dramatically affect the outcome of a visit. Go into the visit with a clear understanding of how you want to come out of it.
- Be very well prepared—with facts and figures and good rationales for why you are what you are.
- Have a vision and be able to articulate how that vision relates to the larger institutional mission and vision.

And finally, be sure that the administration of the institution understands that the library must continue to be supported after the visit.

REFERENCES

Leach, R. G. 1992. "Academic Library Change: The Role of Regional Accreditation." *Journal of Academic Librarianship* 18 (5): 291.

North Central Association of Colleges and Schools. 1990. *A Handbook of Accreditation.* Chicago: North Central Association of Colleges and Schools.

8

The Practical Librarian's View of Accreditation

Joan H. Worley

Academic librarians welcoming visiting committees from regional accrediting agencies for the first time may expect miracles: a sympathetic visitor who, if not a librarian, will be well informed about libraries and have reasonably high standards for facilities, funding, staffing, and service; will praise creative solutions to generic library problems and provide practical ideas for solving those remaining; and will tell the college administration exactly what the library director has been saying for years. Moreover, because the visitor speaks with the authority of the accrediting agency, his or her words will be heeded. The leaking roof will be replaced, the acquisitions budget restored to the level of its glory days, and the superhuman efforts of the library staff receive due credit, at long last.

Bosh, say librarians who have experienced the accrediting process. Don't get your hopes up. Chances are, the visitor will have merely glanced at the library section of the self-study on the plane, will absorb every iota of staff energy and strength for the duration of the visit, will ignore the comprehensive data painstakingly compiled for the occasion, will ask to see timetables for the implementation of multicultural collection development, will recommend that the library provide handicap access to its pencil sharpeners, and will tell the president that the ninety-five hours per week the library is open are woefully inadequate.

DOES ACCREDITATION MATTER?

These anecdotal scenarios represent the extreme ends of a range of practical expectations. In between are any number of opinions of the accrediting enterprise, both hopeful and cynical. Does accreditation matter for the library? *Yes.* Is it relevant? *Yes.* No matter how perfect or imperfect one may deem it to be, the accrediting process is important, if for no other reason than the library is highlighted in almost all of the various accrediting agency standards as a separate component or area of concern. (Regional accrediting agencies publish "standards," "criteria," or "guidelines," variously; *standards* will serve for all three in this chapter.) With such prominence, any deficiencies in the library that are noted in the visitors' report likely will be an embarrassment for the college or university, the more so because the library represents the life of the mind in a tangible way that faculty and classroom cannot. Indeed, the library is a metaphor for the academic program of the parent institution. In this context, the importance of public relations cannot be overstated; presidents and vice presidents associated with institutions undergoing accreditation will have their attention focused on the library for several months, at least. Accreditation may rightly be viewed as a once-in-a-decade opportunity for positive library outreach and advancement, then, in addition to the more commonly held perception of accreditation as a rigorous exercise of data presentation and evaluation.

Much of the criticism leveled at the accrediting process by librarians deals with the relevance of the library to reaccreditation and the currency of present standards, but the busyness and the tension of preparing for the committee's visit often are focused on practical considerations. How will the accreditation be organized? What will the accrediting visitors be looking for, and what can one reasonably expect of the visit?

THE PROCESS

Although the visit of the panel or committee of institutional peers is often seen as *the* accrediting event, in fact, the committee visit is but one step in the multi-step process of accreditation that occurs every ten years at the approximately 3500 accredited two- and four-year institutions of higher education in the United States.

In the Southern Association, for example, the process begins at least 18 months before the committee visit, with correspondence and conversation between campus administrators and the executive officer of the accrediting agency. Dates for the committee visit to the campus are selected; a campus coordinator is appointed; and the executive officer makes a routine visit to the campus to meet with key personnel and outline the process for them. Campus committees, chaired by faculty members and composed of students, staff, and faculty, are appointed to research and write parts of the campus-generated *self-study,* a substantial, year-long undertaking said by many people to be the most valuable part of the accrediting process. The self-study is presumed to be an honest assessment of the work of the college or university, a look at its strengths and weaknesses, its accomplishments, and its needs, more or less based on the standards of the accrediting agency. (The document is usually placed on reserve in the library for the campus community to review.)

The self-study and accompanying documents such as college catalogs, handbooks, etc., are sent to members of the visiting committee for their review, well in advance of the visit. The visiting committee members usually include a college/university president, a chief financial officer, several faculty members, and (perhaps) a librarian. (The regional accrediting agencies always/sometimes/never appoint librarians, according to their differing practices.) The purpose of the committee visit include the following:

1. To verify the authenticity of the information the members have received.
2. To assess the quality of the institutional self-study.
3. To gather additional information through interviews with administrators, faculty, staff, and students.
4. To make professional judgments on the institution's compliance with association standards.
5. To write a report on their findings, with recommendations, suggestions, and commendations.

The latter are usually presented just prior to the committee's departure in an oral report to the president of the college/university and his or her staff or to an open meeting.

Typically, a draft of the report is written before the visit is complete, and the chair of the visiting committee is responsible for editing and submitting the final report to the accrediting association. The visiting committee does not act on accreditation but makes recommendations to a committee, which reviews the report, recommends action, and forwards it to the executive council, which in turn sends it to the full body of the accrediting commission for final action.

The process described here is that followed by the Southern Association of Colleges and Schools for institutional reaffirmation; other regional associations follow similar procedures, and all use the peer review process. Visiting committees are also involved when an institution seeks accreditation for the first time; when an institution changes its status—from two-year to four-year, for example; and when special institutional circumstances are evaluated.

HOW ARE LIBRARIANS INVOLVED?

Librarians have several parts, and sometimes starring roles, to play: They could be asked to coordinate the committee's visit to the campus or to chair the self-study committee and edit its report; they will probably serve on the self-study committee on the library, either as chair, resource person, or member; they will certainly be invited to a formal dinner to welcome the visiting committee on its arrival; they will be interviewed by one or more members of the visiting committee and perhaps asked for additional information; and they may be invited to hear the committee's exit report.

WHAT DO LIBRARIANS WANT?

Librarians want knowledgeable visiting committee members, conversant with contemporary issues facing the profession, with new technologies, and with the social and economic realities of higher education. Faculty visitors are prone to focus on input measures, notably collection strengths or weaknesses, exclusively, ignoring other resources and service. Although they may understand how the academic enterprise works—a desirable insight for any reviewer—few are competent to discuss staffing, hours, technical services, evaluation of services, allocation of resources, or other aspects of library operations.

Librarians would prefer visitors who are able to look with fresh eyes and appreciate the library for what it is doing in the context of the institutional setting, rather than measuring its activities against the visitor's home library and institution or another larger, richer, more nearly perfect model.

Librarians would like some collegiality. The rapport between the committee visitor who coordinates the section or chapter of the report on the library (in the Southern Association, it is always a librarian) and the library director and/ or staff may be warm and friendly...or not. The visitor may simply ask a series of brusque questions while ticking off a list of requirements, but how much better if he or she engages the librarian(s) in real conversation, offering ideas and suggestions as a friendly consultant would do.

Librarians want committee members with reasonable expectations. Veteran library evaluators often approach their task developmentally, as if they were grading freshman English papers, with red ink appearing in reverse correlation to the number of errors—that is, the paper with 100 errors is marked only for the egregious comma splices and subject-verb disagreements, not for every confusion of who-whom, while the brilliant "A" paper is graded for handwriting. Rather than nitpick the library to bits, they concentrate on one or two key issues.

A committee member who doesn't know libraries, one who produces a weak report or a report that is simply off base, is a major disappointment. Some disappointment is perhaps inevitable, however. No matter how enured to a process librarians may be, or how jaded, the momentum of the self-study and the excitement of the committee visit raise expectations, often too high. The visitors are on campus for a short period, gathering snippets and shreds of unfiltered information from every source, interviewing people all day, and meeting in committee till late at night. Their understanding of campus politics, their take on library issues in the institutional context, and their grasp of the complicated dynamics of problems that have their origins in ancient history will be limited. More likely than not, the visiting committee reports will not reflect key issues as perceived by the librarians at the institution.

WHAT DO ACCREDITORS WANT?

The six regional associations alike look for appropriate facilities; quality collections with adequate technical or bibliographic control; instructional services; and qualified, competent staff to carry out the mission of the library. Their overarching statements are similarly general in scope. "An institution must provide sufficient library/learning resources to support the nature, scope, and level of the program offered" (Middle States Association of Colleges and Schools 1993, 2), and "Each institution must ensure that all students and faculty have access to adequate learning resources and services needed to support its purposes and programs" (Southern Association of Colleges and Schools 1992, 45) are representative of these broad requirements.

The North Central Association adheres to this holistic approach, without specific requirements or standards beyond its general statement: "[The institution] provides its students access to those learning resources and support services requisite for its degree programs" (North Central Association of Colleges and Schools 1993, 5). The other five associations include more detailed standards that differ more in emphasis than in the basic requirements. The Southern Association alone includes "must" and "should" statements, clearly stating the detailed qualities and characteristics its accrediting visitors will look for (Southern Association of Colleges and Schools 1991, 11).

Generally, standards reflect the major issues and concerns of the year in which they were written and, to some extent, the interests of the librarians and others who developed them. For example, one may emphasize planning; another, outcomes measures and evaluation or utilization of library resources or the collaboration of faculty members and librarians in collection development.

Interestingly, as of spring 1994, none of the standards have definitive statements on access to electronic or on-line resources. With representative accrediting commissions generally meeting annually, and infrequent revisions of standards, it is difficult for accrediting agencies to respond quickly to changes in the environment. Understandably, librarians in the throes of accreditation are sometimes critical of the standards, claiming that they do not ask the right questions. Given the lumbering pace of their creation and development, and the dynamic nature of library technologies, it is unreasonable to expect them to serve precisely any current reality of the library universe.

In addition to the requirements delineated by the standards, accrediting agencies want a fair and objective evaluation of the library by a professional (librarian or teaching faculty) who can set aside professional or disciplinary loyalties, evaluate the library in its own institutional context, offer expertise informed by experience, and interact with other committee members in a cooperative spirit.

The practical value of the visit, for the library and the institution, in every case, is largely dependent on the competence, diligence, and interest of the visiting committee; the quality of the report and recommendations; and of course, the listening ability of the library staff and institutional officers. The accrediting process may appear to be complete within months of the visit, but even without recommendations directed specifically at improving library services, positive effects can be felt for years.

REFERENCES

Middle States Association of Colleges and Schools. Commission on Higher Education, 1993. *Characteristics of Excellence in Higher Education: Standards for Accreditation.* Philadelphia: Middle States Association of Colleges and Schools, Commission on Higher Education.

North Central Association of Colleges and Schools. Commission on Institutions of Higher Education. 1993. *A Handbook of Accreditation, 1993–94, Working Draft.* Chicago: North Central Association of Colleges and Schools, Commission on Institutions of Higher Education.

Southern Association of Colleges and Schools. 1991. *Handbook for Peer Evaluators.* Decatur, Ga.: Southern Association of Colleges and Schools, Commission on Colleges.

————. 1992. *Criteria for Accreditation Commission on Colleges.* Decatur, Ga.: Southern Association of Colleges and Schools.

PART III

Selected Issues

9

Distance Education and Off-Campus Library Services: Challenges for the Accreditation Process and Librarians

Thomas E. Abbott

In this chapter, I will share a view of the academic world that is focused on the future of higher education as we know it in Maine and, I suspect, for many other parts of the nation. I will base my remarks on our experiences in providing access to higher education for those who have historically been prevented from attending college by barriers such as geography, the need to work, inadequate secondary school preparation, and family obligations. In Maine, we are riding the wave of rapid development of distance education and related technologies that in three years have changed the face of education in the state forever.

With the Education Network of Maine and our statewide Interactive Television (ITV) System now serving eighty-plus locations across the state, we feel that we are on the cutting edge of progress in this area of higher education, yet we continue to face the age-old issue of accountability. Can we show that the services and education we are providing meet the needs of the students of today—not just what they think they want to get a good job? In other words, are our efforts adequate to prepare them for their future as participants in and contributors to society? Can we pass the reasonable person test or even the straight-face test with our constituents?

Among other duties, I chair the campus accreditation process for our upcoming review with the Commission on Institutions of Higher Education of the New England Association of Schools and Colleges (NEASC), and I serve as an evaluator for the NEASC. While the self-study process is a valuable and important one, and my experiences directly bear this out, I am never quite sure that it will have the desired impact—that of providing a wake-up call for the institution to adjust its practices and programs to most effectively meet the educational needs of our students and our society. I suspect that once the team leaves, interest in making difficult change often diminishes. Significant internal change in higher education comes very slowly in spite of all of our organizational restructuring.

In addition to providing traditional classroom instruction on campus, our institution delivers forty courses to 3,500 students in eighty locations across Maine and supports these instructional efforts with a wide range of ever more sophisticated student services, including a nationally recognized Off-Campus Library Services Program. Students, both on and off campus, in our recent independent phone survey, say they are satisfied with our efforts. Yet with all of the progress we have made, the accountability and quality questions remain a concern. Can we as an open-admission institution, chartered to provide statewide access to higher education opportunity, produce an educated person ready to fit into, learn from, and survive in tomorrow's world? Can we prove that we are doing it?

Accreditation, especially by the regional associations, can and should play the all-important role of keeping all of us focused on the future needs of our students and community constituents. The associations as well as the evaluation strategies are created and managed by our peers. It is, in my view, one of the few opportunities for interested colleagues from the region to work together in a supportive atmosphere on the tough questions of who we are and where we are going.

As I understand is the case in virtually all of the regional accrediting associations, the New England Association of Schools and Colleges has recently revised all of its quality measures to include output criteria. The most prominent criterion in our case is 4.19 of the Programs and Instructions section:

Graduates successfully completing an undergraduate program demonstrate competence in written and oral communication in English; the ability for scientific and quantitative reasoning, for critical analysis and logical thinking; and the capability for continuing learning. They also demonstrate knowledge and understanding of scientific, historical, and social phenomena, and a knowledge and appreciation of the aesthetic and ethical dimensions of humankind. In addition, graduates demonstrate an in-depth understanding of an area of knowledge or practice and of its interrelatedness with other areas. (New England Association of Schools and Colleges 1992, 12)

As I have promised our institution, the NEASC Higher Education staff and my president, we will all work diligently toward being able to prove this and the many other new output measures with hard data, but I do not expect it to all come quickly or even in time for this self-study. Nor do I expect it to be an easy transition from what Henry Mintzberg (1983) in his organizational structures study would call the professional bureaucracy's strict reliance on the qualifications of the providers (faculty) as the primary coordinating mechanism of output quality—rather than the more desired common standards of output.

The regional accreditation process utilizing the new focus on output measures can provide the stimulus for discussions of accountability issues as well as provide the leverage to begin the change process.

NEW UNDERSTANDINGS FOR A NEW ENVIRONMENT

We are educating our current students for a future that holds as its central identity accelerating change. The Department of Labor predicts that half or more of the jobs that exist today will be extinct in ten years. Further, most of the new jobs that are developing to replace the dying ones will require some level of advanced education. Systems of information management and education and even ways of thinking about solutions will have to be vastly different to accommodate the higher and higher expectations and complexities required for all organizations to do what is needed with a limited resource base.

In an interview on Maine Public Radio about his book *Nations at Work,* Robert Reich, current secretary of labor, describes the impact of these job changes on individuals (Reich 1991). As the number of jobs requiring advanced skills and education increase and the other low and semiskilled jobs disappear, those individuals with the advanced skills will earn significantly more money and have their choice of positions. On the other hand, with the high schools of our country continuing to graduate underprepared students, the pool of poorly educated and undertrained individuals becomes ever greater. Employers with low and semiskilled jobs now and for the foreseeable future have their choice of employees. And because of the tremendous supply of these individuals, they will be able to pay only the minimum to employ them, thus effectively reducing further their buying power and economic status. Current jobs for the semi- or low-skilled are rapidly disappearing, and competition for those remaining is increasing.

We have lived through a generation since the middle of this century where mechanics have become electronic technologies and information is stored and manipulated to a degree that few imagined possible. As this is written, a court has just approved the delivery of video into homes by telephone companies via telephone that lines that probably go into 99 percent of the homes in the country. The basic four-function calculator has gone from a $300 price tag in 1970 and the size of a cigar box to a multifunction shirt-pocket solar-/room-light-powered version that can be thrown out and replaced for under $10. We can bank and shop by phone, or if you prefer to get out of the house, automatic teller machines (ATMs) provide cash or loan—all curbside. Specialized journals are published on personal computers at home, where many spend much of their workweek. We transmit copies of documents from our offices and homes to anywhere in the world for the price of a phone call. On-line information services are available from a variety of suppliers, and libraries are working together around the world to provide immediate access to their entire collections for anyone with a terminal or personal computer and modem. And American companies are finally making vehicles Americans are willing to buy.

In education, the high-tech change process has begun as well. Computers have added a new discipline for the K–12 curriculum, and some schools have even managed to integrate the computer into all learning processes. Most do agree that there is much room for improvement. At the same time, however, many high school graduates leave their schools without the ability to read, express themselves, or perform basic computations. At my institution, dedicated to providing access and open admissions to a variety of associate and baccalaureate programs statewide, roughly 70 percent of the incoming matriculated students are deficient in one or more of the basics—most often mathematics. Many, but not all, eventually succeed after a round or two of pre-college-level developmental courses that we now routinely offer each semester and summer. Deficiencies, particularly among our highly motivated adult learners, are often quickly remedied. Many express an appreciation for having a second chance at education they know they need to make a new life for themselves. One of the highest-rated reasons (88 percent) for coming to the University of Maine at Augusta, based on a recent survey, was for personal growth and development. Job advancement and new careers rated in the 60 percent range.

From these students, we have learned a valuable lesson that only now seems to be sinking in. The education provided in the 1970s and 1980s to the vast majority of our citizens is no longer serving their needs as citizens in today's world. It can't possibly stand on its own. Our ways of life and work have changed too dramatically for anyone not making an effort to continuously update themselves to remain successful. Looking around at the level and type of education provided by our high schools today, I do not see any significant changes. Certainly the number of students needing developmental support confirms that little has changed. We have only partially faced ourselves in the mirror of accountability on this matter, and few of our institutions are doing much to support educational change in our communities. We seem to have all we can do to deal with our own problems.

In some of our academic programs at the University of Maine at Augusta, we have begun to deal with the issue of what an educated person needs to know and can do. No longer are the academic leaders content to hire full-time or part-time faculty on the basis of credentials and experience alone and turn them loose. Disciplinary faculty meetings in some areas are debates, and agreements about what is taught in each of the courses not just general topics. But the discussions now reach to learning outcomes and specific content. The English Composition faculty recently agreed to include a Library Use and Information Literacy Component in all Basic College Writing courses. The modules were designed in collaboration with the library professional staff and the English faculty.

Administratively, changes are occurring as well. In the library, we are about three quarters of the way through a Continuous Assessment Project designed to follow W. Edwards Deming's approach to managing for quality and continuous improvement. All library employees have been involved in identifying and grouping into four functional units every major function and operation performed in the library. Flow charts have been created for each of the units and shared with all. We brainstormed lists of all the possible ways we would know if we were successful for each of our functions and have sent a random listing in each functional unit to the fourteen-member Faculty Library Committee. Their task was to rate each of these "success or quality delivery" criteria. Next steps will include developing a method of measuring each of the most important success criteria and planning a strategy for sampling the system for results on a regular basis.

When the project is operational, sampling data will allow us to determine if we are meeting our goal of quality service in each area. Where we are not, we will review the criteria to determine if they are still valid. If they are, we will find the best way to improve the system of delivery to meet the outcome goal. Where the criteria can be shown to need revision, they will be adjusted and the criteria measured again. Far from being a bureaucratic nightmare of data collection and employee nonperformance discussions, as suspected by some, this project is designed to measure the operational effectiveness of the library holistically and will enable the entire staff to see how all the pieces of the operation fit together and provide reliable feedback on how their system is functioning. If we come up short on a particular activity or function, everyone will participate in the improvement effort.

We believe such accountability systems will permit us to provide the best possible service as defined by our primary constituents—both patrons and faculty. Certainly it will also make our presentations more effective for the next accreditation report and, I hope, provide very effective data for the next round of budget discussions. We will be able to describe what we do and describe how well we do it and with a reasonable assurance that our constituents have had a hand in creating the level and type of service.

RAPID CHANGES WITH INDICATORS OF SUCCESS

Overall the rapid changes we are making in the delivery of higher education instruction and support services in Maine have been well received. Again this semester (fall 1993), the University of Maine at Augusta campus has broken its old enrollment record by about 12 percent this time over last fall, and more and more institutions, both public and private, are vying for time on a "maxed-out" ITV System. Semifrantic planning is under way for more capacity. Current projections suggest that we will move from our current enrollment of 5,500 to 10,000 in the next few years. This is due specifically to the fact that we are the only institution in Maine capitalized and oriented to providing education to those who now need it the most and cannot get it in the traditional methods of delivery.

New ways of thinking about how we deliver not only education but the accompanying and critical support services will be required. We have just received Title III funding for improving access for staff in remote locations to student information, including academic records and other advising resources, and additional support for computer-assisted learning options for developmental courses. The library is moving to an on-line requestor function for journal articles to parallel the book search and retrieval function already in place, and a gateway on the library system will soon provide access to Internet resources by academic discipline. Similar technological leaps will be needed in the actual delivery of instruction if we are to keep up with the demand. Alternative delivery methods including courses by computer, taped instruction with a variety of faculty interaction options, computer-assisted education, and portfolio assessment are all being considered, tried, or tested.

The quality of the product and service we are providing generally looks good, and we do have some comparison studies to show that our students taking classes on ITV do as well or better as those in campus-based classrooms. And as mentioned, student satisfaction with the experience and academic progress is high. Our main problem at this point seems to be keeping all of our players focused on the issue of quality as things continue to change around us. We continue to be committed to providing access to higher education for the citizens of Maine and taking advantage of this once-in-a-lifetime opportunity we have before us, but we do so with the concern that the programming offered meets the needs of the students and our greater community. Ongoing discussions here about quality have been bolstered and focused with the introduction of the NEASC accreditation self-study process.

OUTPUT CRITERIA IN THE NEW ENGLAND ASSOCIATION

Although it may be years before the full impact of the changes are recognized, it is my view that the New England Association of Schools and Colleges, and their Commission on Institutions of Higher Education, has made an exceptional contribution to the progress of New England higher education with its 1992 revision of the quality standards. The new standards were developed with input from academics from a variety of institutions in New England and reflect the interest and collective concerns of the higher education community.

The most significant change in the NEASC document and the one most important for all of our needs is the overall change from process and input criteria in the old document to output criteria in the new. No longer is the college experience officially viewed by NEASC as a black box where well-qualified faculty and staff and a certain number of library books magically turn out fit and educated college graduates. Too simplistic a description of the old formula, no doubt, but the point is that the college experience is now viewed as one that can be monitored and measured without intrusion and where direction can be provided to make it as effective as possible for all constituents. It recognizes accountability to constituents as an important public policy concern and one to which we are all urged to attend.

NEASC's document, as I suspect other associations', provides guidance for evaluating off-campus distance education activities of colleges. Off-campus educational activities are mentioned in several places, and in general, the references make the point that off-campus programming must be planned, budgeted adequately, and involved in activities and governance, and these students must be adequately supported in all areas of their education. Library services, often mentioned as an area of concern for off-campus programming, receive special mention and require adequate library support.

A COMMON FOCUS FOR OFF-CAMPUS EDUCATION AND LIBRARY SERVICE

If there is a common focus to off-campus education concerns of NEASC, it is that all students, regardless of where they sit for their classes, deserve the same level of support. Some of my experiences working with beginning off-campus programs, especially in the library area, suggest that campus motivation for developing off-campus and distance education programs may not be strictly educational. Clearly, new markets are needed to replace the dwindling recent high school graduate pool, and programs often need to be started in a hurry to beat the competition, but when librarians are the last to hear about a new initiative 100 miles away and no one has considered the need to provide library support, adequate staff, access to the cataloger, or money for phone calls or mailing, there is a serious problem. Here is another reason for librarians to seek out involvement on campus planning, budget, or other committees where there might be a chance to influence the planning process for off-campus education. Today, there are enough good examples of how to do it right to also be able to make a quick referral on off-campus library matters to any vice president on the same day you hear the words "New center in. . . ."

The three-year-old Extended Campus Library Services Section of the Association of College and Research Libraries/American Library Association (ACRL/ALA), now with a membership of over 600, has as part of its mission the education and support of institutions and librarians planning or implementing off-campus library services and would welcome requests for support and guidance from any of the readers. Contact can be made through me by mail, phone, or E-mail.

Additionally, the regional accreditation process can provide a tremendous service to all institutions, their faculty and staff, and especially the students if they are able to raise the flag on delivery of services to support distance education. This area includes library services, advising, information, and instructional support in computing and other essentials.

DEFINING WHAT MUST BE DONE

Librarians themselves need to be sure they have their feet firmly planted as supporters of faculty efforts to educate, in as many academic programs as possible. All too often, librarians are not active enough in promoting their services with the faculty and campus officers. The strongest allies of the librarians are the faculty. Faculty should come to believe that librarians are partners in the instructional process. When a course is scheduled to be delivered at an off-campus site, faculty should be primed to automatically ask: How will we deliver library services and materials to our students?

The accreditation process can also provide a focal point for campus discussions by publicly demanding an answer to the question, What is it the institution hopes to accomplish by delivering education off campus? If the stated goal is to provide access to quality education, anyone listening should ask, what does it look like? Is success for the program defined? Does it include support services beyond instruction? Are there ways to measure the planned outcomes?

In another area of accountability management, the American Library Association Standards Committee approved and published *"ACRL Guidelines for Extended Campus Library Services."* A copy of the document is provided in the appendix to this chapter. These guidelines, developed by a Task Force appointed by the ALA in 1988 and subjected to hearings and input from the Extended Campus Library Services Discussion Group, were published in 1990. The guidelines provide nonprescriptive direction for planning and development of off-campus library services and emphasize provision of quality library services that are part of the campus education planning process, adequately budgeted, and sufficiently staffed so as not to be add-on service without thought or financial support.

The ACRL document supports the need for "equitable services for all students in higher education, no matter where the 'classroom' may be....The parent institution is responsible for providing support which addresses the information needs of its extended campus programs. This support should provide library service to the extended campus community equitable with that provided to the on-campus community" (Association of College and Research Libraries, 1990).

CONCLUSION

I feel we in New England are fortunate to have such a knowledgeable and progressive staff at the NEASC Commission on Institutions of Higher Education. When I began drafting this chapter, my intent was to emphasize the need for accreditation associations and visiting teams to treat off-campus distance education programs as equal partners deserving serious evaluation and that these programs be held to high expectations. At some point, I became aware that in our neck of the woods the plan was working very well, and I revised my comments here to provide more of an overview of the collaborative model we were, and are, working within. The evaluators and staff from NEASC do take their role very seriously and look on distance education initiatives as an integral part of the campus operation and one for which the campus is to be held accountable.

The campus visit to our institution in 1994 may, however, for NEASC, be the watershed experience in distance education assessment. We are just beginning to figure out how to convince the visiting evaluators to set aside enough time to fully appreciate the breadth of what we offer across the state. By way of example, travel to one of the many islands receiving ITV classes is attractive, but as our students remind us, travel to mainland and back can kill the better part of a day. Fortunately, our students are our strongest advocates, so perhaps we can hold a town meeting on ITV for the visitors.

The problem still remains of developing the measurement devices with which to determine outcome success. I am hopeful that with additional collaboration among the colleges involved in distance education the NEASC staff and those who serve as evaluators will develop strategies and training on outcome measurement for all New England institutions long before campus visit time.

We are approaching a crossroad in the evolution of higher education in this country. The main road seems to be headed for distance education alternatives. There will always be a need and room for traditional higher education in face-to-face classrooms, but the success of higher education's future in this state and the country will be made in alternative forms and deliveries of education. And on the assessment side, knowing that what we are delivering is doing its intended job for our constituents will be the challenge for the next ten years.

Meeting the challenge of evaluating these new programs and guiding their development in and out of states and across regional lines and national borders will require new models and new thinking. Some have recommended a national organization or association to oversee boundaryless programs as one new way to look at the picture. I am exploring with the idea of a fully automated national off-campus library consortium, linked by Internet and dedicated to supporting off-campus student library needs. On-line reference support with specialists identified in each discipline, access to journal articles on-line, televised or computer-based instruction on use of the consortium's library resource, shared database, reciprocal borrowing privileges, and free delivery of materials from the nearest library all could help make the idea of a nationally televised or electronic college experience a reality.

How would a regional association respond to such a proposal? Loud applause, I hope. Certainly, we all must be thinking in new ways as we consider how to keep our place, or perhaps better solidify our place, as leaders in education in the world. Minimally, we all need to agree that the off-campus distance education students need the same level of quality instruction and service provided to on-campus students. If that discussion takes us to the question of how we define what we are trying to do and how we measure it, then the process has worked. Change around us occurs so rapidly and each institution is so inwardly focused much of the time that we can never see all of the possibilities. Accreditation bodies can fill the role of connection point with other institutions and for shared ideas and serve as the catalyst for facing the accountability issue head-on.

REFERENCES

Association of College and Research Libraries. 1990. *"ACRL Guidelines for Extended Campus Library Services."* *College and Research Libraries News* 50 (April): 353–355.

Mintzberg, Henry. 1983. *Structures in Five: Designing Effective Organizations.* Englewood Cliffs, N.J.: Prentice-Hall.

New England Association of Schools and Colleges. 1992. *Standards for Accreditation.* Winchester, Mass.: New England Association of Schools and Colleges.

Reich, Robert. 1991. Interview by Andrea de Leon on *Maine Things Considered.* Maine Public Radio. September 6, 1991.

APPENDIX

ACRL Guidelines for Extended Campus Library Services

Prepared by
The Task Force to Review the Guidelines
for Extended Campus Library Services
Mary Joyce Pickett, Chair

ASSOCIATION OF
COLLEGE
& RESEARCH
LIBRARIES

*Approved by the ALA Standards Committee at the
1990 Annual Conference*

This revision of the "Guidelines for Extended Campus Library Services" was prepared by a Task Force appointed prior to the ALA Midwinter Meeting in 1988. The members were Lynn LaBrake, University of Central Florida; Barton Lessin, Wayne State University; Colleen Power, California State University, Chico; Julie Todaro, Austin Community College, Rio Grande Campus; and Mary Joyce Pickett, Illinois Institute of Technology (chair). In establishing the need for revision the task force examined the professional literature, testimony from hearings on the existing guidelines held at the July 1988 ALA Annual Conference and at the October 1988 Off-Campus Library Services Conference, input from previous users and the Extended Campus Library Services Discussion Group, and information received from regional and professional accrediting agencies. The proposed draft revision was published in the May 1989 *C&RL News* and hearings were held at the June 1989 ALA Annual Conference. This draft was revised in response to hearing testimony.

ı

Appendix (*continued*)

Introduction

Library resources and services in institutions of higher education must meet the needs of main campuses, off-campus or extended campus programs, courses taken for credit or non-credit, continuing education programs, courses attended in person or by means of electronic transmission, or other means of distance education. The 1981 "Guidelines for Extended Campus Library Services," designed to assist in the organization and provision of these resources and services, were scheduled for ACRL review. The task force determined that a revision was necessary based on the following factors: non-traditional study becoming a more commonplace element in higher education; an increase in diversity of educational opportunities; an increase in the number of unique environments where educational opportunities are offered; an increased recognition of the need for library resources and services at locations other than main campuses; an increased concern and demand for equitable services for all students in higher education, no matter where the "classroom" may be; a greater demand for library resources and services by faculty and staff at extended campus sites; and an increase in technological innovations in the transmittal of information and the delivery of courses.

These revised guidelines are offered, as the previous guidelines were, in a non-prescriptive manner. They are designed to outline direction, support a process, stress overall coordination and to support the educational objectives of the extended campus program. The audience for the "Guidelines" includes library staff planning for and managing these extended campus services, other library staff working with extended campus library staff, faculty, administrators at all levels within the educational institution, and sponsors of academic programs, as well as accrediting and licensure agencies.

Definitions

"Extended campus community" covers all those individuals and agencies which are directly involved with academic programs offered away from the traditional academic campus including students, faculty, researchers, administrators, and sponsors.

"Extended campus library services" refers to those services offered in support of academic courses and programs offered away from the main campus of the institution responsible for the academic program. These courses may be taught in traditional or non-traditional ways. This definition also includes services to individuals who are involved off-campus regardless of where credit is

given. The definition does not include non-traditional students pursuing on-campus academic programs.

"Parent institution" refers to the institutional entity responsible for the offering of academic courses and programs off-campus.

"Library" denotes the academic library directly associated with the parent institution offering the off-campus program unless otherwise noted.

Philosophy

This document assumes the following statements:

The parent institution is responsible for providing support which addresses the information needs of its extended campus programs. This support should provide library service to the extended campus community equitable with that provided to the on-campus community.

The library has primary responsibility for identifying, developing, coordinating, and providing library resources and services which address the information needs of the extended campus community.

Effective and appropriate services for extended campus communities may differ from those services offered on campus. The requirements of academic programs should guide the library's responses to defined needs.

Where resources and services of unaffiliated local libraries are to be used to support information needs of the extended campus community, the library, or where appropriate, the parent institution, is responsible for the development of written agreements with those local libraries.

The extended campus library program shall have goals and objectives that support the provision of resources and services consistent with the broader institutional mission.

Management

It is the responsibility of library management to identify, plan, and oversee library services and resources in support of extended campus programs. The library administration should:

1) assess the needs of its extended campus community for library resources, services and facilities;

2) prepare a written profile of the extended community's information needs;

3) develop a written statement of immediate and long-range goals and objectives which address the needs and outline the methods by which progress can be measured;

4) involve academic community representatives, including the extended campus faculty and students, in the formation of the objectives and the

Appendix (*continued*)

regular evaluation of their achievement;

5) assess the existing library support, its availability and appropriateness;

6) participate with administrators and teaching faculty in the curriculum development process and in course planning to insure appropriate library resources and services are available;

7) promote library support services to the extended campus community.

Additional areas of management responsibility are covered in the sections on Finances, Personnel, Facilities, Resources, and Services.

Finances

The parent institution should provide continuing financial support for addressing the library needs of the extended campus community. This financing should be:

1) related to the formally-defined needs and demands of the extended campus program;

2) allocated on a schedule matching the parent institution's budgeting cycle;

3) identified within the parent institution's budget and expenditure reporting statements;

4) accommodated to arrangements involving external agencies, including affiliated, but independently-supported libraries.

Personnel

Personnel involved in the management and coordination of extended campus library services may include campus and library administration, the librarian managing the services, additional professional staff in the institution, and support staff from a variety of departments.

The library should provide professional and support personnel sufficient in number and of the quality necessary to attain the goals and objectives of the extended campus program including:

1) a librarian to plan, implement, coordinate, and evaluate library resources and services addressing the information needs of the extended campus community;

2) persons with the capacity and skills to identify informational needs and respond to them flexibly and creatively;

3) classification, status, and salary scales for extended campus library staff that are equivalent to those provided for other library employees.

Facilities

The library should provide facilities, equipment, and communication links sufficient in size, number, and scope to attain the objectives of the extended campus programs. Arrangements may vary and should be appropriate to programs offered.

Examples of suitable arrangements include but are not limited to:

1) access to facilities through agreements with a nonaffiliated library;

2) designated space for consultations, ready reference collections, reserve collections, electronic transmission of information, computerized database searching and interlibrary loan services;

3) a branch or satellite library.

Resources

Access to library materials in sufficient number, scope, and formats should be provided to:

1) support the students' needs in fulfilling course assignments (e.g., required and supplemental readings and research papers) and enrich the academic programs;

2) support teaching and research needs;

3) accommodate other informational needs of the extended campus community as appropriate.

Programs granting associate degrees should provide access to collections which meet the "Association of College and Research Libraries (ACRL) Standards for Community, Junior and Technical College Learning Resources Programs." Programs granting baccalaureate or master's degrees should provide access to collections which meet the standards defined by the "ACRL Standards for College Libraries." Programs offering doctorate degrees should provide access to collections which meet the standards defined by the "ACRL Standards for University Libraries."

Services

The library services offered the extended campus community should be designed to meet effectively a wide range of informational and bibliographic needs. Examples which may help meet these needs include:

1) reference assistance;

2) computer-based bibliographic and informational services;

3) consultation services;

4) a program of library user instruction designed specifically to meet the needs of the extended campus community;

5) assistance with non-print media and equipment;

6) reciprocal borrowing, contractual borrowing, and interlibrary loan services;

7) prompt document delivery such as a courier system or electronic transmission;

8) access to reserve materials;

9) promotion of library services to the extended campus community.

■ ■

Source: Reprinted from *College and Research Libraries News,* April 1990, with permission of the American Library Association.

10

The Concern for Information Literacy: A Major Challenge for Accreditation

Howard L. Simmons

Why should accreditors have a concern for information literacy? One might just as well ask why accreditors should have a concern for student learning. If an accrediting body concludes—as the Middle States Commission has concluded already—that it is important for institutions to produce more information-literate graduates, then information literacy becomes a critical factor in the improvement, evaluation, and assessment of the quality of undergraduate education. But agreement about the importance and value of information literacy to the improvement of undergraduate education is easy when compared with the accreditor's challenge of promoting the development of effective bibliographic instruction and information literacy programs on college and university campuses.

Besides addressing the benefits of information literacy rather broadly, this chapter identifies the various campus constituencies that must be involved in effecting appropriate programs designed to make students more information literate and independent learners. Some observations also are made relative to what information professionals and other educators might do collaboratively to address the concern for information literacy, all within the context of the accreditation process.

Though there are still those who would dismiss the concept of information literacy as yet another educational fad, the concept is slowly gaining acceptance in the academy as one strategy for improving precollegiate and undergraduate education. I would be the first to admit that information literacy is still not well understood by many in higher education, particularly since some confuse the concept with "computer literacy" or assume that *information literacy* is somehow synonymous with *technical applications*. Nevertheless, it has the potential to be more effective in enhancing the teaching and learning process than any other educational strategy in current use.

And just why am I so confident of this? Precisely because I am convinced that until a person *learns how to learn* or until undergraduate students really learn how to find, select from, analyze, interpret, and use information effectively, they will continually have difficulty improving their abilities to think critically and analytically, to use their powers of reason, or to solve problems. I am equally convinced that information literacy programs (or any resource-based learning programs) must be integral components of undergraduate curricula if they are to be effective or taken seriously by faculty and academic administrators.

In her most recent article, Patricia Breivik (1993) comments about the wise use of information technology by suggesting that when "a goal is information literacy among all students, then those students must have access to computers for self-directed use, and training opportunities and software must be available to facilitate their use of computers and networks" (50). She goes on to note, "Students also must have continual practice—both as part of the curriculum and as part of their extracurricular activities—in accessing and using information successfully in all its formats" (50).

EARLY EMPHASIS NEEDED FOR BEST RESULTS

It terms of their undergraduate experience, it is encouraging to learn that some educational leaders (Montgomery 1992) are promoting "the integration of library information skills into curriculum areas" and "suggesting ways in which information skills can be taught naturally within given subject areas" (529). And in a similar fashion, actions now being taken by states (Pennsylvania State Board of Education 1993) and postsecondary institutions (State University of New York 1992) call for the development and improvement of the information literacy skills of students at the K–12 level. Even a portion of the 1994 annual meeting of the American Association of Colleges for Teacher Education will be devoted to the topic "Bringing the Information Age into the Curriculum." This is a significant development, given the influence of this group in the preparation of teachers. As one example of the resolve of teacher preparation institutions to strengthen the information skills of their students, a special committee of the American Library Association (Association of College and Research Libraries 1992) developed a fairly detailed set of recommendations to be followed by prospective and in-service teachers, making it clear that the "document [was] intended to reflect the important role of school library media specialists as partners with teachers in curriculum development and information skills instruction" (586).

Finally, that Patricia Senn Breivik as one of education's leading and well-respected proponents of information literacy is given a proper forum (Breivik and Jones 1993) to open up discourse with other academic colleagues is further evidence of the increasing value being placed on information literacy. In that "discourse," the collaborators not only discuss the new demands of our information age, but they also conclude that "[w]hen a liberal education ... is defined by and supports the goal of graduating information-literate students, it will have renewed power in the Information Age" (27).

INFORMATION LITERACY CANNOT STAND ALONE

From an accrediting perspective, information literacy must be seen as a concept inextricably connected to the improvement of the undergraduate curriculum—and not just a "hobbyhorse" of librarians and eccentric accrediting officials like me. In my judgment, information literacy—when it is narrowly conceived—will continue to be viewed by some as a peripheral activity unless it is an integral component of the teaching and learning process. Broadly construed, information literacy should be seen as a strategy for improving a student's ability to learn how to learn. With an expanded emphasis in regional accrediting bodies on the assessment of student learning outcomes, information literacy is increasing in importance in the Middle States region and elsewhere.

I believe it is in this connection that librarians, chief academic officers, and others will find the basis for extending the concept of information literacy far beyond the confines of the traditional library. Effective use of information resources—within the library and beyond—assumes that students have mastered the skills to exploit these resources fully, that they have learned how to learn. Students who simply look for facts to support their preconceived ideas and conclusions still have not learned how to learn.

While I am encouraged that the winds of change are already beginning to have positive effects on the campuses of our schools, colleges, and universities, there is still much to be done to ensure that information literacy becomes firmly established in self-study, evaluation, assessment, and accrediting processes for the purpose of improving the teaching and learning process in general and student learning outcomes in particular. Therefore, this chapter not only devotes attention to why the development of more information-literate students is necessary, but it also offers some suggestions as to how librarians, other information specialists, chief academic officers, department heads, and faculty might more aggressively promote the value of information literacy. At the same time, I identify some of the challenges—including some "sacred cows" and cynicism—that will have to be confronted and overcome before there is full realization of the benefits of information literacy, especially the difficult challenge of improving undergraduate education.

As I concluded in a recent essay on information literacy and accreditation (Simmons 1992): "Accrediting bodies such as the Middle States CHE need to go a step further in encouraging the colleges and universities that they accredit to view information literacy and other resource-based learning programs as essential elements in assessing quality, student learning outcomes, and institutional effectiveness'' (22).

TAKING THE CHALLENGE SERIOUSLY

What will constitute that further step? What will be the nature of our efforts to encourage a stronger emphasis on information literacy in the undergraduate curriculum? How might we suggest that information literacy be integrated most effectively into the teaching and learning process at the undergraduate level? And who must be involved in assuring that the goal of producing more information-literate graduates will be achieved?

Though I am aware that there are actually an undetermined number of steps—not just one step—that can be taken, my purpose here is to provide the perspective of one who has personally benefited from information literacy skills through years of schooling and career advancement.

Given the enormous opportunity to reinvigorate the undergraduate curriculum through the strategic use of information, it seems particularly advantageous for accrediting bodies to include information literacy in the assessment of institutional effectiveness and student learning outcomes.

As a consequence, for the Middle States Commission on Higher Education (Middle States Association of Colleges and Schools 1990), the following are especially relevant.

Of paramount importance in assessing the effectiveness of library utilization is the ability in the self-study process to describe and document the strategies and activities used to provide an effective program of bibliographic instruction and information literacy. Library instruction can range from the preparation and use of special discipline focused bibliographic instruction to credit courses in bibliography to sophisticated data retrieval systems. Which areas are drawn upon heavily, which slightly? What does analysis of library usage suggest about teaching methods and their effectiveness? These and similar questions, as well as general circulation and acquisition figures, yield valuable insights into library usage. . . . Equally important is the examination of faculty requests for special bibliographies for their courses and the extent to which faculty require students to use learning resources other than the textbook. (8)

It should be clear that the actual development and implementation of effective information literacy programs must be the responsibility of each accredited institution, which should be encouraged by accreditors to view information literacy as important to the improvement of the quality of the undergraduate experience. That will mean that parties participating in evaluation and assessment protocols—including campus constituent groups and others involved in developing and reviewing self-study and assessment results—will need to collaborate with accrediting bodies if the challenge to address the concern for information literacy is to be successful.

COLLABORATION OF ALL CONSTITUENCIES NEEDED

Who are these campus constituent groups? Why is their cooperation and collaboration indispensable to accrediting bodies' efforts to ensure that information literacy is a critical factor in assessing institutional effectiveness and student learning outcomes? And what about those external to the campus? What will be the nature of their efforts to help accrediting bodies address the concern for information literacy? Since campus constituencies and accrediting review groups bring unique perspectives to this challenge, what might be the specific contribution(s) of each? Perhaps the more critical question should be: How will all of these entities, hopefully working toward the same goal of quality improvement at the undergraduate level, collaborate to ensure that undergraduates leave college with more information skills than when they entered?

Every constituent group on campus needs to be involved in any program to improve institutional quality. Therefore, effective information literacy programs must have the collaboration of librarians and other information associates, faculty, students, administrators, and trustees. Each should have a particular role in the process of developing strategies and programs that ultimately should result in more self-directed, independent, information-literate students and graduates. And just as campus constituencies have definite roles to play, so do many outside of the campus who interact with students, professors, and administrators. These might include other universities and colleges, employers, vendors, and a panoply of other information providers and access points. In fact, the very central role played by technology in facilitating information literacy makes it crucial to include these sources.

Now to the special contributions and involvement of the campus constituencies.

Student Involvement?

Since the raison d'être of any college or university is the education of its students, no program of information literacy—however well intentioned—can succeed without the active participation of students. It is simply axiomatic to note that students must take primary responsibility for their own learning, and more *"how"* than *"what."* While availing themselves of every opportunity to pursue truth, students must discern early the importance of enhancing what Adam Robinson (1993) terms "cyberlearning" skills. These skills naturally involve critical thinking abilities that focus on intellectual skills of a higher education order than rote memory. In the process of becoming more independent learners, students must also begin viewing faculty as facilitators of learning rather than as purveyors of specific pieces of information. In searching for information for the resolution of issues related to life and work, students must subject the information to probing questions. Evidence to suggest that students are becoming more conscious of the need to become more information literate might include: the use of course bibliographies prepared for them by faculty; the greater use of reference services; enrollment in courses on library research; and greater utilization of on-line search and computer data banks.

Information-literate students must never be satisfied with an instructional program that is centered almost entirely on that which can be learned from textbooks and lecture notes. In the final analysis, students must become self-directed learners who have mastered the research tools in the search for knowledge and truth.

Faculty Involvement?

Naturally, the faculty, including librarians, should utilize every means available, as the American Library Association admonishes, "to teach users how to take full advantage of the resources available to them." I do not have much worry about what most librarians as teachers will do to implement a sound program of information literacy, but I do have concern that many other teaching faculty have little direct involvement in either helping to develop the collections or in ensuring that they themselves and their students make full use of existing learning resources. It is sad to note that some institutions still rely solely on library instruction programs consisting only of printed brochures on the introduction to the library, or brief orientation sessions at the beginning of each term for students enrolled in English classes.

On the other hand, there are those institutions that provide specially prepared course and program bibliographies on faculty request; credit and noncredit courses in bibliographic instruction and information literacy; various forms of computer access to data (e.g., compact disk read-only memory [CD-ROMs]) and on-line searches; group and individualized instruction; telecourses; special reference services; and videotapes.

At those institutions where faculty build into their instructional programs strong requirements for library research, we find the greatest effectiveness in getting students to take full advantage of the collections and in promoting the use of resources as a means of improving learning outcomes. Requirements as reflected in course syllabi and student learning contracts and in the nature and extent of student and faculty use of library materials give us some indication of faculty commitment to increased effectiveness. Obviously, when faculty members rely almost exclusively on textbooks and make limited or no demands on students to complete library research on topics within a course or program, it is understandable when students also rely heavily on their textbooks, poorly written lecture notes, and limited or no understanding of how to exploit the full range of information available in a number of formats and locations.

Administration Involvement?

Academic and student development administrators in particular, through appropriate and timely planning, must ensure that there are provisions for easy access by faculty and students to needed information resources and instruction in locating and using them. Administrators must be constantly alert to the need for adequate library and other information to support current and proposed academic programs. It will be critical for academic administrators to do everything possible to ensure that the institutional mission statement and the required general education core include expectations for information literacy.

As part of any overall program for institutional assessment of outcomes, chief academic officers, working closely with professional librarians and other faculty, must ensure that the institution's investment in library/learning resources is utilized effectively. Academic deans must ensure that course outlines reflect a requirement for the use of learning resources other than the textbook and should monitor the quality of research papers completed as a partial requirement for course and degree credit.

Self-Study Steering Committee Involvement?

Besides being able to benefit from the cooperation and collaboration of students and faculty, accreditors will likely find their concern for information literacy best addressed through the medium of self-study steering committees, especially since self-study processes stress the evaluation of the institution's mission, goals, and objectives, as well as emphasize institutional assessment goals and the standards of the accrediting body. Moreover, it would be an unusual self-study steering committee that did not focus on information-processing skills or that did not include a relevant focus on the quality of the undergraduate experience. But it is incumbent on library and information specialists to ensure that self-study designs and work plans provide for the review of programs designed to produce more self-directed, information-literate students.

Trustee Involvement?

For example, members of governing boards, according to Middle States Association standards, are "responsible for the institution's integrity and quality" and must view the library as one of the central foci in maintaining and improving quality. Thus, it is the responsibility of the trustees to provide adequate financial resources to allow the library to develop fully in support of the institution's mission.

Accreditor Involvement?

What should be the response of the accrediting body? In addition to ensuring that its standards and policies include appropriate attention to role of information literacy in improving undergraduate quality, accrediting commissions should develop and implement orientation materials designed to give team evaluators and chairs useful guidance in evaluating and assessing information literacy vis-à-vis institutional effectiveness and student learning outcomes. The accrediting commissions should also expect team members to examine course outlines; syllabi; student research papers, theses, and dissertations; the institution's information literacy program; the annual budget devoted to the support of learning resources; the quality and extent of the institution's collections and means of access to other information sources; and evidence that institutional resources are used by students and faculty.

As for accredited institutions, accreditors not only should expect self-studies to reflect an analysis of library collections in relation to the institution's mission and program offerings; in addition, they should expect those documents to show a demonstrable relationship between its program of bibliographic instruction, actual utilization of learning resources by faculty and students, and learning outcomes. And there should be an expectation that course outlines and syllabi reflect a strong component of student research and recommended readings. Therefore, it is important for each accredited and candidate institution to develop and utilize the library or learning resource center, or information resources more broadly, as a central focus of its teaching/learning process.

HOW CAN LIBRARY AND INFORMATION SPECIALISTS HELP?

In the first place, the library profession should take a number of important steps to ensure that the concept of information literacy is fully understood and that measures are put in place to facilitate the implementation of effective information literacy programs. In this regard, the library profession should (1) collaborate with other colleagues in higher education to connect information literacy more closely with the assessment of the undergraduate experience; (2) in consultation with higher education associations (including accrediting bodies) and learned societies, design and implement workshops for target groups of educators, such as chief academic officers, department heads, and faculty; (3) enlist the aid of academic administrators to identify faculty members who can serve as role models in the innovative ways is which they encourage library research and information literacy among their students; (4) collaborate with schools and colleges of education to ensure that teacher training curricula emphasize the role of information literacy in improving students' learning skills; (5) be more assertive in getting accrediting bodies to revise their standards and evaluative criteria to reflect stronger requirements for bibliographic instruction, information literacy, and the essential relationship between information literacy and the assessment of effective teaching and learning processes; and (6) continue efforts already under way to redefine the roles and staffing patterns for academic libraries so that the professional librarian as teacher can devote considerable more time to assisting students and other faculty in improving their information management skills.

I conclude, as I began, with the notion that the effectiveness of the undergraduate curriculum in part is predicated on students' having learned how to learn, the primary thesis of a recently published guide (Robinson 1993) to help students master the learning process. Information literacy is the sine quo non of this process, inasmuch as it signifies the essential skills on how to locate, evaluate, interpret, and use information effectively for the entire range of learning needs.

Whether students are concerned about improving their basic academic skills, about enhancing their general intellectual skills, or about sharpening their technical/professional quotient, information management skills are absolutely essential. And when it comes to assessing whether or not students have achieved their learning objectives, information literacy can become the focal point for the assessment. In each case, there must be critical attention to the degree to which students have developed the ability to formulate analytical questions rather than merely giving descriptive responses to questions. When institutions are able to document in self-study processes and evaluation teams are able to document in their reports that students have improved their information literacy skills significantly, accreditors and institutions alike will probably be able to celebrate real success in improving undergraduate quality and outcomes.

REFERENCES

Association of College and Research Libraries. 1992. "Information Retrieval and Evaluation Skills for Education Students." *College and Research Libraries News* 53(9): 583–88.

Breivik, Patricia Senn. 1993. "Investing Wisely in Information Technology: Asking the Right Questions." *Educational Record* 74(3): 47–52.

Breivik, Patricia Senn, and Dan L. Jones. 1993. "Information Literacy: Liberal Education for the Information Age." *Liberal Education* 79(1): 24–29.

Middle States Association of Colleges and Schools. 1990. *Designs for Excellence: Handbook for Institutional Self-Study.* Philadelphia: Middle States Association of Colleges and Schools.

Montgomery, Paul K. 1992. "Integrating Library, Media, Research, and Information Skills." *Phi Delta Kappan* 73(7): 529–32.

Pennsylvania State Board of Education. 1993. "Rules and Regulations: Title 22—Education (Curriculum)." *Pennsylvania Bulletin Part II* 23(30): 3552–61.

Robinson, Adam. 1993. *What Smart Students Know.* New York: Crown.

Simmons, Howard L. 1992. "Information Literacy and Accreditation: A Middle States Association Perspective." In *Information Literacy: Developing Students as Independent Learners,* edited by D. W. Farmer and T. F. Mech. New Directions in Higher Education Series, no. 78. San Francisco: Jossey-Bass.

State University of New York. 1992. *SUNY 2000 College Expectations.* Report of the SUNY Task Force on College Entry-Level Knowledge and Skills. Albany: State University of New York.

11

The New American College Student and Workforce Competence: Seven Generalizations that Challenge Traditional Accreditation and Licensure

Robert W. Tucker

Despite good evidence to the contrary, the standard of higher education in the United States remains the "youth-centered" institution in which a full-time faculty instruct full-time, often resident students on a campus with physical classrooms, laboratories, libraries, dormitories, gymnasiums, student unions, and other capital-intensive facilities. Like so many other standards that are no longer relevant and impede progress, the standard of the youth-centered university must give way to the reality of higher education at the frontier of the twenty-first century. Youth-centered institutions were designed at a time when virtually all of the nation's college students were nonworking, recent high school graduates. They were not designed to meet the needs of today's 6 million students over twenty-four years of age, especially the more than 5 million working adult students who clearly would be better served by what I call the "adult-centered" university. To better understand the needs of working adult students in relation to the institutional systems that might meet those needs, it is necessary to have a clear picture of the college student population. This population has become more diverse over the past two decades, and with this diversity has come a proliferation of needs. Today, six student groups make up most of large college and university populations.[1]

Group 1. Defining the essence of the image of a college student is the "traditional" undergraduate, age seventeen to twenty-four, who seeks a bachelor's degree and is enrolled full-time at a campus. In 1992, there were approximately 3.9 million of these students, and they made up 27.3 percent of the total college enrollment.

Group 2. The "traditional" graduate student, age twenty-two to thirty-four, who seeks either an academic or professional master's or doctor's degree and is enrolled full-time at a campus. In 1992, there were approximately 650,000 such students, 4.5 percent of those enrolled in a college that year.

Group 3. The "semitraditional" undergraduate student, age seventeen to twenty-four, who seeks a bachelor's degree and is enrolled part-time at a campus, usually working part-time in entry-level jobs. These students comprised approximately 2.9 million (20.8 percent) of the 1992 enrollment.

Group 4. The "semitraditional" graduate student, age twenty-two to thirty-four, who seeks an academic master's or doctor's degree and is enrolled part-time at a campus. (Employment varies among this population. Some have part-time work in a variety of campus and off-campus jobs, and others work in full-time careers, example, schoolteachers, principals and superintendents, or college teachers completing their doctor's degree.) There were approximately 487,000 students, 3.4 percent of total enrollment, in this category in 1992.

Group 5. The "nontraditional" undergraduate student, age twenty-five and up, who usually seeks a first degree in an on-campus or off-campus program, is enrolled full- or part-time and is a career-oriented member of the labor force (whether working or reentering). Approximately 5.3 million students (37.8 percent of total enrollment) fell into this category in 1992.

Group 6. The "nontraditional" graduate student, age twenty-five and up, is enrolled full- or part-time, seeks a professional, master's or doctor's degree in an on-campus or off-campus program, and works full-time in a chosen career. In 1992, approximately 880,000 students (6.2 percent of total enrollment) were in this category.

Groups 1 through 4 of the six student populations are those typically thought of as the consumers of higher education. Today, the traditional students of higher education compose 55 percent of the market. Groups 1 through 4 are served by traditional or youth-centered colleges and universities. Groups 5 and 6 are the new and still growing consumers of higher education—the *New American College Students.*[2] Constituting nearly half of the market, they represent the only segment that is projected to increase significantly through the year 2005. New American College Students are also those who offer the surest and the swiftest economic and societal returns on the nation's educational dollar. More than any other group, these students represent the 28 million agents of change in today's workforce. They are the specialists, supervisors, managers, project coordinators, and others who function to improve the workforce and the economy. When these students are educated in ways appropriate to their need for immediately applicable knowledge and skills, they diffuse their new knowledge and skills to others, improving the quality and efficiency of the nation's workforce. With or without appropriate education, the decisions these individuals make will shape tomorrow's economic future. Given the opportunity for efficient learning, these students will apply to tomorrow's workplace what they learned in last night's class. Equally important, they will take back to class what was learned from the application to enhance the learning experiences of everyone in the class, including the instructor. This knowledge transfer process from classroom to work-place and back creates an urgently needed process of continuous improvement between higher education and the audiences it serves.[3]

It is now time to advance the agenda of the New American College Student. One look across the landscape of higher education reveals a blighted dust bowl called adult education—a worthy but amorphous notion lacking coherence, direction, and prestige; underfunded, understaffed, profitable (but treated as a cash cow to pay for more glamorous but unprofitable programs), relegated to temporary buildings or basements, and carefully ignored in polite conversation among education cognoscenti. I am frequently challenged and occasionally chastised by senior college administrators for my uncharitable characterization of the landscape of adult-centered higher education—until, that is, I ask to see the institution's budget. Perhaps this irritation *cum* ire reveals the community of higher education's tacit understanding of the problem and the latent guilt it feels at ignoring it.

One wonders how institutional wisdom can stray so far from the obvious. Does any other group of college students stand to effect so immediate a reversal in the decline of U.S. global competitiveness through the immediate application of their newly learned skills to the workforce? Is there another sector of college students whose future is more intimately and reciprocally tied to the workplace, families, and communities served by higher education? Is there a class of younger students more certain of their reasons for attending college, more dedicated to succeeding, or more eager to apply what they have learned to their work environment? Can any student keep the classroom as honest and meaningful as can the pragmatic and experience-based appraisal of the adult student? Are these tax-paying, working adult citizens not the students most deserving of priority on the national education agenda? These truths—commonplace to adult educators—seldom rise to shape the administrative agendas of individual institutions, and they are nowhere in evidence at the level of national policy where there is an inappropriate silence on the subject of adult higher education, especially higher education for those already in the workforce. Given the evidence in support of a national system of lifelong education, it is difficult to understand why the education of those five to twenty-five years old consumes 90 percent of the nation's attention to and concern for education and nearly 90 percent of the funds allocated to education.

GENERALIZABLE COMPONENTS OF THE LEARNING ENVIRONMENT FOR THE NEW AMERICAN COLLEGE STUDENT

My studies of the working adult college student have produced findings that do not necessarily coincide with the received view of adult education. First, it seems clear that there are generalizable components of the learning environment for working adults. Second, these components are somewhat different from those of the younger, professionally unemployed student. Third, these generalizations are different from those prescribed by popular "theories" of adult education, many of which commingle models of learning and normative politics. These generalizations about the New American College Student have been drawn less from theoretical presupposition and stipulation (although the former is, to a certain extent, inescapable) than from very clear patterns of evidence derived from the study of tens of thousands of working adult students.

For the past seven years, we have conducted longitudinal studies of the educationally and professionally relevant facets of the working adult student. Facets have included needs, values, attitudes, learning processes, and learning outcomes. To date, over 50,000 working adult students and representative samples of their employers have been studied. Data collection begins at the point of registration in the first class and continues throughout the professional life of the graduate (to date, three or more years postgraduation). As one part of these studies, I have developed and maintained a computerized knowledge base of every comment working adult students write on their end-of-course surveys. Far from being a trivial collection of complaints, as was predicted by some, this knowledge base has become a contextually rich source of insight and understanding into the learning processes, needs, values, attitudes, and preferences of both faculty and students. The knowledge base now contains over 600,000 comments, classified into 535 categories. Each comment can be retrieved in an object-oriented structure to produce a profile for longitudinal or cross-sectional study focusing on any combination of instructor, course, textbook in use, class size, location, grade-point average, and many other educational and demographic considerations. In creating a knowledge base of students' handwritten comments, the typically formidable and overworked distinction between quantitative and qualitative information has been eliminated. The profile reporting system effectively quantifies large amounts of essentially qualitative information.

The findings and generalizations derived from the knowledge-base comment analysis system are revealing of students' attention to the learning environment. Nearly half of students' comments are about instructors and the importance of the role they play (or fail to play) in the learning process; 25 percent of comments are directed toward curriculum; 10 percent focus on fellow students and the role they play in the learning environment; 10 percent address group learning processes and outcomes; and the remaining few percent address everything else (mostly direct administrative services). Of the 50 percent of comments about faculty, for example, nearly 75 percent are positive comments; the 25 percent of faculty-related comments that are negative are constructive and actionable (e.g., "be more clear about grading criteria"). Overall, it is heartening to observe that working adult college students make abundant comments that are constructive, to the point, and that offer educational and professional insights that typically far exceed the written comments of the students falling in Groups 1 through 3. The following are generalizations from the above sources of evidence.

Generalization number one: Working adult students want their educational experiences to be organized around learning outcomes that are both perceived and subsequently have proven to be of direct benefit to the learner. This emphasis on learning outcomes requires that adult-centered universities move away from being structured and evaluated based on the quality of their *inputs* (buildings, physical libraries, tenured faculty with Ph.D.s, etc.) in the fashion of youth-centered universities. Adult-centered universities must be judged by the quality of their *outputs*—measured improvement in the knowledge and skills of their graduates as defined by the needs of the workforce. Redirecting standards of educational quality from their current emphasis on inputs to a genuine emphasis on outputs, especially learning outcomes and impact, will require substantial change in the current regulatory, governance, and management structures that define the nation's institutions of higher education.

Generalization number two: Working adult students prefer to learn from instructors who practice what they teach. With their pragmatic orientation to learning and subject matter selection, the New American College Student has little interest in listening to lectures on untested theories of management from someone who has never managed anything other than a college classroom. They want to learn finance from a financial officer. They want a practicing nurse-manager to teach them the latest in hospital nursing management techniques. When they study research contributed by faculty, they want it to be based on real contexts and cases. They are not at all impressed (perhaps less than they should be) by well-written research based on studies of college sophomores who were asked to pretend that they were corporate executives. As organizational "insiders," they are all too familiar with the unrealistic response accorded visiting academics in search of a study population. The unexamined relationship between full-time faculty and educational quality must be subjected to unbiased empirical study and analysis. The one national study that did examine the relationship between full-time faculty and educational quality produced findings that favor a part-time faculty, especially with adult students.[4] Again, change in the regulatory, governance, and management structures of higher education will be required to approach this question in the public's interest.

Generalization number three: Working adult students prefer to learn in an environment that recognizes and builds on the considerable expertise these students have gained in their jobs. This generalization holds strong implications for the instructor. In addition to being professionally knowledgeable, instructors must be expert facilitators since at least half of their job is to provide a platform for the expression of the relevant knowledge of each working adult in the classroom, helping each to elevate their knowledge to the sum of their individual parts. This process (which I call *horizontal learning*) becomes an ineluctable force when one creates a classroom of working professionals and provides, through structured curriculum, the opportunity for student/workers to teach and learn from each other. However, when the horizontal learning environment is created, working adult students are looking to maximize each other's learning experience by sharing that expertise.

Generalization number four: Working adult students expect curriculum to provide up-to-date information on the discipline as it applies to their job and profession. Moreover, they expect course content to be faithful to the catalog description (truth in advertising). Because students are working adult professionals, curriculum must be carefully designed to accomplish several objectives. First, it must address the central learning objectives of the subject under study in a way that is relevant to the student who hopes to put the learning to work tomorrow morning. Second, it must temper theory with best practice so that the student becomes a critical consumer of information and not merely a skilled practitioner of a particular model or technique. Third, because employers demand it, the infrastructure of curriculum must embed learning outcomes in written and oral communication, group process, and critical thinking and problem-solving skills—skills central to success in the modern workplace.

Generalization number five: Working adult students want time-efficient education. These busy adults have little patience for a process that earns them a college degree, one class per semester over a ten- to fifteen-year period, when there is a faster alternative. Schools that recognize the working adult's ability to benefit from a compressed learning format will find students lined up at their door. Learning for working adults can be accelerated and time formats compressed by emphasizing the horizontal learning process through the strategic use of study groups, group projects, and group accountability. Such group processes not only elevate and accelerate the primary learning process, but they provide invaluable training in group process, leadership, followership, and teamwork skills. Other techniques—such as workplace projects, group field study, and peer teaching—must be employed to accelerate and compress the learning environment.

Generalization number six: Working adult students want a no-nonsense, customer-service-oriented learning environment that recognizes that they have real limits on their discretionary time. Unlike their younger counterparts, working adult students are demanding consumers of goods and services. Commanding disposable income that does not come from their parents, they are accustomed to getting exactly what they pay for, and with a money-back guarantee of quality. Living in a society in which time is *the* central underlying commodity, they have little tolerance for the slow, inefficient, and error-ridden service that characterizes many youth-centered institutions of higher education—especially when needless bureaucracy and disregard for the student's time are at the core of the problem. Because generalization number six can be enabling to the other generalizations, it is worth elaborating upon.

The fundamentals of good customer service in adult-centered higher education are simple. The roles of faculty, staff, and administration should be defined (and evaluated) as service providers. This means that the times and places of class should be arranged for the convenience of the student, not the university or the instructor. Textbooks and supplies should be delivered to the classroom, if doing so is helpful. Everything possible, including the educational process, should be virtualized and freed from the constraints of time and place. Registration, grades, transcripts, and other support services should be available through the mail or over the phone with "instant" response times. Library and other learning resource services should be available in person, on-line through a computer bulletin board system and/or Internet, by facsimile, and by mail. There should be a student-as-customer "bill of rights" with compensation for cases of intentional disregard for the time and convenience of the student. The entire institution should aim for high and continuously improving levels of customer satisfaction.

Generalization number seven: Working adult students want high structure and well-defined "rules of the road" to educational success. In opposition to prevailing theoretical views, I have found little evidence to support the idea that working adult students would choose a self-directed learning environment over a highly structured alternative. To the contrary, I have found abundant evidence that working adult students want well-defined structure and, given an opportunity to exercise their will, will force the institution to impose such structure if the existing structure is too vague or imprecise to meet their needs. This high need for structure seems to be due to several factors, all of them related to their need to project themselves and their families several years into the future and to manage their time and goal attainment accordingly.

MANAGING ACADEMIC QUALITY FOR THE NEW AMERICAN COLLEGE STUDENT

Developing an educational structure that is responsive to the principles embedded in the above generalizations is possible only if that structure is supported by a strong commitment to the principles of academic quality management under which *continuous improvement* becomes the institution's highest goal and *continuous measurement and adaptation* become its way of life. The institution must develop and use an Academic Quality Management System (AQMS) in which both process and outcomes measures are woven into the institution's fabric. In such systems, students are not the only ones to benefit. Faculty and staff find that their jobs are enriched by working in an environment of continuous improvement; not only does it feel better to work with others who are committed to institutional quality, but it feels better to work with responsible, satisfied customers because of the elevated quality of interaction between and among all stakeholders in the education enterprise.

The first tier of the AQMS must focus on all aspects of the educational process, using measurement and management techniques to evaluate service delivery. Are textbooks available when they are needed? Are administrative requirements necessary, friendly, and efficient? Are classes covering the material as promised to students? Are students finding the learning experience worthwhile? Are the study groups effective learning devices? Is the instructor drawing out the knowledge and experiences of the working adult students to the benefit of all? There are a myriad of questions to be asked on a good student end-of-course survey, and adult students are willing to take the time to answer them if they know the information will be put to good use. A faculty end-of-course survey should take parallel measures.

The second tier of the AQMS should focus on educational impact and outcomes. It must assess outcomes in the context of the adult world. Since the development of appropriate professional values and attitudes is a significant variable in adult success in the workplace, the development and change of values and attitudes must be a core component of any outcomes assessment system. Cognitive achievement in the major field is also important. There should be assessments—before and after—in place for every student. Contextually rich measures such as portfolios, simulations, behavioral assessments, and work products must guide and complement the institutionwide assessments. To achieve the objective of meaningful outcomes and impact assessment, employers must be involved in the process; not only do they pay half of the working adult students' tuition, they hold invaluable perspective on workplace competence that cannot be obtained elsewhere. Long-term impact should be determined through studies of alumni and employers.

Both tiers of the AQMS must ensure that they employ the results of those measurements to improve the quality of their educational programs; that they involve employers at each step of the educational process in order to ensure a close fit between the classroom and the workplace; and that, whether organized as public, private not-for-profit, or private for-profit institutions, they hold themselves strictly accountable for efficient results to the primary and secondary consumers they serve.

One significant barrier to the implementation of an AQMS is the fact that the institutional processes of higher education are closed to public inspection. There is little or no robust objective information about how any class, instructor, program, college, or university is performing against appropriate benchmarks or criteria. Hiding behind the robes of academic freedom, the nation's faculty have yet to open their classrooms to rational, scientific inspection. Those attempting to bring the customary tools of scientific measurement and understanding to the classroom are met by a defense squad captained by the faculty senate. It seems all too obvious that the measurement and management of day-to-day educational processes, in situ, as they occur, is a necessary precondition to the management of academic quality. Yet we are asked to believe that there is a sharp line of discontinuity between the activities of knowledge workers that we call professors and the activities of knowledge workers known by any other name. Very few of those who teach the principles of total quality management (TQM) on the college campus will practice it in their own profession. Until the nation's colleges and universities make the transition to an open information architecture in their own backyards, higher education and its stakeholders will continue to suffer from a conspiracy of silence on the topic of academic quality management. The ideals of public and democratic change and improvement cannot be realized in the context of a closed and inscrutable information system.

CHANGING FACE OF ACCREDITATION AND LICENSURE

A very significant barrier to meeting the needs of the New American College Student is that posed by the accrediting and licensing entities. It is an understatement to say that the very essence of regulation in higher education is in a state of flux. The Council on Postsecondary Accreditation, once a focal point for the national agenda and an adjudicator of interregional accreditation issues, no longer exists; the regional agencies are contemplating replacing it with their own creature. The 1992 Reauthorization of the Higher Education Act has hatched a behemoth of state-by-state oversight and regulation of colleges and universities. The effects of this change will devolve to little other than the good sense and restraint of state higher education executive officers (SHEEOs). In any event, the national agenda will be made more difficult. In place of six regions, there are now 50 states to reckon with in the business of establishing and implementing national standards, such as those of Goal 5 of the National Education Goals Panel. And as the regionals try to force colleges and universities into a Procrustean bed of the 1950s with its heavy emphasis on input resources, the six regional accrediting commissions and their growing bureaucracies appear to be defying Thomas Wolfe's maxim that it is foolish to try to find the future in the past. In this state of flux, it would be foolhardy to predict the outcome of the regionals' struggle to survive or the SHEEOs' relationship to the national initiative for outcomes-based educational standards. At the least, we must await the first full round of inspections by the SHEEOs; and we must wonder if the regionals will even survive their quest for meaning and relevance in the Balkanized world of the 50 SHEEOs. Despite the uncertainty about the future of accreditation and state regulation, there are identifiable areas in which current accreditation and licensure do not appear to support either the New American College Student or the national interest these students serve. The short list of these areas includes the following.

Lack of focus on the working adult student. Typical of this lack of focus is the 1993 *Report of the National Commission on Responsibilities for Financing Postsecondary Education.* After two years of studying the issue, the commission produced an eighty-page report that allocates one page to adults. On page twenty-one, the report points out that 45 percent of all college students are twenty-five years or older, and the needs of "both traditional and non-traditional students must be considered." The remaining pages are then devoted to traditional students. Likewise, there is no mention of higher education for working adults in Mandate for Change, the Clinton administration's agenda prepared by the Progressive Policy Institute. The loss accruing to the neglect of the New American College Student is not only economic and societal. This neglect penalizes the educational aspirations of hundreds of thousands of American workers who went to work before beginning or completing their higher education and who now realize the value of education to themselves and to their families.

Blatant disregard for productivity, efficiency, and cost to the taxpayer. It is disheartening to scour the pages of the regional accrediting bodies handbooks, looking for phrases such as "efficient education," "demonstrated cost-effectiveness," and "financial benchmarks against comparable institutions." The cost per unit of service in higher education has risen far beyond plausible economic justification. (The lack of nationwide benchmarks for outcome measures rules out the possibility of a more robust cost per unit of outcome measure.) The federal mandate of SHEEO is also silent on the important issues of productivity. Using figures from the California Postsecondary Education Commission as an example:

The capital cost of new facilities is $1,961 per student in the University of California system and $1,100 per student in the California State University system. The average lead time for planning and building new institutions is 8 to 10 years...the time and cost of planning and building a traditional campus and much of the cost of operating it arises from the need to provide facilities and services that are neither used by nor are useful to working adult students. In sharp contrast, the capital cost of replicating facilities designed to efficiently educate the *New American College Student* can be as low as $140 per student; planning time is three months and construction time (building out leased space) is three months. (Sperling and Tucker 1993, 12)

Preoccupation with inputs and corresponding lack of focus on substantial learning outcomes and impact. Despite the flurry of rhetoric on the assessment of learning outcomes during the mid- to late 1980s, the regional accrediting bodies are paying very little real attention (i.e., the production of scrutable, scientifically based evidence) to learning outcomes, and the SHEEOs are not required to gather any evidence of efficacy based on learning outcomes. In the 1993–94 revision of one regional accrediting body's handbook (North Central Association 1993), for example, there are thirty-two detailed requirements for inputs that overshadow a mere five required measures of outputs. Of the five output requirements, all are stated so loosely that almost any form of assessment (including many that would not pass elementary scientific muster) will satisfy them, and three of the five output requirements have nothing to do with what students have learned.

Self-serving preoccupation with full-time faculty. Despite the evidence that practitioner faculty have the richest perspective to offer the New American College Student, especially in teaching applied, practitioner-focused disciplines, and despite the fact that so many students are now working adults, the regional accrediting bodies are clearly strengthening their commitment to the ideal of the full-time professorate. The historical and continuing reasons for this commitment are not too difficult to trace. Anyone who has read both the collective-bargaining proceedings of the nation's professorate and the regional's accrediting handbooks will see the direct influence of the former on the latter. State licensure requirements regarding the proportion of full-time faculty an institution must have derive from this same source of influence.

Codified Opposition to change and growth. While the world, and our nation within it, changes at a pace that defies comprehension, the regional accrediting bodies appear to believe that they can legislate against change and progress. It remains to be seen whether the SHEEOs will follow suit. Through the "substantive change" clause, the regional accrediting bodies effectively slow innovation in higher education to a snail's pace. This glacial speed limit, in turn, drives business and industry elsewhere for their educational products and makes all but impossible the creation of small, entrepreneurial colleges and universities designed to meet emerging and rapidly changing educational needs. When one looks closely at the rationale for requiring colleges and universities to take years to accomplish what they might achieve in months, there is little to be found but an unfounded concern for maintaining ill-defined "quality." Imagine trying to generalize the principle "Quality must take a long time" to the rest of the marketplace. Were it not for the essentially monopolistic nature of the community of higher education, efficient colleges and universities would have emerged long ago to dominate the landscape. The fact is that there is no necessary relationship between the length of time it takes to develop a product and its quality. Quality does, on the other hand, rest on having open access to information about developmental and production processes—a principle strongly resisted by many institutions of higher education. Unfortunately, the regional accrediting bodies are silent on this point.

MEETING NEEDS FOR HIGHER EDUCATION IN THE TWENTY-FIRST CENTURY

Goal 5 of the National Educational Goals panel states, "By the Year 2000, every adult American will be literate and will possess the knowledge and skills necessary to compete in a global economy and exercise the rights and responsibilities of citizenship.'' Goal 5 goes on to enumerate specific educational objectives including ''strengthening the connection between education and work'' and ''[increasing] the proportion of college graduates who demonstrate advanced ability to think critically, communicate effectively, and solve problems.''

College-educated knowledge workers and those who, through a college education, hope to become knowledge workers require regular knowledge and skill renewal if they are to remain productive over a working lifetime of fifty-plus years. In addition, a very large portion of workers and soon-to-be workers who are classified as ''non–college bound'' in relation to the youth-centered system of higher education would in fact avail themselves of useful college education, were an adult-centered institution near their home or place of work. Our projections (Sperling and Tucker 1993) show that some 900,000 working adults would immediately enroll in, and derive benefits from, an educational institution designed to serve the New American College Student, had they one near their home or place of work. Over the next five years, 2 million additional working adults would also enroll. In addition to these new students, at least 50 percent of the new entrants to Groups 5 and 6 would choose the adult-centered option rather than force themselves into an ill-fitting form of youth-centered education. Without repeating the now widely discussed statistics on higher education regarding declining state financial support, inflationary budgets, steeply rising tuition, declining research and education budgets, and declining teaching loads, the nation's public and private institutions of higher education are already operating at or beyond capacity, and they cannot afford to build additional facilities to accommodate growth in the adult market. There is a better alternative.

To implement this better alternative, the regional accrediting bodies, the state SHEEOs, and the institutions themselves must undergo a major, and lifesaving, self-transformation. Their roles must become one of collegial advocacy for quality and productivity. Through a lengthy public process, they must redefine and narrow their goals to (1) facilitate through public and professional dialogue a broad and common core of educational outcomes associated with each of the major disciplines of study, (2) ensure that institutions identify educational outcomes unique to their missions, academic programs, learning systems, students, and other stakeholders, (3) ensure that institutions measure and manage their operations to the achievement of both the core and the unique educational outcomes, (4) ensure that institutions make known to their customers and potential customers the core and unique educational outcomes of their institution as well as the efficiency with which they achieve these educational outcomes, and (5) encourage and reward institutional innovation in the interest of quality and productivity. When compared with their current roles as keepers of the guard, this will be a sea change.

NOTES

1. This taxonomy owes to the work of John Sperling. By design, it omits classification by purpose and thereby slights attention to controversial student categories such as mid-

career reentrants in favor of showing the sheer size of the heretofore undefined Groups 5 and 6.

2. This material draws on the author's work published in *Adult Assessment Forum* (see Tucker 1992).

3. Of course the New American College Student does not represent the majority of the nation's workers. The system that educates these students must teach them the new agendas for quality and productivity. It must teach them specific principles that support the value of a well-educated and continuously educated workforce. It must show them the shortsighted thinking inherent in corporate training budgets that provide weeks of highly generalizable education each year to senior managers and a day or so per year of job-specific training to workers.

4. A study by Jeffrey Gilmore (1991) examined a number of variables relating to educational quality, and two of the findings run counter to the commissions's rationale: (1) The percentage of faculty holding doctoral degrees has no significant effect on student performance, and (2) the most significant factor that was negatively associated with educational quality was the percentage of full-time faculty.

REFERENCES

Gilmore, Jeffrey. 1991. *Price and Quality in Higher Education.* Washington, D.C.: Office of Educational Research and Improvement, U.S. Department of Education.

North Central Association of Colleges and Schools. 1993. *A Handbook of Accreditation 1993–94.* Chicago: North Central Association of Colleges and Schools.

Sperling, J. G., and R. W. Tucker. 1993. *For-Profit Higher Education for Working Adults: The Least Cost Way to a World Class Workforce.* Phoenix, Ariz.: Center for the Study of Higher Education and the Economy.

Tucker, R. W. 1992. "A New Agenda for a New American Student." *Adult Assessment Forum: Journals of Quality Management in Adult Centered Education* 2(2): 3–5.

12

Challenges to Accreditation Posed by Nontraditional Models of Information Delivery

Cynthia Hartwell and Edward D. Garten

During the 1980s and now into the 1990s, American higher education has continued its long-standing tradition and history of innovation and desire to serve ever-changing and diverse constituency. While demonstrating a desire for flexibility and responsiveness to a new and often foreign environment, traditional colleges and universities have often done so under severe economic constraints, staffing limitations, and in some instances, retrenchment.

Numerous nontraditional programs sponsored by a range of institutions have arisen within the last several decades. In some instances, the nontraditional programs have been extensions of traditional universities, taught in new ways via new vehicles. Others have been unique, stand-alone programs aimed at specific target groups such as professional working adults or industrial production workers. Some nontraditional programs such as Walden University and Nova University have been directed primarily toward graduate study including the doctorate. Distance learning, computer conferencing, and other mediated and often self-directed approaches to education have characterized many of these traditional programs. Many of these programs are openly entrepreneurial in their attempts to target specific clientele who desire and respond to the flexibility of the academic programs offered.

Many academics and information professionals, however, have held little appreciation for the ways in which these institutions operate. This is especially true with respect to the more entrepreneurial in spirit among nontraditional universities. Unhappily, it would seem also that even among those individuals where some basic appreciation for these programs exists, there is often present a high degree of skepticism relative to both the intent and the integrity of such programs. As Millard (1991) recently observed, there is a "basic assumption that nontraditional higher education is essentially second-rate, of lower quality than traditional residential education" (148).

In the summer of 1992, one of the authors, a consultant-evaluator for the North Central Association of Colleges and Schools, served on the comprehensive visit to the University of Phoenix, an entrepreneurial, for-profit institution of higher education serving the educational needs of working adults at twelve campuses in five southwestern states, Hawaii, and Puerto Rico. While an experienced consultant-evaluator with more traditional institutions, he approached the assignment with some anxiety and, it must be admitted, several preconceived notions about this type of institution. The preconceptions proved to be unfounded. Indeed, this institution proved to be a useful and innovative model for other entrepreneurial and nontraditional universities in its approach to the provision of learning resources.

The intent of this chapter is threefold. First, it will explore the educational approach taken by one entrepreneurial university, that of the University of Phoenix. As part of this discussion the information access and delivery model used by the University of Phoenix will be explained. Second, the chapter will suggest some of the major challenges that entrepreneurial and other nontraditional institutions pose to library managers associated with more traditional universities. Finally, this chapter will suggest several areas for discussion and collaboration between this niche of higher education and more traditional libraries and information agencies.

NONTRADITIONAL EDUCATION AND THE
ENTREPRENEURIAL MODEL

American higher education has a long history with nontraditional and experimental education, and that history will not be reviewed here. Recent years have seen a revitalization of interest in nontraditional models of higher education as well as new models for the diversity of instruction. At least in the last fifteen years, librarians have had some record of engagement with the provision of information services to many of these nontraditional programs. One has only to read the literature associated with the "off-campus library services" movement to quickly recognize that librarians have had a strong and growing interest in the delivery of academic information to educational participants in off-site and nontraditional learning sites. Educational and informational technologies, in partnership with libraries, are being used successfully in such places as the Intermountain Community Learning and Information Services Project funded by the W. K. Kellogg Foundation (Millard 1991, 58). Among model nontraditional educational programs serving the needs of employees within major corporations could be noted the College and University Option Program sponsored by the United Automobile Workers and Ford Motor Company and the Pathways to the Future program supported by Mountain-Bell and the Communications Workers of America (Millard 1991, 58). Notable in its support of these and other programs has been the work of the Council for Adult and Experiential Learning (CAEL).

One must note, as well, the fairly sustained history of entrepreneurial university outreach to military installations around the country. Certainly institutions with more traditional "home" missions such as Central Michigan University have had a long history in delivering academic programs at military installations. Numerous other less traditional institutions, including the University of Phoenix highlighted in this chapter, have a strong record for such programs.

While here we have used the term *entrepreneurial university* to identify many nontraditional programs, today this term may be somewhat of a misnomer. The emerging reality is that senior administrators at many more traditional universities are being asked to become more "entrepreneurial" in the sense that many campus units, including libraries, are being urged to seek creative solutions to the funding of programs or are being asked to target their students (customers) in a far more intentional fashion than in the past. In addition, they are being asked to be more outcomes oriented and more responsive in their delivery of educational programs. If being asked to become more of a profit center, if being asked to focus more closely on customer expectations, and if being asked to share a more outcomes orientation and can be considered at least three of the traits often associated with what we are calling the entrepreneurial university, then we might, in the future, allow that many more universities will embody the entrepreneurial model. As Gareth Williams (1992) has observed, "[The] idea of the university as an economic enterprise, selling academic services to federal and state governments, to business and to households, is much more widespread in the United States than in any other country" (844).

THE UNIVERSITY OF PHOENIX EDUCATIONAL MODEL

Wanted: A College/University That Specializes in Educating 26- to 45-Year-Olds with 10+ Years of Professional Management Experience. Seeking university program that acknowledges my personal/professional goals, including increasing my level of work-related knowledge, gaining skills pertinent to my job, and assisting me in progressing in my career. Need small class size, workshop-type format, group discussion, use of class studies, and emphasis on applied research fitting my job. Factors important for enrollment in a degree program include short time frame, ability to coordinate work with school, convenient scheduling/location of classes, faculty with current/relevant experience, and curriculum tailored to adult needs.

This ad reflects the educational needs, wants, and expectations of a student enrolled at the University of Phoenix, a postsecondary educational institution focusing on the provision of needed educational services to working adult learners. The cornerstone of the university's educational philosophy and practice is the recognition of the distinction between the younger college student still deciding on a career and the experienced adult student who has established professional goals and has had experience in achieving them. As an institution that has served nearly 70,000 working adults, the university knows that working adult students tend not to respond to educational programs that fail to acknowledge the proper role and place of the experience of the students in the learning process. This important distinction is reflected in the content of the University of Phoenix's curriculum, instruction, student services, and administrative infrastructure.

The university's curriculum design and operational structure are based on recognized principles of adult learning espoused by Malcolm Knowles, the pioneer adult educator. These principles embody a participative, collaborative, and applied problem-solving orientation in the educational process. Education is facilitated by faculty whose advanced academic preparation and current professional experience help integrate academic theory and practical application.

In recognition of the distinction between younger college students and the adult learner, the University of Phoenix has established, among others, two critical learning objectives to help students achieve their academic goals: (1) enhance self-directed learning through the use of small group dynamics; and (2) develop interpersonal skills needed for effective participation in small groups.

To achieve these learning objectives, the university uses the "study group" process as an integral element of its educational and delivery system. Each study group is composed of three to five students and meets weekly outside of class. Study groups function as an extension of classroom activities and as a mutual support mechanism through which students learn efficient problem solving from exposure to the professional expertise of peers. Study groups not only help students accomplish the rigorous workload in an accelerated format (four hours per week for five weeks for undergraduates; four hours per week for six weeks for graduate students), but they also help students apply interaction skills to achieve a common objective. Through the sharing of talents, experiences, and learning resources of the study group, adult students assume a greater self-direction and responsibility for their own learning. The study group process demands active participation by students in their educational development and places greater responsibility for knowledge and skill acquisition on the learner.

Curriculum development at the University of Phoenix reflects the principles of adult learning that are embedded in the university's teaching/learning model. Each course in every degree program specifies goals, learning activities, and learning outcomes. Students are required to demonstrate the achievement of the outcomes of each course in their degree program. These principles are translated into instructional elements included in a module, an annotated syllabus that is distributed to all faculty and students. A module exists for each course offered and includes learning objectives, expected outcomes, and activities and assignments that support the learning objectives.

THE UNIVERSITY OF PHOENIX INFORMATION SERVICE MODEL

Learning resource services at the University of Phoenix are designed to support the university's mission of serving adult learners and to assist in the achievement of the educational objectives of programs as delineated by the learning outcomes in the university's curriculum. To this end, the university develops its learning resource services in much the same fashion as corporate/special library/information centers within business and government. Owing to the structured nature of the curriculum and the professional nature of most course offerings, learning resource services are highly specialized, relying on a coordinated mixture of on-line database searching and a well-selected periodical collection.

Learning resources are provided by the corporate-based Learning Resources Services Center, headquartered in Phoenix, Arizona. From this centralized location, literature and information services are provided to the university's 15,000 students enrolled in business, management, education, computer science, and nursing programs at twelve campuses in five southwestern states, Hawaii, and Puerto Rico. In addition, students enrolled in two distance education programs— computer-based and teleconferencing/directed study—use the services of the Learning Resource Services Center.

The Learning Resource Services Center operates three programs: (1) Academic Information Services; (2) an article retrieval/document delivery service; and (3) a resource referral services program. The first service, Academic Information Services, provides computer-based bibliographic searching in topic areas for students and faculty. Searches are requested by phone, an 800 toll-free number, voice mail, or fax or through the use of the university's E-mail/bulletin board system (Academic Library Exchange [ALEX]). Regular mail, campus courier, or in-person requests also may be made. The full range of databases are searched for students. Owing to the accelerated nature of the university's instructional delivery system, turnaround time for search results is critical. Seventy percent of searches (the Center averages completing 700-plus mediated searches per month) are completed and returned to students within twenty-four hours.

The Learning Resource Services Center completes searches via on-line clearinghouse databases, that is, Dialog, BRS Afterdark, and Datatimes, as well as various CD-ROMs (compact disks read-only memory). The center depends on four part-time librarians (referred to as learning resource specialists) to retrieve citations from a wide variety of databases. In addition, these librarians provide feedback to students, faculty, and staff regarding resources to consult for additional information.

The center's article copy service is based on the maintenance of a core collection of 840 journals in business and management, nursing, education, counseling, and computer/information sciences. Students access the copy service through the same mechanisms as the search service. The center uses a variety of on-demand document delivery vendors as well. Finally, it offers a resource referral service providing additional assistance to students and faculty in identifying and locating general reference sources, books, and local library facilities that may be of benefit. The center maintains an ongoing resource list that delineates information about community borrowing privileges for various libraries, fees/restrictions, and services pertinent to academic and public libraries in the communities where the university delivers its programs.

The center produces and disseminates a *Learning Resource Manual* that is provided to every incoming student. The manual provides the student with information on how to conduct library research and how to do on-line literature searching. It includes descriptions of machine-readable databases. Beyond the support provided through the Learning Resource Services Center, additional information support is provided via the curriculum module that each student receives upon registering for a course. When appropriate and necessary, supplementary literature and information are provided in the form of journal articles, case studies, and book chapters (with copyright permission).

ADVERSARIES OR COLLEAGUES? ISSUES FOR CLARIFICATION

Accreditation Issues

Library administrators have long been troubled by the belief that the nontraditional and entrepreneurial university has not met fully the standards or has skirted the standards promulgated for library services by the regional accreditation commissions. There is some evidence to suggest that the six regional commissions long have struggled with how to approach this type of institution. Increasingly, however, the regional commissions have become firm in their wording of standards and criteria with respect to the provision of library services with respect to off-campus and distance learning programs. For example, the Southern Association's most recent standard concerning library resources at offsite locations notes that "an institution must ensure the provision of and access to adequate learning resources and services required to support the courses, programs, and degrees offered. The institution must own the learning resources or provide them through formal agreements." In addition, it notes that when "formal agreements are established for the provision of library resources and services, they must ensure access to library resources pertinent to the programs offered by the institution" (Southern Association 1992, 48). The Middle States Association is clear in its most recent draft criteria when it states that an "institution's library/learning resource center can augment its existing learning resources and draw upon the special strengths of other institutions by collaboration and resource-sharing through formal networks and cooperative agreements" (Middle States Association 1992, 18). Also clear in intent is the Western Association's standard that "basic collections held by the institution [be] sufficient in quality and quantity to meet substantially all the needs of the educational program on and off the campus.'' With respect to the use of others' resources, Western goes on to note that ''institutions have formalized agreements to supplement their own collections with those of other institutions, have mutually agreed upon arrangements with those other institutions, and contribute appropriately to the maintenance of those resources'' (Western Association 1988, 62).

Clearly, the intent of the regional accreditation bodies is that those individuals who propose offering academic work in remote or off-site locations be especially responsive to the ways and means through which they provide learning resources to their students. When institutions are using the locally held resources of others, evidence of formal contracts, letters of understanding, and other documentation is being given increased attention.

Fair Use

The most controversial issue in need of attention in the relationship between the entrepreneurial and the more traditional university-based libraries concerns fair use. The entrepreneurial university would describe fair use as affording their students who live and work in the local community access to the same array of services (on-site research, use of the public catalog) as is offered to all local residents. The traditional university-based library would respond to this viewpoint with some reservation, asserting that outside students are placing a hardship on an already overburdened system. These two opposing positions place the traditional university-based library in a challenging situation: responding to local citizens/businessmen/professionals who happen to be enrolled in an entrepreneurial university program while at the same time ensuring that sources of information are readily available for their own users.

For fair use to be truly fair, entrepreneurial universities must fully recognize the substantial investment that traditional university-based libraries have made in their collections and technologies over a long period of time. Both private and public university libraries have been hard hit economically in recent years to such a degree that serving the needs of their own users has become impossible without the effective sharing of information via collaborative arrangements. Entrepreneurial universities should also be involved in such collaborative efforts, whether through formal reciprocal agreements or fee-based contract structures.

Many individuals in both the public and private sectors applaud the emerging ''virtual'' library as an answer to fair use and open access to information for all citizens. However, it seems that only a few people are asking the question of who is going to pay for its production and support. In some sense, it would be easy to fall into an electronic version of the access versus ownership debate. We are all for access, but who is going to pay for resources development and technical support? We probably all will agree that the current government support for an information superhighway open to all citizens in the United States is highly commendable, but its full realization may well be somewhat in the future. Nevertheless, the notion that libraries don't really need to be funded and that they are just out there waiting to be used is a tragedy.

Fee-Based Structures

One avenue for dealing with the controversial issue of fair use of traditional university-based libraries by entrepreneurial universities is the development of formal contractual arrangements. Essential to developing formal contractual arrangements are fee-based structures. Well-thought-out fee-based structures ensure that there will be equitable and satisfactory renumeration for the services to be delivered by the traditional university-based libraries to the entrepreneurial university libraries.

If the traditional library or library consortia offers the possibility of full or associate membership, then the entrepreneurial university can simply seek membership. If fact, in many instances students enrolled in entrepreneurial university programs financially participate in the traditional university-based library's "community borrower card" program. If, however, the entrepreneurial university needs to establish a more systematic relationship with the traditional library, then an appropriate letter of understanding detailing the conditions of membership and library use, including specific services to be afforded students, should be developed. The principal academic administrator responsible for the proposed program that will use these library services should make contact to set the stage for a strong and mutually supportive relationship. Finally, appropriate contractual letters, which again state the relationship and accompanying fees, are communicated.

In instances where no established fee for access at an institution level is available, the entrepreneurial university and the anticipated host library will need to discuss at length what services will be offered (bibliographic instruction books on reserve, use of CD-ROMs/other computer equipment) so that duplication between home and host university is kept at a minimum. In addition, a cost study will need to be conducted. A realistic and equitable financial arrangement must be reached so that the host library is being fully compensated for the realistic use of services, and the entrepreneurial university is paying for the services that are truly needed.

One option not often considered in a payment schedule might be a combination of financial renumeration and services/purchases. For instance, many entrepreneurial universities offer a broad range of courses that might serve the continuing education needs of library department heads. The entrepreneurial university could offer a set of courses, tuition free. Given the fact that many entrepreneurial universities cater to the working adult, their accelerated and conducive delivery formats (weekends, evenings) could prove to be quite advantageous for personnel at the traditional university-based library. Indeed, many entrepreneurial universities are often willing to customize training courses. If training or education is not what is needed, providing resources/services to the traditional university-based library possibly might be investigated as an alternative or supplement to the fee arrangement. This type of arrangement is quite common with those entrepreneurial universities operating educational programs at military installations. In many cases, additional books, journal titles, or CD-ROM subscriptions are provided to the local military base library in order to enhance the collection to meet the specific information needs of the military personnel enrolled in the entrepreneurial university programs.

Who Is to Be Served?

Another perhaps less difficult issue is, Who is to be served by the host institution and for how long? Do library administrators at the host institution work out of the model whereby the entrepreneurial university provides a list of registered students during a particular instructional period? Or do they work out of the model that simply says "We will serve all of your students for a fixed period of time," perhaps one calendar year, and then renegotiate the agreement. The latter model appears to be the most popular, given the typically short-term periods associated with many distance and nontraditional learning programs and the fact that the former may be less than manageable considering that entrepreneurial institutions may have dozens of courses in one geographic area and in overlapping fashion. Having lists of students registered at any one point in time may be unreasonable. Clearly, however, the question of blanket coverage of all students for a specific period or individual student coverage for students in designated courses over the life of the course will need to be resolved if the host institution is not to suffer resource losses. Whatever arrangement is reached needs to be incorporated into the letter of understanding.

By way of practical concern is the need for a conversation between the principal information specialist at the entrepreneurial university and library administrators at the host institution with respect to what level of library use and when that use can be expected by students associated with the entrepreneurial university. Will most of the students be using the host library during evening hours and on weekends, as might be the instance with nontraditional and entrepreneurial universities catering to working adults? Does this period of more intense use pose a problem for students associated with the host university?

OPPORTUNITIES FOR COLLABORATION AND UNDERSTANDING

Nontraditional colleges, by definition, depart from more traditional notions of educational practice. There is a special burden on the part of these institutions' representatives to engage in open dialogue with library administrators associated with more traditional institutions so that myths are dispelled. In this climate of open dialogue, the entrepreneurial university will be given the opportunity to describe clearly its mission, practices, and use of personnel. In these contexts of discussion between principals of these institutions and library and other administrators associated with traditional universities, a clear understanding of the mission, intentions, and aims of the entrepreneurial institution will go a long way toward dispelling the often-held notion that this sector of higher education is, because of its difference, suspect.

Information professionals associated with traditional colleges need to gain a broader appreciation for the way entrepreneurial universities use pedagogical language. Quite often, faculty and administrators at the entrepreneurial university have their own assumptions and definitions to describe the pedagogical orientation and set of educational values. Concepts like *self-directed learning, collaborative learning, delivery of instruction,* and others have often taken a different slant at the nontraditional school from how those terms might be used at the more traditional school. Learning the language of a nontraditional, entrepreneurial school can go far toward understanding and appreciation.

Administrators and academics associated with more traditional universities need to understand, too, that many of the entrepreneurial-type institutions display a remarkably different organizational culture than what they typically might encounter. Some programs, and in particular, the University of Phoenix program described in this chapter, consciously take on a strong corporate flavor ranging all the way from the way people dress to the type of faculty employed. Faculty at these institutions may not resemble traditional faculty in many dimensions. Practice-based orientations and connections typically will be stronger with those faculty associated with the entrepreneurial institution serving the needs of working adults.

Nontraditional and entrepreneurial universities like the University of Phoenix and others can teach academics and information professionals at more traditional institutions useful ideas about customer service, outcomes assessment, and the measurement of educational accomplishment. Several studies, most importantly those conducted under the auspices of the Council on Postsecondary Education in 1978, emphasized the head start that many nontraditional institutions have over more traditional ones in effectively measuring outcomes (Millard 1991, 54).

Traditional universities and their associated library and information services should not be threatened by the entrepreneurial university as long as both institutions provide contexts for the achievement of a better understanding of what each is about and what expectations there are for the provision of services. There will continue to be a growth in what Tucker (1992) has called the New American College Student, that is, the largely adult student who is "not served well by the institutional mechanisms established to serve the younger student" (3–4). This growing legion of students, observes Tucker, includes "people who want to learn in an environment that recognizes and builds upon the considerable experience they have gained in their jobs. They want to learn in a no-nonsense, customer service–oriented environment that recognizes that they have real limits on their discretionary time'' (4). These students "view higher education as but another service industry that should emulate the high standards set by companies such as Federal Express and WalMart'' (4).

CONCLUSION

We are at a point in American educational history described as one in which "the emergence of an educative society in which lifelong learning is essential for social, political and economic well-being and progress for individuals and society" is taken for granted (Knox 1987, 2). In this environment it is likely that we will see a steady emergence of new forms of alternative and nontraditional education. In the past, some individual, institutional nontraditional and often entrepreneurial-type education has been viewed with suspicion by library administrators. This has been true when those institutions gave appearances of using others' resources with little thought of quid pro quo. Today there is growing evidence that traditional and nontraditional entrepreneurial-type institutions can coexist and mutually benefit each other. We must first recognize that the traditional student is no longer the norm and that a group of culturally unique, nontraditional institutions have arisen that are meeting concretely and needs of both working adults and those students who want an education but not under the time and location constraints imposed by more traditional institutions. Library administrators within traditional academic institutions need to see these programs not as threats to their own institutional models but as unique challenges to greater innovation within their own institutions and libraries.

The model of providing information resources and support services to faculty and students at the University of Phoenix is based on several principles. The most important is the clear and direct aligning of information needs of students and faculty with educational objectives delineated in the curriculum. Some critics, including some academic library managers, will continue to argue that the entrepreneurial and often for-profit institution is largely a taker of others' resources with little thought given to reciprocity. Responsive entrepreneurial universities such as the University of Phoenix have demonstrated, however, that they will continue to direct their students to a broad spectrum of library resources including those found in the general vicinity of the distance learner's residence. Verduin and Clark (1991) have observed that while many technologies will become common in the support of distance and nontraditional learning, print will continue to be an important element in this form of education. They note that "learning centers, consortia, and other cost-sharing innovations will be needed to maximize access" to educational opportunities (211). Mainstream universities and their associated academic libraries can become partners with the newly emergent and entrepreneurial forms of higher education so that both reap benefits that are based on clear perception of expectations.

REFERENCES

Knox, A. B. 1987. "Implications of Societal Myths and Realities for Planning Responsive Continuing Opportunities in Oklahoma." In *Oklahoma Network of Continuing Higher Education, Annual Report, 1986–87*. Oklahoma City: Oklahoma State Regents for Higher Education.

Middle States Association of Colleges and Schools. 1992. *Characteristics of Excellence in Higher Education: Standards for Accreditation (draft)*. Philadelphia: Middle States Association of Colleges and Schools.

Millard, R. M. 1991. *Today's Myths and Tomorrow's Realities: Overcoming Obstacles to Academic Leadership in the 21st Century*. San Francisco: Jossey-Bass.

Southern Association of Colleges and Schools. 1992. *Criteria for Accreditation: Commission on Colleges*. Atlanta, Ga.: Southern Association of Colleges and Schools.

Tucker, R. 1992. "A New Agenda for a New American Student." *Adult Assessment Forum: Journal of Quality Management in Adult-Centered Education* 2(2): 3–4.

Verduin, J. R., and T. A. Clark. 1991. *Distance Education: The Foundations of Effective Practice*. San Francisco: Jossey-Bass.

Western Association of Colleges and Schools. 1988. *Handbook of Accreditation*. Oakland, Calif.: Western Association of Colleges and Schools.

Williams, G. 1992. "Introduction to Analytical Perspectives." In *The Encyclopedia of Higher Education*, edited by Burton R. Clark and Guy Neave. Oxford: Pergamon Press.

13

Rethinking Library Self-Studies and Accreditation Visits

Ralph A. Wolff

INTRODUCTION

It is time to fundamentally rethink and restructure the involvement of libraries and librarians in the accreditation process. Libraries participate in all comprehensive institutional self-studies and usually prepare a separate chapter. Librarians and members of the library staff participate actively in this process. Librarians also participate in nearly all comprehensive accreditation visits and are typically assigned to evaluate the library. Yet despite this extensive involvement, the library portions of self-studies and team reports are usually among the weakest and least analytical sections.

Indeed, a study of sanctions issued by the Accrediting Commission for Senior Colleges and Universities of the Western Association of Schools and Colleges (WASC) from 1977 to 1981 found that library concerns were rarely, if ever, cited as a primary reason supporting an institutional sanction (probation or show cause), whereas institutional finances, governance, or concerns about academic program quality were nearly always cited (Cole 1985). While no accrediting agency explicitly ranks its standards in importance, the implicit characterization of library concerns as less important than other issues has continued even in the face of significant budget cuts at many libraries.

In many respects, the library increasingly has become less connected to the central concerns of the accrediting process. This may be a result of emerging new concerns for accrediting agencies, such as increased attention to assessment of student learning or diversity issues, but it is more likely a reflection of realities occurring on the campus. Libraries are less connected to the central concerns of many campuses.

This is not as it should be. As discussed further in this chapter, there are many new exciting challenges for libraries that are significantly linked to broader institutional issues of educational quality and effectiveness. Indeed, libraries may be able to assert a new leadership role that can help institutions redefine the process and content of learning. Nonetheless, the library is not now seen as a major force for or locus of academic leadership and innovation on most campuses.

Significant changes will need to take place for libraries to thrive and become directly connected to the central functions of teaching and learning. The accrediting process has not traditionally been a stimulus for developing new roles for the library, but changes in accreditation now provide significant opportunities for libraries to define and chart new futures. This chapter will explore the current state of library self-studies and visiting team reports, discuss methods for improving both, and suggest fundamental new approaches for libraries to consider through the accreditation process.

THE CURRENT STATE OF SELF-STUDIES AND VISITING TEAM REPORTS

There are many factors that affect the limited role libraries currently play within the accrediting process. Regional accrediting standards simply do not challenge libraries to address the most significant issues. Some progress has been made with the Middle States Association's attention to bibliographic instruction (Middle States Association of Colleges and Schools 1990; Lutzker 1990), but the primary emphasis of all accrediting associations continues to be on inputs and resources, such as the size of library collections, staff, and budgets, rather than on evidence of library usage and other indicators of effectiveness. Indeed, in this regard accrediting agency standards reflect the traditional views of the higher education community that library quality and status are largely determined by comparative quantitative ranking of holdings, staffs, and budgets.

Library self-studies and team reports too often carry forward this emphasis on inputs and resources. Ironically, by following such standards so narrowly, libraries rarely engage in thoughtful analyses of important issues or use the self-study as a platform for charting the major changes needed to prepare for the future. Self-studies tend to be heavily—if not exclusively—directed to *descriptions* of holdings, bibliographic and other services, staffing, hours of operation, facilities, budgets, and operational issues. Little evidence is typically available about actual library use by students and faculty, or of student and faculty perceptions about the library. Rarely do self-studies address the role the library *really* plays in the life of students and faculty (Wolff 1992).

Team reports often follow the descriptive tenor of the self-study chapters on the library, breaking little new ground. They address only what has been described and do not challenge libraries to develop meaningful evidence of library effectiveness. Instead, team reports continue to emphasize resource indicators.

In this regard, neither accrediting associations nor library evaluators challenge libraries enough (Wolff 1992). Two recent studies bear out these conclusions. The first, conducted by Ronald Leach (1992), reviewed the self-studies and visiting team reports of forty institutions within the North Central accrediting region. The research sample included institutions at all degree levels, from associate to doctorate. While Leach attempted to evaluate the extent to which the accrediting process encouraged the application of new technologies and resource sharing, what he found was a consistent emphasis on collection size, space, and budget issues. This was especially true of team reports, which emphasized resources and inputs even more than self-studies.

Another investigation was conducted during the summer of 1992 by the author and Susan Perry, director, Departmental Systems Group, at Stanford University. All self-study and team report sections dealing with library issues were reviewed for institutions that had comprehensive visits during the 1991–92 year by the Accrediting Commission for Senior Colleges and Universities of the Western Association.[1] Materials for twenty-four visits were reviewed. While the scope of the review was more general than Leach's, the conclusions were similar. Self-studies and team reports followed in general order the topics covered by the WASC standards but in a heavily descriptive and resource-oriented mode. Topics most frequently described in both self-studies and team reports were aggregate quantity of holdings; general but undifferentiated statements about the quality of collections; use of such broad terms as *adequate* or *inadequate* without further analysis; information on the size of the library staff; and information about the library facility, budget data, and hours of operation. When usage data were available, they were often presented without analysis in the self-study appendixes.

The following were typically not included in these reports: analysis of the library's relationship to the mission of the institution and evidence of how effectively the library was accomplishing its role; analyses of usage data, especially in a desegregated format by school, program, or discipline to establish appropriate comparative benchmarks; data and analyses of faculty usage or surveys of faculty perceptions of the library; analysis of the faculty's relationship to the library and the role of the library in curriculum and program development; analysis of student perceptions of the library; analyses of the interlibrary loan system—typical users, time for delivery, cost issues, and the like; evaluations of bibliographic instruction efforts; the impact of new technology on the library; and the relationship of the library to the institution's computer center. These were significant omissions and areas worthy of extensive and thoughtful engagement.

One of the most disappointing aspects of this review of self-studies and team reports was the insularity of discussions about the library. Rarely were library issues raised outside the sections of the self-study or team report on the library. Discussions of the quality and effectiveness of academic programs were devoid of information about, or analysis of, the role and value of the library. Similarly, discussions of institutional or program learning expectations, including general education requirements, ignored expectations for library usage. Discussions of institutional planning in both self-studies and team reports similarly failed to incorporate consideration of library issues. Given the major educational and financial implications of technological changes under way, no institutional strategic vision or long-range plan could be complete without full consideration and integration of library and information technology issues. In a similar vein, the library assessments being conducted were not coordinated with campus assessment activities, nor were the data generated by the library integrated with campus assessment findings.

While many issues were common to both self-studies and team reports, a number of special issues emerged from this review of team reports. Team recommendations for improvement of the library frequently focused on the need for increased resources. (A similar finding was made in the Leach study.) When recommendations were made, they typically did not go beyond funding increases and staffing issues. Praise for the library or commendations for model programs also were rare. Teams often failed to identify the basis for findings. Thus, a number of reports commented that ''students report...'' without identifying whether the basis of this information was team interviews with students throughout the visit, a single group interview, or a campus survey or another data source.

Given that in most cases the library staff had a large hand in the preparation of the self-study section on the library, and that a librarian on the evaluation team was assigned to evaluate the library, it is not surprising that many self-studies and team reports about the library read as if they were written by librarians to librarians. The lack of critical evaluation in both self-studies and team reports gives credence to the charge that peer review of libraries is tainted by an ''I'll scratch your back if you'll scratch mine'' attitude. The failure to include library issues in other sections of the self-study or team reports also bespeaks of the isolation of the library from other academics. Changes and improvements in the self-study and visit process with regard to library issues are crucial and will need to come from both librarians and others involved in the accrediting process.

MEASURES TO IMPROVE LIBRARY SELF-STUDIES AND VISIT REPORTS

Inevitably, one place to improve the accrediting process with respect to libraries is in the formulation of accrediting standards. Revising accrediting standards is a lengthy and complex process because accrediting commissions need to balance the interests of the wide range of institutions they accredit—from large research universities to small church-related to specialized institutions. Accrediting standards are revised comprehensively by each regional commission every five to seven years, and in between, revisions often are made piecemeal to specific standards. Leach (1992) concluded his study: ''[The North Central

Association] needs to review its criteria and accompanying instructions to accommodate changes that are occurring in academic libraries. The current criteria consist of general and often vague statements that require extensive interpretation. More emphasis should be given to the significance of performance (or 'outcomes') in the areas of resource sharing, networking, and expedited document delivery. Additionally, more training should be provided for the consultants/evaluators concerning the changes that are occurring in libraries'' (291).

The WASC study noted here was undertaken as background for discussions about the direction of needed changes in accrediting standards for libraries, especially in light of the impact of new technologies. Still, any changes in these standards will be several years off as they go through the drafting and institutional consent process. As discussed in the remainder of this chapter, while revisions to the standards of regional associations will need to incorporate a greater emphasis on outcomes, there also is reason to go well beyond outcomes and for future accrediting practices to include a fundamental rethinking of the role of the library within institutions.

Notwithstanding the need for revisions to accrediting standards and the time that will take, there is much that could be done now to improve the quality of library self-studies and team reports. Accrediting agencies and institutions can give different emphasis to existing provisions of all the regional associations' accrediting standards for libraries, such as those focusing on outcomes assessment. Similarly, the self-study processes of all regional associations permit wide flexibility in self-study formats and encourage in-depth analysis of issues rather than descriptive presentations. Library issues can easily be introduced into the format of training workshops for evaluation team members.

Six elements are essential to change the quality and effectiveness of library self-studies significantly:

1. Seek an open—or even critical—attitude for the evaluation of the library. In the eyes of many, accreditation reviews can hurt more than help. Critical comments can affect already restricted funding. Library evaluations often are viewed as personal evaluations of the effectiveness of the librarian and library staff. Thus, there is increased sensitivity to critical comments. While lip service may be paid to the desire for searching reviews of the library, the fact that so few self-studies actually probe and analyze issues relating to the library and engage in thoughtful, critical discussions is sufficient evidence of the need for a far different orientation to the self-study. For library self-study to be effective, there needs to be a genuine attitude of inquiry and openness. Rather than describing library holdings and services, the self-study should be a thoughtful engagement of the key issues affecting the effectiveness of the library. The self-study might begin with the question, How do we learn how effective the library is and thereby improve its effectiveness? The goals of the self-study can then be increased learning, new plans, and specific recommendations.

2. Significantly broaden the range of people involved in library self studies. Most self-study chapters on the library are developed by library staff, regardless

of who serves on the self-study committee preparing the library chapter. Typically, these sections reflect the views of the librarian about key issues and do not offer a wide range of views. Meaningful and substantive involvement of faculty is critical. Students also have an important role to play. The self-study should actively solicit identification of key issues for the library to address from the president, academic vice president, deans, faculty and student leadership, and other appropriate leaders of the institutional community. Drafts of the self-study section should be circulated not just for consent but for encouraging on-going dialogue about the issues raised. Have the key issues been identified? Have they been appropriately and fairly treated? Are the recommendations consistent with the issues raised? The broader the inclusion of institutional leadership in this process, the more successful the self-study section.

3. Develop a candid and realistic portrayal of the library as the basis for the self-study. We can no longer hold on to the illusion that the library serves as the intellectual center or the academic heart of the institution. The modern library is one subset of the total network of information resources available on and off campus. Too often the library is view as a *place to study or socialize* rather than as a rich, intellectual resource crucial to a student's education or a dynamic learning center where important lifelong learning skills are developed (Wolff 1992). Moreover, expectations that all graduates of an institution are at least library literate are challenged by statistics of low library usage. Earnest Boyer (1987) cites such statistics in *College: The Undergraduate Experience in America*: "And yet we found that today, about one out of every four undergraduates spends no time in the library during a normal week, and 65 percent use the library four hours or less a week" (160). Our reviews also suggest there is a wide gap in library use among students of different majors within an institution, making aggregated institutional usage figures of limited value. In addition, the isolation of the library from key academic developments and decision making within institutions is rarely surfaced during the self-study process. If not raised, how can such an issue be addressed? A self-study can only raise institutional awareness of issues and identify appropriate recommendations if a realistic portrayal of the library is candidly presented and discussed in the self-study.

4. Create a "culture of evidence" that underlies analysis of the library's effectiveness and quality. Libraries, more than most other departments of the institution, have data readily available. But are the data about the right things that affect quality and effectiveness? Statistics on holdings, number of periodical subscriptions, staff positions, facility size, and hours of operation are important but not determinative of quality. The library needs to develop evidence of outcomes of the application of these resources. What is the impact of the library on the lives of students, faculty, and other patrons? What evidence exists that the educational goals of the library are being accomplished? How universal is bibliographic instruction? What evidence is there of its effectiveness? Evidence about these matters is difficult to generate only in anticipation of an accrediting

visit. Core questions about quality and effectiveness are difficult to frame and answer. The capacity to ask penetrating questions and analyze resulting evidence grows over time and with experience. Thus, the collection and analysis of evidence need to be instituted on an *ongoing,* rather than episodic, basis. A *culture* of inquiry, data collection, and analysis provides the proper basis for an outcomes-oriented self-study.

How can a library provide such a culture? Beyond the typical existing data, librarians can collect data on usage by program, discipline, or student year, for example. Periodic surveys of students and faculty addressing types of library usage, satisfaction with services, or areas of needed improvement would provide not only useful data but comparative benchmarks over time. Focus groups of students and faculty would provide an effective technique for learning about opinions and attitudes in greater depth. Exit interviews with graduating students at both the undergraduate and graduate levels would provide perspective on library usage and satisfaction over the different stages of degree programs. A sample of students could be asked to develop a ''library portfolio'' of library assignments and a journal of library interactions. Syllabi reviews would provide important information about the existence and extent of library assignments. Analyses of the involvement of the library in program reviews would highlight the interaction of the library with this important quality assurance process.

In addition to creating its own ongoing process of evidence gathering, the library should link its efforts with ongoing institutional assessment efforts. For example, a few questions might be added to an alumni survey already in use. In this way, costs can be minimized and information sources substantially increased.

5. Focus the self-study on relationships—the relationships of the library to key academic goals and processes, as well as other academic divisions—rather than on resources. Most self-studies reinforce the insularity of the library by focusing primarily on resource issues and internal concerns for the administrative operation of the library. Yet the effectiveness of the library is more a consequence of the success of the library's relationships with other parts of the institution. What relationships deserve attention in the self-study process? While others can readily be added to this list, several seem the most important:

a. *The relationship to the educational mission and goals of the institution.* If libraries are no longer at the heart of the academic enterprise, what is their role and relationship to the educational mission of the institution? Libraries have become in many ways more of a support service than a direct provider of the educational mission of the institution. Is this an intended consequence? It is perhaps easiest for the library to provide evidence of its support for the research mission of the institution through data on collection size and usage statistics. But how is the library linked to the teaching and learning goals of the institution, especially as these areas get increasing attention? Many institutions cite lifelong learning as one of its intended educational outcomes. Does the library consciously link itself to the fulfillment of this goal through programs and services? Is there evidence of accomplishment of the expectations of these programs?

b. *The relationship to program and curriculum review processes.* Nearly all institutions have (or should have) periodic reviews of each academic program or department, as well as of the general education program for undergraduate degree programs. Increasingly, regional accrediting commissions encourage or require such reviews, as it is impossible for accrediting teams to evaluate each program at an institution. Accrediting teams are able to review and evaluate the effectiveness of the institution's program review process as a key element of the institution's internal quality assurance process. The relationship of the library to the program review process should be a fundamental part of any self-study: To what extent does the program review process consider library issues? Does the program identify information technology and library usage expectations? Is there evidence that these expectations are met? Does the program review go beyond consideration of holdings to consider syllabi requirements for library usage and information retrieval? Are the bibliographic instruction programs of the library adequate for the department's needs?

c. *The relationship to the curriculum development process.* The self-study should review how the library is involved in course and curriculum development, in terms not only of process but also of *substance.* Many institutions have formal course and curriculum review procedures that include consideration of library resources as part of the review and approval process. However, such reviews often emphasize the availability of collections but not the library and information expectations of the course or program. Self-studies also should review the level of involvement of library staff with faculty in curriculum development. Typically, this is sporadic and depends on the initiative of individual faculty. The explosion of information resources and technology places the library staff in an indispensable position for assisting in the development of pedagogy.

d. *The relationship to computing centers, media centers, and other learning support services of the institution.* One of the key developments in higher education over the past fifteen years has been the growth of academic and administrative computing within colleges and universities. Typically, computing services are separated administratively from the library, resulting in inadequate coordination of planning. Communications between these two areas also is often limited, or even strained. The self-study should examine the relationship between the library and computer centers. No longer can the library be viewed as separate from the total network of information services and telecommunications infrastructure available on campus. As students and faculty engage in research and information retrieval as much from individual workstations as physical presence in the library, the meaning of the term *library* warrants serious exploration. In his study of forty institutional self-studies, Leach found that only two associate degree–level institutions even reported formal relationships between the library and the computing center and that team reports ignored this important area as well (Leach 1992). Similarly, coordination and communication with media centers and other learning resource centers of the institution are important, especially as the library attempts to become more involved in pedagogical support. CD-ROMs and other technologies that blend text with graphics, video, and sound raise new possibilities for instruction. At the same time, these new technologies raise issues of identifying who is responsible for financing their acquisition, housing them, and providing access to them.

6. *Consider issues of efficiency as well as effectiveness in the self-study process.* Existing assumptions of higher education, mirrored by accrediting standards and practices, consider that spending more money increases educational quality. By this line of thinking, reductions in funding inevitably cause a decrease in quality. With the likelihood that resources available to higher education in general, and libraries in particular, will not significantly increase in the foreseeable future, it is important to identify the most important goals to be accomplished and how more can be achieved with fewer dollars. In addition, care is needed to ensure that self-study recommendations do not become a "wish list" without consideration of cost implications. One institution that recently completed its self-study in a period of severe financial strain creatively separated recommendations with and without cost implications. The self-study also should consider issues of efficiency: Are there ways of doing the same things more efficiently? A number of cost management techniques are available to assist in such an endeavor. It would be a worthy accomplishment if a self-study resulted in recommendations for reducing costs while maintaining or improving services.

Together these six elements form a powerful lens for refocusing library self-studies. They give far greater attention to substantive issues in assessing library quality and effectiveness, and they would engage self-study participants in a far more candid and searching process of reflection and analysis. Resources and input data should be considered in the service of these six areas but not as ends in and of themselves. They also provide a meaningful vehicle for drawing other campus constituencies into the dialogue about library goals, services, and relationships to key parts of the institution.

These six elements also form a substantive agenda for visiting teams. There are no barriers to implementing any of these suggestions under the existing accrediting standards of each regional accrediting association. Moreover, discussions with numerous team chairs and evaluators and direct observation of dozens of visiting teams suggest that there is great room for improvement in the performance of those team members assigned to evaluate the library. Librarians serving on evaluation teams tend to focus most of their time during a visit within the library, meeting almost exclusively with members of the library staff (Wolff 1992). In meetings with personnel outside the library, library evaluators are frequently silent and tend not to raise critical matters affecting the library as well as the broader issues such as those raised in this chapter. By such reticence, fellow team members and the institution lose the benefit of discussing these issues and relating them to the central educational functions of the institution.

Training programs of accrediting agencies should highlight the need to expand the range of library and information technology issues expected to be addressed by visiting teams. These issues should not be the exclusive province of the team member(s) assigned to evaluate the library; they are responsibilities of those team members focusing on planning, academic programs, program review procedures, assessment, finances, and faculty affairs. Librarians also must attempt to become more integrated into the functioning of evaluation teams, and more proactive in raising issues that relate the library to other parts of the institution.

Improvements in both the self-study process and team visits for libraries must occur simultaneously. Without an improved self-study, it will be difficult for team members to address these issues and gather any independent evidence in the short time spent in campus interviews. Conversely, evaluation team members who persist in emphasizing resources and inputs will frustrate those who develop more substantive and analytical self-studies focusing on outcomes and effectiveness data. Both self-study participants and team evaluators must be willing to challenge libraries and encourage them to become more connected to the academic quality debate within institutions.

USING ACCREDITATION TO BUILD A NEW VISION FOR LIBRARIES

Even as institutions and accrediting agencies act to improve the self-study and team visit processes, events within and outside higher education are changing our fundamental conceptions of the library, as well as the very nature of the content and methodologies of learning sponsored by the institution. These changes could catapult the library into a central role within the teaching/learning enterprise if appropriate adaptations are made; if not, they could further remove the library from the institutional center. Accreditation self-studies and reviews provide libraries an opportunity to explore these issues with colleagues within the institution and from peer institutions.

Technological changes are fast rendering obsolete our historic models of libraries. First, we will need to redefine what we mean by *libraries*. No longer should we think primarily in terms of a library as a place or as a depository of print media. We must expand our thinking to a total institutional information environment, which extends through networks and interlibrary loan and on-line databases regionally, nationally, and internationally. Within a bigger institutional information infrastructure, the word *library* as we have come to know it serves only some of the many information needs of faculty and students. Institutions will need to address how all of these needs will be fulfilled, organize themselves administratively, and develop the means to evaluate the effectiveness of these services and the organizational arrangements created to support them.

The current organizational separation between the library and computing and telecommunications functions at many institutions, compounded by less-than-ideal patterns of communication, stands as a significant barrier to creating an integrated information resources environment. Still to be worked out is where the library will fit in such a total institutional information infrastructure. Transitions to an integrated information resources environment will need to be planned and managed. There will be major investment costs, which are already occurring on a piecemeal basis.

In addition to definitional and organizational implications for the library, there are significant consequences arising from the emerging worth of information. New technologies are only a means to an end. Changes in our society have made the timely availability of relevant information of great economic value. Users of information place great weight on accessibility to information whose content is relevant to a problem, as well as an information format that is accessible whenever or wherever it is needed. Not only are these attributes significant to manufacturing and service industries and the professions; they are of real value to educational institutions. For example, there is value to having necessary information readily accessible from the classroom, laboratory, or field site.

The importance of timely access to information to economic development is underscored by Robert Reich, former professor of economics and current secretary of labor, who writes in his book *The Work of Nations* (1992) that just as our society has moved from high volume to high value, so, too, must our educational systems. In a highly industrialized economy, mastery of "facts" was considered essential, and institutions developed a "standard assembly-line curriculum divided neatly into subjects, taught in predictable units of time, arranged sequentially by grade, and controlled by standardized tests intended to weed out defective units" (226).

To Reich, leaders in the information age are those whom he characterizes as "symbolic analysts," people whose primary skills are problem solving and problem identifying and who broker services nationally and internationally. These skills require ready access to a wide range of information resources and the ability to apply and tailor information in ways that have value to clients and consumers. Colleges and universities prepare students for this role by providing training and experience with problem solving and information retrieval and can bring together a critical mass of like-minded symbolic analysts who learn from one another. According to Reich, the demand for timely and accessible information increasingly will be linked to any country's economic well-being.

Thus, facility with new technology is a critical skill for today's graduates. The ability to recognize when information is needed and to locate, evaluate, and effectively use needed information is defined as *information literacy*. The American Library Association's President Committee on Information Literacy further defines information-literate people as "those who have learned to learn. They know how to learn because they know how knowledge is organized, how to find information, and how to use information in such a way that others can learn from them. They are people prepared for lifelong learning, because they can always find the information needed for any task of decision at hand" (American Library Association 1989, 1).

Embracing information literacy is more than a responsibility of the library. It is an *institutional* concern. The faculty should play a vital role in defining the content and place of information literacy within the curriculum. It cannot avoid this issue if students are to be prepared effectively for the future. Every program should determine the appropriate information skills needed for graduates. Information literacy also should be a key element of the institution's general education program at the undergraduate level.

It may not be realistic, however, to expect faculty to be knowledgeable about all available information technologies or the broad range of information resources that would support individual courses or whole programs. Librarians can assist in developing research assignments, identifying appropriate materials supporting course or program objectives, or developing ways of promoting information literacy (Breivik 1992). However, the capability to retrieve information does not develop the ability to discriminate between useful and useless information. Because users have the freedom to access information directly, they need to exercise the judgment that has historically been expected of trained librarians. Who will provide the training to distinguish between the useful and useless? This is another area of shared responsibility between the library and the faculty.

Perhaps the most significant and long-term implication of information literacy is its potential impact on the very definition of learning—both in terms of content and process. The Presidential Report on information literacy of the American Library Association is quite direct in stating this implication: "Education needs a new model of learning—learning that is based on the information resources of the real world and learning that is active and integrated, not passive and fragmented....To any thoughtful person, it must be clear that teaching facts is a poor substitute for teaching people how to learn, i.e., giving them the skills to be able to locate, evaluate, and effectively use information for any given need. What is called for is not a new information studies curriculum but, rather, a restructuring of the learning process" (American Library Association 1989, 4).

The issues involved in addressing the implications brought by the information revolution and the need for information literacy are deep and pervasive. They will require the thoughtful involvement of all within the institution and could eventually lead to a rethinking of the very content and methodologies of learning. Partnerships among faculty, library, and telecommunications staff will be needed to explore these implications and to develop institutional capabilities. Developing faculty-librarian partnerships, however, will not likely happen on its own. In many institutions, relationships between library staff and faculty are individual and not systemic; for information literacy to become embedded, a far more structural relationship between the faculty and the library will need to be established.

Forging such partnerships will require new roles for librarians and a level of leadership and initiative that has not traditionally been asserted or recognized within the institution beyond the orb of the library itself. Librarians will need to become, and be seen by members of the faculty and administration as, educational leaders and innovators, not just custodians of the institution's print media.

The accrediting process can be a vehicle for exploring these issues throughout the institution as well as within the library. Since it is expected that self-studies involve a wide range of participants from the institution, it can provide the basis for considering such cross-institutional issues as information literacy. The self-study also can provide a more neutral forum for exploring the often sensitive organizational issues associated with developing an integrated information infrastructure within the institution and for exploring new patterns of involvement with the faculty leading toward structural partnerships. Additionally, the self-study can provide a significant platform for the inauguration of new leadership by the library.

CONCLUSION

Rethinking the participation of libraries in the accreditation process would lead to more thoughtful analyses of the library's current status and the quality of its relationships with other parts of the institution and to substantive recommendations about the library's future. Since the accreditation process expects and provides the basis for drawing together representatives of the many constituencies of the institution, it may be possible to draw others into more effective partnerships. Certainly a major task for the library and the faculty is to explore the implications of information literacy. New technologies and learning needs give promise for an exciting potential expansion of the library's role in the life of the institution.

Accrediting agencies and team members assigned to evaluate libraries will need to pay more attention to these issues as well. Accreditation teams and commissions can play an important leadership role in stimulating deeper analyses of these issues without dictating a single course for all institutions.

NOTE

1. The Senior College Commission accredits only institutions awarding the baccalaureate or higher degree.

REFERENCES

American Library Association Presidential Committee on Information Literacy. 1989. *Information Literacy, Final Report*. Chicago: American Library Association.

Boyer, Ernest. 1987. *College: The Undergraduate Experience in America*. New York: Harper & Row.

Breivik, Patricia. 1992. "Information Literacy: An Agenda for Lifelong Learning." *American Association of Higher Education Bulletin* 44 (7): 6–9.

Cole, D. 1985. *Study of Negative Actions: 1977–81*. Oakland, Calif.: Western College Association.

Leach, Ronald. 1992. "Academic Library Change: The Role of Regional Accreditation."
    Journal of Academic Librarianship 18 (5): 288–91.
Lutzker, M. 1990. "Bibliographic Instruction and Accreditation in Higher Education."
    C & RL News 51: 14–18.
Middle States Association of Colleges and Schools. 1990. *Characteristics of Excellence
    in Higher Education: Standards for Accreditation.* Philadelphia: Middle States
    Association of Colleges and Schools.
Reich, Robert. 1992. *The Work of Nations.* New York: Vintage Books.
Wolff, Robert. 1992. "Rethinking the Librarian's Role on Accrediting Teams." *C&RL
    News* 53: 450–51.

PART IV

Current Standards for Libraries, Information Technologies, and Academic Computing

14

Current Regional Commission Standards and Guidelines

Edward D. Garten

The six regional accrediting commissions for senior colleges and universities, enumerated in Table 14.1, have set forth specific standards for academic libraries, learning resource centers, and audiovisual and instructional technology support. Increasingly, recognition is being made in these standards and expectations for the newer information technologies and the entire area of academic computing. Nearly all of these standards have received some revisions within recent years to reflect changes in information technologies and instructional delivery systems.

Several of the commissions offer standards or expectations that might be viewed as more prescriptive in nature. The Western and Southern associations fall primarily at one end of a spectrum, while the other end of a spectrum might be illustrated by the new criteria developed by the North Central Association. In the latter association's criteria, few specifics are noted with respect to libraries and information technologies. Rather, concern for these areas is subsumed under "academic resources and equipment," Criterion Two: "The institution has effectively organized the human, financial, and physical resources necessary to accomplish its purposes." A more middle ground might be found in the Middle States Association standards, which are written in a highly narrative form and are at points more prescriptive while at other points, more open-ended. This chapter, then, simply brings together in one place the current standards for libraries, information technologies, and academic computing. An analysis of these standards and expectations is found in Chapter 16.

Table 14.1
Regional Accreditation Associations for Senior Colleges

North Central Association of Colleges and Schools

Middle States Association of Colleges and Schools

Southern Association of Colleges and Schools

New England Association of Schools and Colleges

Northwest Association of Schools and Colleges

Western Association of Schools and Colleges

WESTERN ASSOCIATION OF SCHOOLS AND COLLEGES

The Western Association's Standard Six on library, computing, and other information and learning resources is prefaced with a general statement: "Information and learning resources, including the holdings and any equipment needed to access the holdings of libraries, media centers, computer centers and any other repositories, are sufficient to support institutional offerings at appropriate levels" (Western Association of Schools and Colleges 1988, 61). Under the general standard are subsumed seven expectations:

The curriculum is supported by appropriate learning resources.

Learning resources are readily accessible to all students and faculty.

Special equipment, software, or telecommunications necessary for access to learning resources are regularly available to students and faculty in appropriate type, number, and quality.

Professional staffs with appropriate expertise are available to assist users of the library, computer center, and other learning resources.

Provisions are made for the security and preservation of all learning resources.

Institutional planning recognizes the need for service linkages among complementary resource bases (e.g., libraries, computer centers, learning resource centers).

Learning resources available in the institutional bookstore support the educational program, contribute to the intellectual climate, and serve other student needs. (61)

With regard to academic libraries, the Western Association subsumes five statements under the general concern with quality of holdings: "Library holdings and media resources are sufficient in quality, depth, diversity, and currentness to support the Institution's academic offerings" (61). The five concerns here are:

Basic collections held by the institution are sufficient in quality and quantity to meet substantially all the needs of the educational program on and off campus.

The institution provides services and holds readily available basic collections at all program sites not serviced by the main library. Interlibrary loan or contractual use arrangements may be used to supplement basic holdings, but are not used as the main source of learning resources.

Collections are structured in direct relationship to the nature and level of curricular offerings, and they include adequate holdings in non-book materials as appropriate.

Written collection development and weeding policies are documented, updated, communicated to the faculty, and implemented. These policies include the bases for accepting gifts.

Institutions having formalized agreements to supplement their own collections with those of other institutions have mutually agreed upon arrangements with those other institutions and contribute appropriately to the maintenance of those resources. (62)

The concern with adequate library acquisition and bibliographic services is stated: "Library and learning resource materials are kept current; bibliographic services meet the needs of institutional users" (62). Under this expectation are subsumed four subconcerns:

Annual budget allocations for acquisitions provide sufficient learning resources to support degree programs. Faculty participate in the selection and evaluation of resources.

All materials are catalogued or appropriately listed so as to make them easily available to their users. Where appropriate, a union catalog is established to provide a central listing for all resource centers serving the institution.

Bibliographic records for machine-readable data files are included in appropriate catalogs, and their use is facilitated to the same degree as are book and media resources. (62)

The Western Association's concern for the availability and use of library collections is noted in the following standard: "Collections are readily available for use by the institution's academic community on-campus and where, by virtue of program or distance from the main campus, they are needed off-campus." Under this standard, Western subsumes six expectations:

Open hours provide for convenient access to library collections and resource centers.

An efficient circulation system facilities the expeditious checking out and reshelving of library resources.

The intensive-use service is available for reserve materials required by the curriculum.

The interlibrary loan service provides the academic community with needed resources that are otherwise unavailable in the library's collections.

Where off-campus programs exist, students are provided ready access to basic collections held by the institution.

Comprehensive training programs to promote library use are available to both students and faculty. Library orientation is responsive to the needs of the nontraditional as well as the traditional student. (63)

The final section of the Western Association standards concerns facilities and is broadly stated in the following fashion: "The library facilities accommodate the collections, readers, and staff so as to foster an atmosphere of inquiry, study, and learning" (63). Four concerns are subsumed under this expectation:

The size of the central library structure and other decentralized units, as required, is adequate and appropriate to the nature of academic programs, student enrollment, the size and character of the collections, the specialized equipment, and the size of the staff.

Adequate space is provided for immediate growth and plans have been laid for the future. As new technology is adopted for library functions and services, adequate space is provided for equipment.

Space and furnishings have been laid out for efficient use; needs of the physically disabled are accommodated.

Collections and services are readily accessible, yet provision has been made for adequate security and the long-range preservation of library materials. (63)

In the area of academic computing, the Western Association makes the following general statement about information technologies: "Computing and data communication services are provided as learning resources to the academic community in sufficient quantity and quality to support the academic offerings of the institution" (64). Seven specific expectations are noted under this standard:

A variety of computing resources (e.g., professional support staff, hardware, software, and, as appropriate, network access on- and off-campus to databases and computing resources) supports the instructional and research needs of students and faculty.

Access to computing resources is convenient for faculty and students.

The institution provides adequate computer support services (including consulting, documentation, and software) to meet academic needs.

The appropriate software and databases are available to support curricular needs of disciplines.

The computing and data communication services adequately ensure security and privacy of records and data developed by faculty and students.

Data communication services provide access to information and services both locally and where appropriate, nationally.

Information technology and academic resource planning assess the need for computing resources. Strategies are established for acquisition of hardware and software to meet institutional and program needs, and for replacement to prevent obsolescence from impeding educational objectives. (64)

The Western Association provides a list of items that are required in the documentation of Standard Six.

Printed materials that describe for students the hours and services of learning resource facilities such as libraries, computer labs, and audio-visual facilities.

Statistics on use of library and other learning resources.

Statistics on library collection and inventory of other learning resources.

Data regarding number and assignments of library staff.

Vitae of professional library staff.

Formal written agreements with other libraries.

Collection development and weeding policies.

Policies regarding security and privacy of research data.

Information on computer usage statistics and rate structures.

Printed information describing user services provided by the computing facility. (65)

NORTH CENTRAL ASSOCIATION OF COLLEGES AND SCHOOLS

Library, information technologies, and academic computing resources are covered within Criterion Two of the Commission's Criteria for Accreditation. The criterion states: "The institution has effectively organized the human, financial, and physical resources necessary to accomplish its purposes" (North Central Association of Colleges and Schools 1993, 19). The commission has a precise definition of the phrase *effectively organized,* which is taken to mean both the requirements established in the General Institutional Requirements and the common understanding within the higher education community relative to the structures and processes that contribute to effective governance, administration, and communication (19).

The commission also defines the word *necessary* with respect to resources. The 1993 criterion makes clear that the commission is not guided by mathematical formulas. This guideline also applies to the number of learning resources held by an institution. The commission believes that if a college or university cannot accomplish its mission and purposes without certain resources, then these resources clearly must be necessary. the 1993 criterion goes on to say that a college or university is in a position to evaluate itself against this criterion when it employs a definition of *necessary* that is shared by the higher education community. What are the resources needed by an institution with similar purposes in order for the institution to accomplish its mission and purposes (21)?

In looking at this criterion, the commission, among other things, looks for evidence that the institution's "decision-making, administrative, and communications structures and processes are well-understood and appropriately used by the institution's constituencies'' (21). The commission also looks for ''each of the various human resources'' at the institution to determine whether they are ''appropriate to the institution's purposes'' as well as the ''economic strength of the institution'' to determine whether it ''is sufficient to undergrid appropriately all of the institution's programs and activities.'' Finally, the commission looks for evidence that ''the institution's means of obtaining income and its distribution of human, financial, and physical resources reflect values consistent with those widely held by institutions of higher education'' (22).

The 1993 North Central criterion places emphasis on the determination of a pattern of evidence supporting the criterion. Item ''j'' within suggested areas where a pattern of evidence might be developed says: ''Academic resources and equipment (e.g., libraries, electronic services and products, learning resource centers, laboratories and studios, computers) adequate to support the institution's purposes'' (23).

SOUTHERN ASSOCIATION OF COLLEGE AND SCHOOLS

Within the 1992 Southern Association standards, Section V, ''Educational Support Services,'' notes expectations for libraries, information technologies, and computer centers. The standards begin by suggesting the scope of what is termed *support services*: ''Each institution must ensure that all students and faculty have access to adequate learning resources and services needed to support its purposes and programs. Because these resources and services are an integral part of the learning experience of students, they must be available to all students enrolled in programs wherever they are located or however they are delivered'' (Southern Association of Colleges and Schools 1992, 45).

The Southern Association Commission begins its standards on educational support services with libraries by noting that ''library resources and services are essential to learning. Priorities for acquiring materials and establishing services must be determined with the needs of the users in mind. Thus, with the active cooperation of the administration, faculty, students and library staff, each institution must develop for its library a mission statement consistent with its purpose. The library must be evaluated regularly and systematically to ensure that it is meeting the needs of its users and supporting the programs and purpose of the institution'' (45).

The Southern Association then precedes standards on library services by noting that

each institution must ensure that all students and faculty have access to the primary and secondary materials needed to support its purposes and programs. Basic library services must include an orientation program designed to teach new users how to obtain individual assistance, access to bibliographic information and access to materials. Any one of a variety of methods, or a combination of them, may be used for this purpose: formal instruction, lectures, library guides and users aids, self-paced instruction and computer-assisted instruction.

The library should offer point-of-use instruction, personal assistance in conducting library research and traditional reference services. Adequate hours must be maintained to ensure accessibility to users. Professional assistance should be available at convenient locations when the library is open.

The library must provide adequate records of materials through catalogs, indexes and bibliographies; access of information sources, regardless of location, through standard indexes and bibliographies; and, where appropriate, access to external bibliographic data bases.

The library must have adequate physical facilities to house, service and make the library collections easily available; up-to-date equipment in good condition for using print and non-print materials; provision for rapid access to any remotely stored materials; provision for interlibrary loan agreements; and an efficient and appropriate circulation system. The library must provide students with opportunities to learn how to access information in a variety of formats so that they can continue life-long learning. Librarians must work cooperatively with the teaching faculty in assisting students to use resource materials effectively. (46)

Next the commission looks at library collections and sets forth the following expectations:

The library collections and data bases must be sufficient to support the educational, research and public service programs of the institution. The collections of print and non-print materials must be well organized. Institutions offering graduate work must provide library resources substantially beyond those required for the bachelor's degree. Librarians, teaching faculty and researchers must share in the development of collections and the institution must establish policies defining their involvement. Each library must have a policy governing resource material selection and elimination, and should have a procedure providing for the preservation, replacement or removal of deteriorating materials in the collection. (46–47)

The commission follows its expectations on library collections with its expectations on staff and notes:

The library must be adequately staffed by trained professionals who hold graduate degrees in library science or learning resources. In exceptional cases, outstanding professional experience and demonstrated competency may substitute for this academic preparation. Such exceptions must be justified by the institution on an individual basis. Because professional or technical training in specialized areas is increasingly important in meeting user needs, professionals with specialized non-library degrees may be employed, where appropriate, to supervise these areas.

The library support staff must be adequate to carry out the responsibilities of a technical nature. Qualifications or skills needed for these support positions should be defined by the institution.

Organizational relationships, both external and internal to the library, should be clearly specified. Institutional policies concerning faculty status, salary and contractual security for library personnel must be clearly defined and made known to all personnel at the time of employment. (47)

The Southern Association is concerned with library relationships with other libraries and institutions in its section on institutional relationships. It notes that "[c]ooperative relationships with other libraries and agencies should be considered in order to increase the ability of the library to provide the resources and services needed by its users. However, these cooperative relationships must not be used by institutions to avoid responsibility for providing their own adequate and accessible library resources and services. In all cases of cooperative arrangements, formal agreements must be established, thereby safeguarding the integrity and continuity of library resources and services. The effectiveness of such cooperative arrangements must be evaluated regularly" (47).

Finally, under its section on library requirements and expectations, the commission notes its expectations for library resources provided to off-campus sites.

At any off-campus location where credit courses are offered, an institution must ensure the provision of, and access to, adequate learning resources and services required to support the courses, programs and degrees offered. The institution must own the learning resource or provide them through formal agreements. Competent library personnel must be assigned duties in planning and providing library resources and services and in ascertaining their continued adequacy.

When formal agreements are established for the provision of library resources and services, they must ensure access to library resources pertinent to the programs offered by the institution and must include provision for services and resources which support the institution's specific programs, in the field of study and at the degree level offered. (48)

The Southern Association's expectations for audiovisual and media resources are found in the portion of Section V titled "Instructional Support." This area also includes other instructional support facilities including laboratories.

To support its curriculum, each institution must provide a variety of facilities and instructional support services (e.g., educational equipment and specialized facilities such as laboratories, audiovisual and duplicating services, and learning skills centers). These services should be organized and administered so as to provide easy access to faculty and student users, should be adequate to allow the fulfillment of institutional purpose to support the educational process, and should contribute to the effectiveness of learning and to the wise and efficient use of resources. This requirement applies to all programs wherever they are located or however they are delivered. (48)

The Southern Association's expectations for computer resources and services can also be found in Section V of the Criteria.

Computer services are essential to many educational programs and should be available to support the institution's management and administrative functions. Policies for the allocation of computing resources and the assignment of priorities for computer use must be clearly stated and consistent with an institution's purpose and goals. These policies should be evaluated regularly to ensure that academic and administrative needs are adequately served. Since the range of available computing services often requires a compromise between the needs of the various users and what is realistically affordable, the administration must establish priorities for computer usage and must balance the services provided among the user groups. Records should be kept to determine an accurate profile of computer resources use. These requirements apply to all programs wherever they are located or however they are delivered.

Although the diversity of educational programs and goals will be a major determining factor in the type and size of computer resources selected by an institution, all students should be encouraged to make some practical use of these available resources. (49)

NORTHWEST ASSOCIATION OF SCHOOLS AND COLLEGES

The Northwest Association requirements for libraries, information technologies, media services, and telecommunications can be found in their Standard IV titled "Library and Information Resources." These standards were last revised in 1992. Standard IV begins with an overview purpose and scope statement:

The purpose of the library and information resources and services is to support and improve instruction and learning in ways consistent with the philosophy and evolving curricular programs of the institution. The institution ensures that all students, faculty, and staff have access to adequate information resources and services needed to support their efforts in learning, instruction, and research. Information resources include the holdings, equipment, and staff expertise of libraries, media and production centers, computer centers, telecommunication centers, and other repositories of information significant to the accomplishment of the institution's educational mission. The goals and objectives of these information resources and services are compatible with, and supportive of, the institutional mission and objectives. These information resources are sufficient to support the curriculum, faculty, and student scholarship to the level of degrees offered, and the intellectual, cultural, and technical development of students, faculty, and staff.

An essential part of the learning environment, these resources and services, at the appropriate degree levels, are available to all students enrolled in courses and programs wherever located and however delivered. Faculty, in partnership with library and information services staff, are responsible to ensure that information resources are integrated, where appropriate, into the curriculum.

Institutional culture and climate contribute toward an environment that supports faculty and staff to make appropriate and innovative uses of information technology to improve the curriculum. (Northwest Association of Schools and Colleges 1992, 1)

Turning specifically to physical library resources and services offered, the commission notes:

The library and related information resources and services are critically important to students, faculty, and staff toward the development and the achievement of information literacy. Types, formats, and location of information resource materials will depend on the nature of the institution and its educational programs.

Policies, regulations, and procedures for development and management of educational information resources in all formats, are systematically documented and updated. Major policy changes are routinely communicated to the institution's constituencies. Opportunities are provided for faculty, staff, and students to participate in the planning and development of these resources. Further, providing assistance to students and faculty in the effective utilization of information resources is an institutional priority.

Resources in libraries, computer labs, media centers, and other instructional information locations are readily available to students, faculty, and staff. Computing and data communications services are used to extend the boundaries in obtaining information from other sources, including regional, national, and international databases.

Cooperative relationships and links with other institutions and agencies are encouraged in order to increase the ability of the institution to provide the resources and services needed by users. In cases of cooperative arrangement with other libraries, formal agreements are established. However, these cooperative relationships and external information services are not a substitute for an institution's responsibility to provide its own adequate and accessible core collection and services.

A core collection is defined as materials that are sufficient to support the curriculum and student and faculty scholarship to the level of the degrees offered. A core collection also includes materials which contribute to the intellectual, cultural, and technical development of students, faculty, and staff.

Through the institution's ownership or guaranteed access, sufficient collections, equipment, and services are available to students wherever programs are located or however they are delivered. These collections and services are sufficient in quality, level, scope, quantity, and currency to meet the needs of the institution's educational programs.

Institutions which provide instruction at off-campus locations ensure the provision of, and access to, adequate learning resources and services required to support the courses, programs and degrees offered. (2)

The commission's expectations relative to space and technical services note the following:

The institution provides facilities adequate to house and use information resources and equipment which foster an atmosphere conducive to inquiry, study, and research among students, faculty, and staff.

The organization and management of collections through appropriate technical services that include cataloging, acquisitions, serials management, etc., is an institutional priority. Adequate and dependable financial support is provided to assure the maintenance of quality information resources and services. (2)

Requirements for personnel and library organization are put forth as follows:

Library and information resources personnel are adequate in number and in areas of expertise to manage and provide assistance in the use of these services by students and faculty. Instructional support services (such as bibliographic instruction, research assistance, technical consultation, curriculum development, etc.) are provided to faculty and to students to meet their curricular and educational program needs. Information resources personnel exercise initiative to inform faculty about new and changing developments in teaching and learning technologies.

Personnel include qualified professional and technical support staff, who demonstrate required competencies. Staff responsibilities are clearly defined and current job descriptions are maintained. The institution provides appropriate opportunities for the professional development of staff, including continuing education for professional staff and training for support staff. Like faculty, information resources staff play an active role in planning and governance and are involved in the life of the campus community.

Evaluation criteria are appropriate and in conformity with the standards of the respective library and information resource professional fields.

While each institution is organized in such a way to accomplish its unique mission and objectives, the responsibility to provide for appropriate cooperation, collaboration, and communication among institutional library and information resource entities remains a critical priority. The institution's organizational structure facilities and fosters innovation and integration of information resources and services in the teaching/learning environment. The centrality of the library and information services to the function of the institution is recognized through the close involvement of appropriate professional information resources staff in curriculum development, facilities planning, budgeting, and other related activities. (2)

And finally, under the category of "Planning and Evaluation," the Northwest Association notes the following expectations:

The institution's educational information resources are adequately supported in relation to the total budget and needs of the institution. Annual budget allocations are sufficient to support the needs of faculty and students for the library and information resources. Provisions are made for proper maintenance and adequate security of equipment and facilities. The protection of records and data developed by faculty, staff, and students is consistent with state and federal public disclosure laws.

The institution, in its planning and organization, provides for cooperation, efficient management and coordination of resources among various information resource areas (libraries, academic computing resources, media production resources, resource programs, and telecommunications/network services). A planning process at the policy-level is in place involving users, faculty, senior administrators, library and computer professionals, and students. Information resources planning is integrated into the institution's strategic long-range planning, including assessment of need for print and non-print resources, bibliographic utilities, resource sharing technologies, networking capabilities, electronic resources, media programming and production, telecommunications, and access to remote sources of information.

The institution regularly and systematically evaluates the adequacy and utilization of its information resources, including those provided through cooperative arrangements, and at all locations where courses, programs or degrees are offered, and uses the results of the evaluation to improve and increase the effectiveness of these resources. (3)

NEW ENGLAND ASSOCIATION OF SCHOOLS AND COLLEGES

Standard Seven of the New England Association 1992 standards concerns library and information resources. New England includes six sections under this standard.

The institution makes available the library and information resources necessary for the fulfillment of its mission and purposes. These resources support the academic and research program and the intellectual and cultural development of students, faculty, and staff. Library and information resources may include the holdings and necessary services and equipment of libraries, media centers, computer centers, language laboratories, museums, and any other repositories of information required for the support of institutional offerings. The institution ensures that students use these resources as an integral part of their education.

Through the institution's ownership or guaranteed access, sufficient collections and services are readily accessible to students wherever programs are located or however they are delivered. These collections and services are sufficient in quality, level, diversity, quantity, and currency to support and enrich the institution's academic offerings. The institution provides facilities adequate to house the collections and equipment so as to foster an atmosphere conducive to inquiry, study, and learning among students, faculty, and staff.

The institution provides sufficient and consistent financial support for the effective maintenance and improvement of the institution's library and information resources. It makes provision for their proper maintenance and adequate security. It allocates resources for scholarly support services compatible with its instructional and research programs and the needs of faculty and students.

Professionally qualified and numerically adequate staff administer the institution's library and information resources. The institution provides appropriate orientation and training for use of these resources. Clear and disseminated policies govern access, usage, and maintenance of library and information resources.

The institution participates in the exchange of resources and services with other institutions and within networks as necessary to support and supplement its educational programs.

The institution regularly and systematically evaluates the adequacy and utilization of its library and information resources, and uses the results of the data to improve and increase the effectiveness of these services. (New England Association of Schools and Colleges 1992, 23–24)

The instructional development aspect of media services can be construed to be assumed under Standard Six, "Instruction," which states, in part: "Instructional techniques and delivery systems are compatible with and serve to further the mission and purposes of the institution as well as the objectives of individual courses. Methods of instruction are appropriate to the students' capabilities and learning needs'' (15).

MIDDLE STATES ASSOCIATION OF COLLEGES AND SCHOOLS

The Middle States Association standards can be found in *Characteristics of Excellence in Higher Education: Standards for Accreditation* (1992). In the preface to the standards, Middle States notes that all accredited institutions hold a number of important common denominators. These "characteristics of excellence" include Middle States' concern that institutions have "library learning resources sufficient to support the programs offered'' (1).

In discussing the centrality of library and learning resources to the educational mission of a college or university, *Characteristics of Excellence in Higher Education* notes:

Students and faculty, and other users should have access to the broadest range information resources and services wherever they might be and in whatever form, both at primary and off-campus instructional sites and through other means. While access to these resources is customarily gained through a library or learning resource center, access is not limited to a single place. Whatever the source, learning and research of students, faculty, and other constituents.

While such broad access to the world of information resources should be available, it is still the obligation of each institution to provide critical reference and specialized program resources at or within easy reach of each instructional location. The types of service and the varieties of print and non-print media available depend on the nature of the institution. The development of services, collections, and other resources must relate realistically to the institution's educational mission, goals, curricula, size, complexity, degree level, resources, and the diversity of its teaching, learning, and research requirements. (17)

In discussing the scope of resources and nature of services that libraries should provide, Middle States standards assert:

The scope of library/learning resources holdings, the nature of services provided, and the form of access must be in reasonable proportion to the needs to be served, but numbers alone are no assurance of excellence. Of more importance are the quality, accessibility, and availability of the services and holdings on site and elsewhere; their relevance to the institution's current educational programs; the means by which an institution enhances use of library/learning resources; and the degree to which resources are actually used. (17)

The library/learning resources center needs to promote, through its collections and services, the general scope of learning, inquiry, and creativity. Teaching faculty, librarians, and other information providers should collaborate on the selection of materials, chosen for intellectual depth as well as breath. They should work closely together to plan for collection development and evaluation and for the utilization of resources. Basic and interpretive books and periodicals and standard reference works should be included. Materials such as videotapes, videodiscs, audiotapes, records, CD-ROMs, and film should be available, as well as electronic databases and instruction in their use. (17–18)

The Middle States Association has maintained a strong posture with respect to the development of information literacy among students and, in its standards, states: "Each institution should facilitate optimal use of its learning resources through a variety of strategies designed to help students develop information literacy—the ability to locate, evaluate, and use information and to become independent learners. It should encourage the use of a wide range of non-classroom resources for teaching and learning. It is essential to have an active and continuing program of library orientation and bibliographic instruction, developed collaboratively by teaching faculty, librarians, academic deans, and information providers" (17–18).

The standards impose an expectation that the library will be continually evaluated when they say that "[c]areful evaluation of all learning resources available to the institution's educational program, including on-site collections and services, should be an ongoing process. Therefore, a system for assessing the effectiveness of library and learning resources, including utilization, accessibility and availability of materials; quality and relevance of the collections; and effectiveness of reference and referral services must be an integral part of the library/learning resources center's self-assessment program. Ultimately, the most important measure will be how effectively students are prepared to become independent, self-directed learners" (18).

Concern with collaboration and resource sharing and off-site support of instruction is found in the Middle States standards.

An institution's library/learning resources center can augment its existing learning resources and draw upon the special strengths of other institutions through collaboration and resource-sharing through formal networks and cooperative agreements. Access to external as well as internal information resources is essential for students and faculty. Computer and other technological systems, including voice/data/facsimile transmission, can assist in providing convenient access. Interlibrary loan services should be available, well supported, and structured to ensure timely delivery of materials. Multi-campus institutions and those with off-campus programs should design special procedures or systems to provide sufficient on-site access to learning resources and services. (19)

With respect to library staff, the Middle States Association asserts: "Librarians and other resource center staff must demonstrate their professional competence on the basis of criteria comparable to those for other faculty and staff. Status should be commensurate with the significance and responsibilities of their positions" (19).

And finally, the commission notes its expectations for facilities and hours of operation when it says: "The collections and other resource materials must be readily accessible at convenient hours and housed in a building designed to facilitate such access for all library users. Such features as seating, lighting, arrangement of books and materials, and acoustical treatment are important and are to be judged by their effectiveness in making the center an attractive and accommodating place for study. Nothing else matters if the resources are not used'' (19).

REFERENCES

Middle States Association of Colleges and Schools. 1992. *Characteristics of Excellence in Higher Education: Standards for Accreditation.* Philadelphia: Middle States Association of Colleges and Schools.

New England Association of Schools and Colleges. 1992. *Standards for Accreditation.* Winchester, Mass.: New England Association of Schools and Colleges.

North Central Association of Colleges and Schools. 1993. *A Handbook of Accreditation 1993–94.* Chicago: North Central Association of Colleges and Schools.

Northwest Association of Schools and Colleges. 1992. *Accreditation Handbook.* Seattle, Wash.: Northwest Association of Schools and Colleges.

Southern Association of Colleges and Schools. 1992. *Criteria for Accreditation, Commission on Colleges.* Decatur, Ga.: Southern Association of Colleges and Schools.

Western Association of Schools and Colleges. 1988. *Handbook of Accreditation.* Oakland, Calif.: Western Association of Schools and Colleges.

15

Current Disciplinary and Professional Association Standards and Guidelines

Edward D. Garten

In spring 1993 the executive directors of forty-three professional and disciplinary accreditation associations affiliated with the Council on Postsecondary Accreditation (COPA) were asked to submit their current accreditation criteria, guidelines, or standards for incorporation into this chapter. While this comprises nearly all of the disciplinary and professional accreditation associations affiliated at that time with COPA, I chose to exclude a few associations such as those that accredit occupational and technical programs and that typically are not found at four-year colleges and universities.

Forty-one associations chose to submit materials for the development of this chapter. Association documents were read, with all references to libraries, instructional media support, and academic computing identified. In some instances, expectations for libraries, computer centers, and other learning resources, while minimal relative to actual commentary devoted to the areas, are augmented by accreditation manual material that offers observations about libraries and other academic support areas or offers checklists for on-site evaluation. Thus, while a few accrediting associations appear to offer only a few sparse words relative to standards or expectations in these support areas, they often make observations, offer guidelines, or suggest the use of checklists to be used in tandem with their specified criteria or standards.

It should be noted that in several instances the standards are excerpted from draft documents, and in these instances, the final wording of the standards may have changed slightly. In some instances, statements that reflect library, information technology, and learning resource support are found embedded in a larger discussion of academic support, facilities, or institutional resources. An attempt has been made, in most instances, to heave pertinent statements to this chapter in their original context.

This chapter comprises, then, the current requirements and expectations relative to libraries, academic computing, and media/instructional support services for forty-one disciplinary and professional accrediting associations. These associations have been categorized under the following major headings: "Arts and Sciences," "Professional," "Law," "Engineering and Construction," "Theological," and "Medical and Medical-Related" (see Table 15.1). An analysis of this material appears as Chapter 17 of this book.

ARTS AND SCIENCES

Computing Sciences Accreditation Board

This accreditation agency was established as a result of several years' work by the Joint Task Force on Computer Science Program Accreditation and the Computer Society of the Institute of Electrical and Electronics Engineers. The board's scope of accreditation includes postsecondary baccalaureate programs that prepare students for entry into the various computing sciences professions (Computing Sciences Accreditation Board 1992, 1).

The board's expectations for libraries are stated as follows:

The library that serves the computer science program must be adequately staffed with professional librarians and support personnel. Sufficient financial support must be provided to acquire and maintain an adequate technical collection and an appropriate nontechnical collection. The technical collection must include up-to-date textbooks, reference works, and appropriate publications of professional and research organizations such as the IEEE Computer Society and the Association for Computing Machinery. The collection should also include a representative number of trade journals. (62)

The board's expectations with respect to laboratory and computing resources are stated as follows:

Programs in computer science require substantial laboratory and computing resources for class work and individual projects. Such resources will normally involve a blend of computing facilities of varying capabilities. Sufficient facilities must be available so that each student has adequate and reasonable access to the appropriate system for each course. Where scheduled laboratory instruction is required, sufficient equipment must be available so that no more than two students share a laboratory station.

Appropriate facilities must also exist to support scholarly activities of the faculty. Depending on the nature of such activities this may require additional and desperate facilities. In any event this requirement must be considered in addition to the equipment needed to support the student activities. At a minimum, all faculty members should have access to computers from their offices for class preparation and research purposes.

Adequate and reasonable software to support the program must be available. Typically,

Table 15.1
Disciplinary and Professional Accreditation Associations

ARTS AND SCIENCES

American Psychological Association
Computing Sciences Accreditation Board
National Association of Schools of Art and Design
National Association of Schools of Dance
National Association of Schools of Music
National Association of Schools of Theatre

PROFESSIONAL

Accrediting Council on Education in Journalism and Mass Communications
American Assembly of Collegiate Schools of Business
American Association for Marriage and Family Therapy
American Dietetic Association
American Home Economics Association
American Library Association
American Physical Therapy Association
American Speech-Language-Hearing Association
Council for Accreditation of Counseling and Related Educational Programs
Council on Rehabilitation Education
Council on Social Work Education
Foundation for Interior Design Education Research
Landscape Architectural Accreditation Board
National Architectural Accrediting Board
National Association of Schools of Public Affairs and Administration
National Council for Accreditation of Teacher Education
National Recreation and Park Association
Planning Accreditation Board
Society of American Foresters

Table 15.1 (continued)

LAW

> American Bar Association
> Association of American Law Schools

ENGINEERING AND CONSTRUCTION

> Accrediting Board for Engineering and Technology
> American Council for Construction Education
> National Association of Industrial Technology

THEOLOGICAL

> American Association of Bible Colleges
> Association of Advanced Rabbinical and Talmudic Schools
> Association of Theological Schools in the United States and Canada

MEDICAL AND MEDICAL-RELATED

> Accrediting Commission on Education for Health Services Administration
> American Dental Association
> American Optometric Association
> American Osteopathic Association
> American Veterinary Medical Association
> Committee on Allied Health Education and Accreditation
> Liaison Committee on Medical Education
> National League for Nursing

this includes current versions of at least one structured language, one or more languages in "common" use, one or more assembly languages, an operating system, and a database management system. Students must have appropriate expendables to work with the system. Complete documentation of available hardware and software must be readily accessible to faculty and students.

It is critical to have adequate support personnel to implement and to maintain the laboratory component of the program. Appropriate instructional assistance must be provided for the laboratories. (60–61)

National Association of Schools of Art and Design

The constitution of the National Association of Schools of Art and Design was adopted in 1948 with the association being formed to establish "a closer relationship among schools and programs of art and design for the purpose of examining and improving practices and professional standards in art and design education" (National Association of Schools of Art and Design 1991, 8).

The association's expectations for libraries and other instructional support are stated as follows:

The institution shall place importance on the development and maintenance of library resources which support its curricula in art and design. Holdings in art/design may be part of the general institutional library, or they may be a separate library unit. Whatever the structure, the art/design library or collection should be considered an integral part of the art/design program of the institution. The institution shall have policies concerned with but not limited to the following aspects of library operation: governance, collections and their development, personnel services and access, facilities, and finances. These policies should support both the number and scope of curricular objectives and should be developed in a manner which demonstrates coordination between the library staff and the art/design faculty.

1. Governance. The functional position of the art/design collection within the total library structure shall be clearly identified, and the responsibilities and authority of the individual(s) in charge of the art/design library shall be defined. There should be a close administrative relationship among all libraries within the institution so that art/design students and faculty may make the best use of library resources.

2. Collections. Institutions must maintain library holdings in art and design of sufficient size and scope to complement the total instructional program of the institution, to provide incentive for individual learning, and to support research appropriate for its faculty.

There shall be evidence that a systematic acquisitions program compatible with appropriate needs has been planned, and that some form of faculty consultation and review is a continuing aspect of this program. Materials in all formats required for the study of art and design—books, slides, periodicals, microforms, and video recordings—shall be the basis of the acquisitions program. These shall be of good quality, appropriately catalogued, and regularly maintained.

The library serving an institution with "professional" undergraduate programs should contain no fewer than 10,000 volumes on art, design, and related subjects, and 50 periodicals. Such institutions should own a minimum of 30,000 slides.

The library serving an institution with "liberal arts" undergraduate programs should contain no fewer than 5,000 volumes on art, design, and related subjects, and 25 periodicals. Such institutions should own a minimum of 15,000 slides.

Large departments should have proportionately larger library resources, and schools with graduate degree programs should have holdings substantially in excess of the minimum stated above.

Whenever possible, cooperative arrangements should be established with information sources outside the institution to augment holdings for student and faculty use. (The books, slides, and video recordings held by the libraries of municipalities, broadcast stations, historical societies, and other schools often can provide a breadth of coverage far beyond that of the institution.)

3. Personnel. The art/design library shall be staffed by professional qualified personnel sufficient to meet the various needs of the art and design program. Institutions are encouraged to engage specialized personnel whenever feasible to organize and maintain the art and design holdings.

4. Services. The institution shall maintain appropriate hours of operation for the library.

There should be convenient access to the library holdings in art and design through complete and effective catalogs, indexes, and other appropriate bibliographic tools. There also should be access to the holdings of other institutions through union catalogs, cooperative network facilities, photoduplication, and interlibrary loan.

Instruction in the use of the art/design library shall be provided.

5. Facilities. The institution shall provide an effective environment for study. Facilities should be as centralized as possible to provide convenient access to all library holdings devoted to the study of art and design. For example, slides and books should be easily accessible for effective use in conjunction with one another.

The institution shall provide and maintain equipment that allows reasonable access to the resources of the library, including but not limited to video equipment, microform units, and computer terminals. (47–49)

Standards for Non-Degree-Granting Institutions (Art and Design). The National Association of Schools of Art and Design accredits non-degree-granting institutions. Programs that are offered by these schools may or may not lead to a professional diploma or certificate. For these non-degree-granting institutions, the association states that ''[t]he institution shall have either library space and holdings adequate for its educational programs, or shall have made arrangements for its students and faculty to have access to appropriate library facilities in the immediate area'' (93).

The association states specific requirements for these non-degree-granting programs with respect to libraries and slide libraries:

Adequate art library resources should be readily available to support both the programs offered and the curricular/research needs of faculty and enrolled students. Library materials must be kept current and of high quality. The size and scope of the collection, including slides, is related to the size, scope, and objectives of the various programs offered by the institution. The standards for library holdings for specific areas of study are the same as those required for degree programs at the same level of the specific non-degree-granting program.

Institutional libraries must have adequate resources to maintain and enlarge the collections and to provide professional and support staff. Institutions which provide access to library facilities in the immediate area must demonstrate that the library used has a collection adequate to support the programs, and that policies and procedures for access are appropriate to the needs of students and faculty. (93)

National Association of Schools of Dance

The association was established "to develop a closer relationship among schools and programs of dance for the purpose of examining and improving practices and professional standards in dance education and training" (National Association of Schools of Dance 1991, 2). The association recognizes many programs that do not lead to a degree. Some programs may or may not lead to a professional certificate. Many of these programs are professional studio schools. Among the basic criteria for membership is included the statement that "[t]he institution shall have either library space and holdings adequate for its training programs, or shall have made arrangements for its students and faculty to have access to appropriate library facilities in the immediate area" (34).

In addition, the association states as a standard for professional studio schools:

Adequate dance library resources should be readily available to support both the programs offered and three curricular/research needs of faculty and enrolled students. Library materials must be current and relevant to the programs offered.

Institutional libraries must have adequate resources to maintain and enlarge the collections and to provide professional and support staff. Institutions which provide access to library facilities in the immediate area must demonstrate that the library used has a collection adequate to support the program, and that policies and procedures for access are appropriate to the needs of the students and faculty. (36)

The association has promulgated standards for degree-granting institutions. Degree-granting institutions include those that offer two-year, four-year, five-year, and graduate-level programs. The association states the following library standard for degree-granting institutions: "The institution shall have library space and resources commensurate with the needs of its educational program" (38).

The association notes the following with respect to audiovisual equipment:

Appropriate audio-visual equipment for the instruction program should include the following:

A. A piano in each studio.
B. Video, film, and slide projection equipment in appropriate teaching stations.
C. Sound systems (record players, tape recorders, etc.) in each studio and in production areas.
D. A variety of percussion instruments in appropriate teaching stations.

E. An adequate, secure, and well-equipped facility for producing performance-quality audio and video tapes. (42)

Specifically, with respect to the library, the association notes:

The institution shall place importance on the development and maintenance of library resources to support its curricula in dance. The dance library or collection should be considered an integral part of the dance program of the institution.

The institution shall have policies concerned with but not limited to the following aspects of library operation: governance, collections and their development, personnel services and access, facilities, and finances. These policies should support both the number and scope of curricular objectives and should be developed in a manner which demonstrates coordination between the library staff and the dance faculty.

1. *Governance.* The functional position of the dance collection within the total library structure shall be clearly identified, and the responsibilities and authority of the individual in charge of the dance collection shall be defined. There should be a close administrative relationship among all libraries within the institution so that dance students and faculty may make the best use of library resources.

2. *Collections.* Institutions must maintain library holdings in dance of sufficient size and scope to complement the total instructional programs of the institution, to provide incentive for individual learning, and to support research appropriate for its faculty.

There shall be evidence that a systematic acquisitions program compatible with appropriate needs has been planned, and that some form of faculty consultation and review is a continuing aspect of this program. Materials in all formats required for the study of dance—books, periodicals, microforms, audio recordings, notated dance scores, video tapes, films, and slides—shall be the basis of the acquisitions program.

Whenever possible, cooperative arrangements should be established with information sources outside the institution to augment holdings for student and faculty use. (The books, films, and audio recordings held by the libraries of municipalities, radio stations, historical societies, and other schools often can provide a breadth of coverage far beyond that of the institution.)

3. *Personnel.* The library shall be staffed by qualified personnel sufficient to meet the various needs of the dance program. Institutions are encouraged to engage specialized personnel whenever feasible to organize and maintain the dance holdings.

4. *Services.* The institution shall maintain appropriate hours of operation for the library. There should be convenient access to the library holdings in dance through complete and effective catalogues, indexes, and other appropriate bibliographical tools. There should also be access to the holdings of other institutions through union catalogues, cooperative network facilities, photoduplication, and interlibrary loan. Institution in the use of the dance collection shall be provided.

5. *Facilities.* The institution shall provide an effective environment for study. Facilities should be as centralized as possible to provide convenient access to all library holdings devoted to the study of dance.

The institution shall provide and maintain equipment that allows reasonable access to the resources of the library, including but not limited to audio and video equipment, microform units, and computer terminals.

6. *Finance*. Budgetary support shall be adequate to provide appropriate services, carry out necessary operations, and satisfy stated requirements of the programs offered.

Although fiscal policies may vary among institutions, it is desirable that the allocation for the dance collection be an explicit element in the institution's library budget. The management of this allocation should be the responsibility of a designated staff person.

An organized system of involvement by dance faculty and students should exist to advise the librarian in planning short- and long-term fiscal needs most effectively. (42–43)

The association notes expectations for libraries in their section "General Standards and Guidelines for Graduate Programs in Dance" (44): "A considerable investment, far beyond that for an undergraduate program in faculty, library, space, and equipment is required to qualify an institution to offer graduate study....The dance library should provide facilities and holdings appropriate to the degree programs offered" (44).

National Association of Schools of Music

Founded in 1924, this organization provides, among other things, "a national forum for the discussion and consideration of concerns relevant to the preservation and advancement of standards in the field of music in higher education" (National Association of Schools of Music 1991, 5). The association recognizes many types of programs in baccalaureate and graduate degree–granting institutions. As part of the basic criteria for membership, the association states: "The institution shall have library space and holdings adequate to the needs of its educational program" (43).

Under its standards section for facilities and equipment, the association asserts: "The following facilities shall be provided as appropriate to the size and objectives of the music program in each particular institution: classrooms, faculty teaching studios, student practice rooms, ensemble rehearsal rooms, auditoriums for concerts, a music library, storage facilities, and administrative offices" (43).

Specifically, with respect to libraries the association states:

The institution shall place importance on the development and maintenance of library resources which support its curricula in music. The music library should be considered an integral part of the music program of the institution. The institution shall have policies concerned with but not limited to the following aspects of library operations: governance, collections and their development, personnel services and access, facilities, and finances. These policies should support both the number and scope of curricular objectives and should be developed in a manner which demonstrates coordination between the library staff and the music faculty. (46)

Under the area of governance, the association states the following:

The functional position of the music library within the total library structure shall be clearly identified, and the responsibilities and authority of the individual in charge of the music library shall be defined.

There should be a close administrative relationship among libraries within the institution so that music students and faculty may make the best use of library resources. (46)

Relative to collections, the association instructs:

Institutions must maintain library holdings in music of sufficient size and scope to complement the total instructional programs of the institution, to provide incentive for individual learning, and to support research appropriate for its faculty.

There shall be evidence that a systematic acquisitions program compatible with appropriate needs has been planned, and that some form of faculty consultation and review is a continuing aspect of this program. Materials in all formats required for the study of music—books, periodicals, microforms, audio recordings, scores, and parts—shall be the basis of the acquisitions program.

Whenever possible, cooperative arrangements should be established with information sources outside the institution to augment holdings for student and faculty use. (The books, scores and audio recordings held by the libraries of municipalities, radio stations, historical societies, and other schools often can provide a breadth of coverage far beyond that of the institution.) (46)

Under the area of staffing and personnel, the association observes that: ''The music library shall be staffed by qualified personnel sufficient to meet the various needs of the music program. Institutions are encouraged to engage specialized personnel whenever feasible to organize and maintain the music holdings'' (46).

Under a category termed ''services'' the association notes:

The institution shall maintain appropriate hours of operation for the library.

There should be convenient access to the library holdings in music through complete and effective catalogs, indexes, and other appropriate bibliographic tools.

There should be access to the holdings of other institutions through union catalogs, cooperative network facilities, photoduplication, and interlibrary loan.

Instruction in the use of the music library shall be provided. (46)

Under the area of ''facilities'' it is noted that

[t]he institution shall provide an effective environment for study. Facilities should be s centralized as possible to provide convenient access to all library holdings devoted to the study of music. For example, scores and recordings should be easily accessible for effective use in conjunction with one another.

The institution shall provide and maintain equipment that allows reasonable access to the resources of the library, including but not limited to audio equipment, microfilm units, and computer terminals. (47)

The association observes the following relative to library finance and budget:

Budgetary support shall be adequate to provide appropriate services, carry out necessary operations, and satisfy stated requirements of the programs offered. Although fiscal policies may vary among institutions, it is desirable that the allocation for the music library be an explicit element in the institution's library budget. The management of this allocation should be the responsibility of a designated staff person.

An organized system of involvement by music faculty and students should exist to advise the librarian in planning short- and long-range fiscal needs most effectively. (47)

The association's *Handbook*, in Appendix B, notes special considerations with respect to the joint guidelines between the National Association of Schools of Music and the National Association of Schools of Theatre "Standards and Guidelines for Opera and Musical Theatre Programs." Appendix B states: "In addition to the standards for degree and diploma programs, institutions with comprehensive objectives in opera or musical theatre must provide: (1) specialized faculty appropriate to the scope and level of the program; (2) complete opera or musical theatre production facilities available and accessible for full productions; (3) library resources for the study of roles through scores, recordings, and analytical texts. These should cover all standard works" (app. B, 105).

The association, in its *Handbook*, Appendix C, notes its "Standards and Guidelines for the Education and Training of Orchestral Conductors." A specific reference to music libraries is found in Section C: "In addition to the standards for all degree and diploma programs, institutions with comprehensive objectives in orchestral conducting must provide: (1) specialized faculty appropriate to the scope and level of the program; (2) a complete symphony orchestra available and accessible for rehearsals and concerts; (3) library resources for the study of scores, recordings, and analytical texts. These should cover all standard works and a cross-section of lesser-known works, including contemporary compositions" (app. C, 115).

In Appendix C, dealing with advanced graduate degrees in orchestral conducting, the association notes that "[r]esources for the study of the orchestral literature through recordings, scores, and analytical texts must be available. These should cover all standard works" (app. C, 117).

In Appendix E, dealing with "Standards for Baccalaureate Curricula Combining Studies in Music and Electrical Engineering Prepared by NASM and ABET [American Board for Engineering and Technology], the association notes that for the bachelor music with an emphasis in electrical engineering, "[i]n addition to the holdings appropriate to the music component the library should contain appropriate engineering texts and technical journals" (app. E, 129).

The National Association of Schools of Music had developed a preliminary report as of October 1992 to consider the future of music libraries. Major topics under consideration by the Music Library Association and the National Association of Schools of Music were: Technologies, Collections and Services, Operations and Administrative Issues, Relationships with Curriculum, and the Multiple Forms of Scholarship (National Association of Schools of Music 1992, 1).

National Association of Schools of Theatre

Founded in 1975, the association's mission is to secure "a better understanding between institutions of higher education engaged in teaching theatre, establishing a more uniform method granting credit, and setting minimum standards for the granting of degrees and other credentials" (National Association of Schools of Theatre 1991, 84).

This association's library expectations are as follows:

Adequate theatre library resources should be readily available to support both the programs offered and the curricular/research needs of faculty and enrolled students. Library materials must be current and relevant to the programs offered.

Institutional libraries must have adequate resources to maintain and enlarge the collections and to provide professional and support staff. Institutions providing access to library facilities in the immediate area must demonstrate that the library used has a collection adequate to support the program, and that policies and procedures for access are appropriate to the needs of the students and faculty.

American Psychological Association

The American Psychological Association accredits doctoral and predoctoral internship training programs in professional psychology.

Under its 1986 criteria found in the *Accreditation Handbook*, the association notes the following with respect to libraries, audiovisual equipment and facilities, and computing services in Criterion VI: Facilities:

Training in professional psychology requires adequate facilities. Although the specific facilities may vary depending upon the program specialty (e.g., clinical, school, counseling) and the geographical area (e.g., rural, urban), adequacy of the following will be assessed in relation to program goals:

A. Teaching facilities, including classrooms, seminar rooms, observational facilities, and laboratory space for studies of individuals and small groups;
B. Library facilities, including books, journals, reprints, microforms;...
I. Data analysis and computer facilities, including consultants;
J. Audio-tape and video-tape recorders, and closed-circuit television. (B–9, B–10)

The association also notes: "Site visitors will be given the opportunity to visit all physical facilities available to the program, including those for teaching, research, practicum training, and internship training, and to inspect the relevant library holdings. In addition, they will have an opportunity to form impressions of the apparatus and materials available, the adequacy of secretarial and clerical support provided, and access by faculty and students to data analysis facilities, as well as to professional settings for practicum land internship training when nearby'' (26).

The American Psychological Association encourages its site visitors to visit all physical facilities and services that support psychology education programs. Site visitors are urged to comment on the general adequacy for the purposes of the affected programs and call attention to any special facilities or equipment provided by the institution in support of its programs (American Psychological Association 1986, 26). Site visitors use a check sheet that asks for their comments on the areas noted above as well as others noted under facilities.

PROFESSIONAL

National Architectural Accrediting Board

The origins of architectural accreditation extend to 1897 with an architectural registration act in Illinois. In 1912 the Association of Collegiate Schools of Architecture was established, and in 1940, the American Institute of Architects, the National Council of Architectural Registration Boards, and the Association of Collegiate Schools of Architecture created the present National Architectural Accrediting Board (National Architectural Accrediting Board 1991, 4).

The board recognizes libraries, information technologies, and computing under its standard 3.11: Information Resources that states:

An institution must provide evidence of adequate information resources and their integration into the program. These resources must be of sufficient substance to support the curriculum and the scholarly and research objectives of the program: not less than 5,000 Library of Congress NA or Dewey 720–729 volumes and additional technical and support volumes to provide a balanced architectural collection as described by the Art Libraries Society of North America and the Association of Architecture School Librarians. An ample collection of periodicals and slide and video collections must be located in easy assess for the students. (22)

The board asks schools who are currently being reviewed and undergoing self-study to supply the number of volumes in the:

Departmental Library Architecture Collection

Departmental Library NA or 720–729 Collection

University Library Architecture Collection

University Library NA or 720–729 Collection

Department Library Architecture Slides

University Library Architecture Slides (54)

Visiting teams are asked, in their report, to describe how the institution conforms with each of the board's criteria, including the area of Information Resources. Specific library and information technology guidelines note:

An architecture library is defined as that library collection or branch library which supports the primary instructional and research needs of the architecture program. The architecture library generally falls into one of the following types:

A separate branch library designed to serve a school or department of architecture within a university, college, or institute, which is able to draw on the resources of the larger central library;

A separate branch within a university, college, or institute with collections devoted to several related subjects including architecture (e.g., art and architecture, architectural and planning, architecture and engineering, etc.);

A collection of architecture-related materials housed and serviced within a central library;

An independent library that performs all library operations (e.g., ordering and cataloging library materials, interlibrary loan, etc.) for a school or institution physically or administratively unconnected with a parent institution. (62)

The guidelines go on to note that "administratively, the architecture library can report to the institution's library system or directly to the head of the architecture program" (62).

To achieve accreditation an architecture program's library collection should be adequate in size, scope, content, currentness, retrospectiveness, and availability, and its staff and services should be adequate and appropriate to support the goals, objectives, and curriculum of the architecture program. The architecture library must be a responsive and active force within the educational life of the architecture program. Access to other architecture libraries in the region is not a substitute for an adequate library. Since visual resources and other non-book materials are an integral part of an architecture program, the accreditation process should include the evaluation of these collections whether they are within the architecture library or in a separate collection. (62)

The board offers the following specific criteria that must be met:

1. Library Collections.
   a. Context: Is the library collection appropriate to the mission, goals, programs, and curriculum of the architecture program and its parent institution?
   b. Funding: How do collection funds, size, and growth rate compare with peer institutions? Does the librarian have input into the collections budget process? Does the librarian have authority for selection decisions and expenditure of the budget? Is there a regular pattern of growth?
   c. Subject coverage: Are the breadth, scope, and complexity of subjects relevant to the practice, history, theory, and criticism of architecture, both current and retrospective, sufficient to support the architecture program? And where library support of faculty research and professional development is specified in the institutional goals, is the collection adequate?
   d. Levels of coverage: Is there sufficient depth in the collection to adequately support

programs taught? Compare to the "comprehensive, research, study, basic, and minimal levels" defined by the American Library Association in *Guidelines for Collection Development* (Chicago: American Library Association, 1979, 3–5).

e. Number of volumes: Does the architecture library have sufficient collections to meet the needs of the architecture program and the number of students?

f. Serials: Is the serials collection sufficient in coverage and scope? Are sets current, retrospective, and complete? What periodicals indexes are available for access to the collection? What percentage of serial titles indexed in the major architectural periodical indexes (*Architectural Periodicals Index, Art Index, Avery Index to Architectural Periodicals, Construction Index*) are available?

g. Visual resources and non-book resources: Are sufficient non-book materials appropriate for the teaching and instructional needs of the school (slides, videos, drawings, photos, models, materials samples, electronic databases, or other formats, etc.) available and readily accessible? Are they produced or purchased in a timely fashion? If housed and serviced in a separately administered collection, visual resource/non-book collections should also be evaluated against these guidelines by their librarians for inclusion in the *APR* (1991, 64–67).

h. Access: Does the organization and cataloging of the collections provide adequate physical, bibliographical, and intellectual access to information? Are collections organized or cataloged using the national standards MARC, AMC, and AACR2? Does the architecture library participate in national cataloging networks? Are library materials cataloged within a reasonable time of receipt?

i. Conservation and preservation: Is there adequate physical care of the collection through appropriate housing, storage, binding, mending, encapsulation, and other means?

j. Policy statements: Are there written collection development policy statements that are regularly used and reviewed? Was there participation by faculty in the development of the policy? Is the policy appropriate for the mission, goals, and curriculum of the architecture program?

2. Services.

a. Access to collections and services: Is there barrier-free and equal access to the architecture library? Is there student access to course reserve or other intensively used materials? Is there ready access to non-book materials?

b. Circulation: Are there appropriate written loan policies?

c. Reference: Is there guidance in the use of library materials? Is knowledgeable, professional, and personal guidance available? Are reference publications for quick consultation available? What about computerized reference services?

d. Bibliographic instruction: Is an architecture librarian available for library orientations, instruction in library skills, and research methods? Are there reference guides/pathfinders to aid in use of collection? Is bibliographic instruction incorporated into the architecture program curriculum?

e. Hours open: Are hours of collection availability and reference services convenient for the architecture library's primary users?

f. Current awareness: Are new book and journal lists, notices or displays, SDI, exhibits, or other current awareness practices available?

g. Cooperative agreements: Are formal interlibrary loan and other cooperative agreements to augment or extend access to library materials regionally and/or nationally in practice?

3. Staff.

a. Numbers: Is there sufficient staff to successfully accomplish library goals and services?

b. Professional: Does the architecture library have sufficient professional librarians with master's in library or information science and subject expertise in architecture or closely related fields? What is the status of librarians within the architecture program or institutional administrative structure? Are there written position descriptions: What is the education and experience of architecture librarians?

c. Support staff: Does the architecture library have sufficient paraprofessional, clerical, and student staff? What are the job training and academic preparation required of paraprofessionals? Are there written job descriptions?

d. Reporting structure: What is the administrative structure of the library? How does the library relate to the architecture program? Is the architecture library and its staff considered a part of the architecture program educational team?

e. Professional development: Are opportunities for professional development and continuing education (conferences, workshops, courses, etc.) available for all architecture library staff?

f. Salaries: Are library staff salaries commensurate with training and experience of comparable others in the institution?

4. Facilities.

a. Space: Is there adequate square footage for all architecture library activities and services? If not, are there realistic plans to ameliorate any inadequacy? Is the location convenient to the architecture students and faculty? Is there an attractive, welcoming environment for users and staff? Are there proper environmental controls for library materials? Is there regular access to collections in remote storage facilities?

b. Equipment: Is there sufficient and appropriate storage and housing systems for all types of library materials? Are there sufficient numbers of photocopiers, microform readers/copiers, slide viewers, projectors, computer workstations, etc., for public and staff use?

c. Furnishings: Are there sufficient numbers of appropriate workstations for staff and users, including adequate lighting, electrical supply, heating, and ventilation?

d. Security: Is there adequate protection for library users and materials from theft, fire, and natural hazards? Are there emergency procedures, disaster plans?

5. Budget/Administration/Operations.

a. Funds: Are funds sufficient to achieve goals, missions, programs, and operations, and to develop and maintain resources and services? What is the source of funding (endowment, institutional allocation, gifts, etc)? Does the librarian have control over expenditure of the budget? How does the budget compare with peer institutions? What is the reliability and regularity of annual funding?

b. Evidence of planning: Are there written goals and objectives for the architecture library and realistic plans to achieve them?

c. Intra-institutional relations: How does the architecture library relate to the architecture program and to other libraries on campus or in the community?

d. Efficiency of operations and services: Does the architecture library function smoothly and systematically?

e. Participation of faculty and students: Is there a library advisory committee or other means for user particulation in the development and evaluation of the architecture library services, resources, and programs? (64–67)

American Assembly of Collegiate Schools of Business

The American Assembly of Collegiate Schools of Business (AACSB) is the official accrediting agency for all bachelor's and master's degree programs in business and administration. It was formally established in 1916, and its membership has grown to encompass not only educational institutions but business, government, and professional organizations as well. The assembly's standards for libraries, information technologies, instructional technologies, and computing services may be found in its 1992 publication *Achieving Quality and Continuous Improvement Through Self-Study and Peer Evaluation: Standards for Business and Accounting Programs* (American Assembly of Collegiate Schools of Business 1992, 1). The AACSB accreditation review focuses on an institution's mission determination, its faculty, its curriculum planning, and the quality of its instructional delivery systems (1). Specific expectations in the areas noted above may be found in the standard dealing with Instructional Resources:

Standard: The school should provide and manage resources to meet the instructional responsibilities created by the programs offered.
Basis for Judgment: To meet this standard, the school must demonstrate that the available instructional resources are sufficient to meet the instructional objectives of the programs offered. A summary assessment concerning instructional resources should consider the items identified below:

• Appropriate instructional technologies and related support should be available and utilized by faculty.

• Students should have access to and be required to make use of library and computing facilities.

• Schools with heavy emphasis on graduate programs or applied and basic scholarship must augment library resources, data bases, and information technology appropriately to support those mission elements.

• When on-campus resources cannot be duplicated reasonably for off-campus programs, comparable access should be provided through inter-library loans, electronic delivery systems, agreements with other libraries, and by other means.

• Space, facilities, and staff support should be adequate to meet program goals and objectives. (25)

AACSB accredits accounting programs separately and notes that "the accounting unit must meet the business instructional resources and responsibilities standards" (48)

National Council for Accreditation of Teacher Education

The National Council for Accreditation of Teacher Education, or NCATE, was founded in Washington, D.C., in 1954. There were five organizations that were instrumental in the founding of NCATE: the American Association of State Directors of Teacher Education, the National Association of State Directors of Teacher Education and Certification, the National Commission on Teacher Education and Professional Standards of the National Education Association, the National Council of Chief State School Officers, and the National School Boards Association (National Council for Accreditation of Teacher Education 1992a, 2).

NCATE holds as its mission: (1) requiring a level of quality in professional education that fosters competent practice of graduates and (2) encouraging institutions to meet rigorous academic standards of excellence in professional education (1). The council carries on a systematic program for the evaluation and revision of its accreditation standards, setting forth eighteen standards and ninety-four criteria against which professional education units are evaluated (1, 6). Criteria for Compliance in the area of library resources, equipment, materials, and supplies are noted below:

Library holdings provide adequate scope, breadth, and currency to support the professional education programs.

Systematic reviews of library and media materials are conducted periodically and are used to make acquisition decisions.

An identifiable and relevant media and materials collection is accessible to education students and faculty.

Modern equipment is available to support administration, research, service, and instructional needs of the unit.

Necessary supplies are provided to support faculty, students, staff, and administration in the operation and implementation of programs, policies, and procedures.

National Association of Schools of Public Affairs and Administration

This accrediting association is dedicated to the advancement of education, training, and research in public affairs and administration. Approval of master's degree program standards was initiated in 1977, and in 1986 the association officially accredited programs. The association is a specialized agency for master's degree programs only (National Association of Schools of Public Affairs and Administration 1991, 1).

Master of Public Administration standards, effective in September 1993, noted the following with respect to library services:

8.0 Supportive Services and Facilities...

    8.2 *Library Services.* All students and faculty shall have reasonable access to library facilities and services that are recognized as adequate for master's level study in public affairs and administration. This would normally include texts, monographs, periodicals, serials, pamphlets, and research reports. The program faculty should have a major role in selecting library acquisitions for its program. (7)

As part of the team visit to determine the adequacy of this standard, visitors are asked to consider the following:

The team may wish to visit the placement office and library. It may be helpful to see the documents that relate to the placement activities, e.g., career counseling, student vitae, and to interview appropriate library officials and look at the library's record of yearly book acquisitions in subject fields offered by the program. The list of regularly maintained periodicals and journals may be obtained and reviewed, if necessary.

In order to check intended library usage, required reading lists of courses, which should also be included in the Self-Study Report, may be compared to reserve lists in the library....

Obviously, an on-site review of library resources and services is important. The team's tour of the school's library and those ancillary services, such as the university computer center, etc., is important to an effective visit. (National Association of Schools of Public Affairs and Administration 1990, 12, 13)

American Association for Marriage and Family Therapy

This is the national accrediting agency for the field of marriage and family therapy. It sets standards for and accredits master's, doctoral, and postdegree clinical training programs (Commission on Accreditation for Marriage and Family Therapy 1991, 1). The association accredits programs located in various university academic departments as long s those programs demonstrate integrity through a commitment to marriage and family therapy as a profession (5). Library standards are found under Section 200 of the standards: Administration and Organization Structure:

Resources necessary to meet program and institutional objectives must be evident. The program should have a clearly defined financial policy and budget. It must have sufficient funds to ensure the retention of a well-qualified faculty and staff, the maintenance of library resources, and the effective operation of facilities. These factors will be examined by comparing the balance between the program's resources and facilities and the resources of the institution. The effectiveness of library resources will be judged by student, faculty, and staff usage, by the availability of sufficient quantities of books and pertinent journals, and by sufficient expenditure for new accessions. The faculty and staff should plan the educational program around a reasonable projection of need for space and equipment, and personnel. (9–10)

Council on Rehabilitation Education

Formed in 1971, the council is unique among accrediting agencies in that it is not specifically or solely academic in orientation. From its inception, the council has included a major concern for the delivery of services. There are five organizations represented in the council: the American Rehabilitation Counseling Association, the Council on Rehabilitation Counselor Educators, the National Council on Rehabilitation Education, the Council of State Administrators of Vocational Rehabilitation, and the National Association of Rehabilitation Facilities. These constituent organizations of the council "represent the professional and organizational constituencies concerned with the training, evaluation, and employment of rehabilitation counselors (Council on Rehabilitation Education 1991, 1).

Concern for library, media, and academic computing support can be found in the council's standards, Section G: Program Support and Resources:

The program shall have reasonable access to resources and facilities necessary for effective implementation of the program, including:

- Adequate support staff, office space for support staff, office equipment and records/data processing;
- Instructional classrooms, student and research facilities, faculty office space with sufficient privacy for confidentiality;
- Individual counseling rooms with assured privacy and provisions for audio- and video-tape recording and feedback;
- Facilities to house and make available Rehabilitation Counselor Education materials, instructional media, occupational information materials, testing materials, microcomputer equipment, and other appropriate equipment, including audio-tape, videotape, and instructional resources. (37–38)

Accrediting Council on Education in Journalism and Mass Communications

Having established its structure for evaluating and accrediting journalism and mass communications programs in 1945, the council attempts to stimulate and encourage strong educational programs in these fields (Accrediting Council on Education in Journalism and Mass Communications 1992, 1–2). Concern with libraries and instructional equipment is found in Standard 8: Equipment/

Facilities. The standard reads: "The unit must have facilities and equipment in sufficient quantity and quality to carry out its stated educational objectives" (12).

The council explains this statement through the following statement:

A professional program worthy of accreditation should have the equipment and facilities necessary for carrying out the educational mission that it has assigned itself. The library should have at least the standard books and current periodicals in the field, and its holdings should be not only accessible to, but used by, the students and faculty. Faculty members should have offices with sufficient privacy for their own study and for conferring with students. Laboratories should have ample space and equipment for efficient instruction. Students in print journalism should have training in the use of the basic equipment that they will need in their careers. (12)

For this standard, the council suggests the need for the following evidence:

a. Inspection tour of quarters and equipment.

b. The evaluation made of the equipment and facilities in the self-study report.

c. Observation of the adequacy, availability, and use made of equipment.

d. Student responses to questions by the visiting team about the adequacy and accessibility of necessary equipment and facilities.

e. Basic reference works in main library and unit reading room.

f. Utilization of current periodicals by students in keeping abreast of the field. (12)

Council for Accreditation of Counseling and Related Educational Programs

The council grants accredited status to graduate-level programs in the professional counseling field. Programs accredited by the council include those preparing master's-prepared students for work in community counseling, marriage and family counseling, mental health counseling, school counseling, and student affairs practice in higher education. It also accredits programs offering doctoral-level work in counselor education and supervision (Council for Accreditation of Counseling and Related Educational Programs 1991, 11).

Entry-level program standards promulgated by the council in the area of library resources and services are:

Library facilities and resources are appropriate for scholarly inquiry, study, and research by program faculty and students. The library facilities and resources:

1. Include basic resources (i.e., books and journals) directly relevant to the program as well as resources from related disciplines such as psychology, sociology, education, business, economics, and anthropology.
2. Are open evenings and weekends.

3. Provide services including computerized searches, inter-library loans, reserved books/materials, microfiche and microfilm reviewing, and photocopying.
4. Hold multiple copies of resource materials frequently used by program faculty and students. (44)

Under the area of clinical instruction, the council notes the following with respect to audiovisual equipment and resources and microcomputer equipment:

Individual counseling rooms, with assured privacy and sufficient space for appropriate equipment (e.g., videotape and audiotape).

Portable and permanent audio and videotape recording, and playing equipment.

Technical assistance for the use and maintenance of audio and videotape, and microcomputer equipment is available. (52–53)

Under the standards for doctoral-level programs the council notes the following with respect to library resources and services: "Library facilities and resources are appropriate for doctoral level scholarly inquiry, study, and research by students and program faculty" (65).

American Home Economics Association

The association is dedicated to improving the quality of home economics programs in institutions of higher education. A committee of the association in the 1940s led to the publication in 1949 of *Home Economics in Higher Education*, which included an appendix titled "Criteria for Evaluating Undergraduate Programs in Home Economics" (American Home Economics Association 1990, 1). Today, current standards are found in *Accreditation Documents for Undergraduate Programs in Home Economics*. Standard 8: Library and Related Educational Resources discusses the areas of concern to librarians and media professionals. The standard notes: "The library is adequate in terms of scope and depth of holdings related to the general and professional components of the program(s). Library holdings and services are accessible to students. Instructional media and related educational resources are maintained as a part of the library or as a separate unit" (75). Under Standard 7, Subsection 7.1 notes the intent of this standard: "The print and non-print materials are authoritative, up-to-date, and of adequate coverage to support the program(s) being offered and the professional development of students and faculty" (75).

Specific criteria under this intent are as follows:

Policies, procedures, and budgets for the purchase of books, periodicals, and other educational materials are defined and are adequate to meet the needs of the program(s).

The library holdings, both contemporary and historical, in home economics and related disciplines are appropriate for program(s) offered.

Research and other primary sources of data are available.

The faculty and professional library staff cooperate in building the library collection(s), evaluating services, and developing long-range plans.

The budget allocation is responsive to special needs such as: new programs, enrollment increases, and program redirection.

Reciprocal arrangements are made with libraries in the other communities, as needed by faculty, students and practitioners (inter-library loan). (75)

Subsection 7.2 notes additional intent of the standard: "The library services, facilities, and related educational resources are adequate, functional, accessible, and used by faculty and students in the unit" (75). Specific criteria under this intent are:

The library services and related educational resources assure students and faculty access to materials and equipment. Circulation procedures and user guidelines, including those relating to reserve materials, are such as to achieve optimum use.

Information services for facilitating usage are provided to students and faculty.

There is evidence that students and faculty are aware of, and use, the resources for reference, study, and research.

Equipment for faculty and student use is up-to-date, adequate in quantity, and readily available. (75)

American Dietetic Association

Dietetic accreditation extends back to 1923 when the Education Section of the association first discussed plans for courses for student dietitians. In 1924 the minimum specifications for a course of study for student dietitians was introduced (American Dietetic Association 1991, 1). Development of standards in the field has continued since that time. Today, the association notes the following with respect to libraries, information technologies, and learning resources:

Principal. Minimum resources are necessary for effective education to occur in a dietetic education program. Minimum resources include competent administrators and faculty, sufficient support personnel, and adequate services to provide for the planned education of students.

Standard Three. Resources available to the program shall be identified and their contribution to the program described.

Criterion 3.1
The program shall provide evidence that the administrative support, learning resources, physical facilities, and clerical and technical support needed to accomplish stated goals and objectives are available.

Guideline:
For example, evidence may include a description of the following:

- Library resources, such as numbers, recency, and accessibility of books, journals, and other pertinent materials.
- Learning resources, such as audio-visual equipment, computers, etc.
- Other support such as data processing; assistance in development of instructional materials, including media; public relations; and assistance with the development of grants. (23)

Society of American Foresters

The society is the national organization representing all areas of the forestry profession including both public and private practitioners, researchers, administrators, educators, and forestry students. From its founding in 1900 the society has sought to advance the science, technology, education, and practice of professional forestry (Society of American Foresters 1990, ii).

In its eight standards, the society describes the essential elements of a professional forestry education program. Standard VII: Physical Resources and Facilities notes the following with respect to library resources: "[s]tudent appraisal of library, adequacy and use" and "[p]rogram conducts regular assessment of adequacy of resources/facilities" (13).

Self-study coordinators are asked to answer the following questions related to library and computer resources:

Describe the institution's library in terms of meeting the needs of forestry students and faculty members.

Describe the forests, summer field facilities, and other special facilities (such as special library collections) available for forestry education, and the extent to which these are used.

Specify the computer services and independent study facilities available, and the extent to which these are used.

Describe the adequacy of the above resources to meet the needs of the forestry program in light of the stated program goals and objectives. (39)

The society provides a checklist for evaluation of library and related facilities. This checklist would appear to be used in conjunction with the standard noted above and during the on-site visitation.

Books and Related Materials

Identity: Is there discrimination among subject fields, and some attention paid to needs of individual courses?

Scope: Is the full scope of course and research interests covered by current books, both as to geographic distribution and degrees of subject specificity, including primary and secondary works, and a fair quantity of collateral and even minor works in the major fields?

Quantity: Is there a reasonable quantity of books, including duplicate copies of heavily used titles, and are they relevant to the range and level of the curricula offered?

Currency: Is the collection kept current? Is there evidence of a substantial and continuing infusion of new books discriminately selected in the major fields?

Condition: Is the physical condition of the collection adequate to assure its availability for the next generation of students, especially in bibliographics, reference works, primary sources and journals?

Facilities and Related Staff

Location/Use: Are students taking advantage of personal, career and other provided student services? Are methods/procedures evident to describe these services?

Hours: Are hours of related facilities (library, computer, placement, etc.) conducive to meeting student needs?

Computer Search Capabilities: If available, are these services explained and utilized by the students? What is the availability and use of inter-library loans for students? Faculty?

Staff: Are there qualified and effective professional staff to assist the student in these areas?

Orientation: Is the formal orientation program in library, computer, placement, financial aid, and other services provided or otherwise available?

Budget: How do the faculty assess the adequacy of the annual appropriation for acquisition of forestry books and periodicals, for maintaining educational supplies, and to maintain facilities and field locations? Is there comparison with other similar services in other academic units on campus?

Evaluation Method

Personal observation and direct discussion with both faculty members and students on the above points is usually most helpful. (8)

Landscape Architectural Accreditation Board

This association promotes quality education in first-professional-degree programs in landscape architecture and encourages programs to regularly review their academic objectives and the adequacy of their curriculum, faculty, and facilities to meet those objectives. The standards set forth for libraries and academic computing are found in Standards 11 and 12.

11. Facilities and Equipment
    Technical Equipment. Computers and other current technical equipment are available to support the program.

12. Library
    An accessible library collection shall be provided to support the program.

    Indicators:
    Extent of Collection: The collection is adequate to support the program.
    Guideline: The collection should include bound volumes, periodicals, microform, video, slides and other materials pertinent to the study of landscape architecture.
    Acquisition of New Materials: Regular acquisitions supplement the existing collec-

tion, and faculty have a role in recommending them.

Areas of Concentration: The collection supports any program areas of concentration.

Integration with Curriculum: Course syllabi and problem statements integrate library use with course work. (Landscape Architectural Accreditation Board 1990, 10)

Planning Accreditation Board

The planning accreditation program, initiated in 1984, provides formal recognition that a planning program measures up to the profession's educational standards and qualifies individuals as future practitioners. In 1989 the criteria for accreditation were substantially revised and, currently, reflect the experience that has been gained in assessing the quality of programs (Planning Accreditation Board 1992, 3). The Planning Accreditation Board "accredits educational programs leading to bachelor's and master's degrees in planning" (1).

The board subsumes the concern with libraries, instructional resources, and computing facilities under its Criterion 10: Resources. It states the intent of this criterion as: "The Self-Study Report and the accreditation review are directed toward determining that the program has sufficient resources to support and advance its goals and objectives and to ensure that the criteria of the PAB are met. Thus, planning programs are expected to provide adequate organizational and physical resources in order to deliver an accreditation-worthy program. They are expected to strive to make efficient use of the resources provided by the institution and to generate resources external to the program and larger institution" (23).

The criterion is further illuminated by the following:

The resources available to the program shall be adequate for fulfilling the goals and objectives of the program and for meeting the criteria for accreditation. Resource areas include: faculty salaries and adjustments; program budgets for operating and equipment needs; and the physical plant in which the program is housed, including classrooms, studios and laboratories, computational facilities, and the planning library (its currency, as well as the extent of its holdings). Resources also include other facilities in the institution, such as centers, institutes, or libraries on which planning faculty and students depend. These resources shall reflect the program's emphases and the professional interests of the faculty and students, shall serve the program's functional needs, and shall encourage academic endeavors and institutional responsibilities appropriate to the program. (23–24)

Foundation for Interior Design Education Research

Founded in 1971, the Foundation for Interior Design Education Research ensures a high quality of program in interior design to meet the needs of students, the interior design profession, and society. Specific standards are set forth for programs that provide a first professional degree or a preprofessional assistant-level education (Foundation for Interior Design Education Research 1988,

1). Specific library-related requirements are found within Standard 5: Resources and Facilities. These requirements are:

The library of the institution has a strong reference collection on design, interior design, architecture, construction and the arts, as well as relevant literature from supporting academic areas such as sociology, psychology, management, and environmental design.

Current and high quality reference materials, professional magazines, samples and catalogues are available and should be in close proximity to the studios.

The physical facilities including buildings equipment and library are appropriate to serve the stated objectives of the program.

Library facilities are easily accessible.

An audio-visual library and necessary equipment are readily available.

A suitable yearly budget allocation is made to ensure the up-dating of the library reference material and the audio-visual collection. (11)

National Recreation and Park Association

The Council on Accreditation of the association held its first meeting in 1974, and in 1976 the council began to accept applications for accreditation from colleges and universities. The council accredits academic programs preparing recreation and park educators.

Library, instructional resources, and computer support expectations are found under the council's 1992 Standard 6: Instructional Resources:

There shall be adequate instructional resources available to implement properly the curriculum of the academic unit, including special services for individuals with disabilities.

There shall be adequate library materials available including, but not limited to, books, periodicals, reports, microfilms, and other unpublished reference materials.

There shall be adequate computer and statistical services available to faculty and students of the academic unit for instructional, research, and administrative applications. (National Recreation and Park Association 1992, 11)

Council on Social Work Education

This association is charged with establishing standards for the accreditation of social work education programs at the baccalaureate and master's degree levels. The council reviews undergraduate programs to determine the quality of their preparation of students for entry into social work practice at the beginning level, while it reviews graduate programs to determine adequacy of preparation of students to enter practice at an advanced level (Council on Social Work Education 1991, V). Within candidate status, expectations for libraries, information technologies, and computer support may be found under the council's Baccalaureate Candidacy Criteria Standard 4.0: Resources:

The application must describe the program components, facilities, and resources that are in place, or that will be in place at the date designated for the opening of the program.

The application must include a statement of the institution's commitment to provide the program with adequate financial support, a clearly specified position in the institution's administrative structure, and adequate physical facilities and computer and library resources....

There must be adequate library holdings of basic social work literature including a range of social work and social science journals necessary for the educational support of an undergraduate social work program. (3–4)

The council notes its evaluative standard for the above through its "Guide to Library Evaluations and Reports." That document is designed as an aid in judging the adequacy of the library that supports the social work program. It was prepared in response to Baccalaureate Evaluative Standard 14.3 and Master's Evaluative Standard 12.3 above. The document is organized into sections of descending importance:

1. Prime evidence—books and related materials, library physical facilities, and professional staff and staff services.

2. Secondary evidence, including budget and planning documents.

3. Special activities.

The guide document lists the following library expectations for baccalaureate programs under Evaluative Standard 14, Resources:

Since books, facilities, and staff are the ingredients that can make a library excel, there is often no need to document or consider the secondary points of special activities. Local circumstances determine the advisability of using these subordinate data to clarify the evaluation.

In applying these evaluation methods to the well established library, it is important to watch for signs that the library may be slipping on one or another index or failing to meet new conditions posed by evolving instructional or research patterns and practices. In evaluating a library that has not yet established its quality, it is emphasized that the most important condition is a strong rate of improvement; the mere fact of meeting minimum quantitative standards is of far less importance.

Various sets of minimum standards exist and can be discriminatingly applied in library evaluations. These have been established by the Association of College and Research Libraries and by the several regional accrediting associations. This guide does not contradict any of these standards; nor does it purport to set standards. Rather, it suggests the criteria for judging the library program for any institution of higher education that provides baccalaureate or graduate social work education.

Standards can be of use in judging threshold cases, but even for these libraries, the momentum of library development and the effective use of available resources is of far greater significance than are quantitative data alone. The published ranges of actual library statistics may also serve as benchmarks. (119)

The guide document goes on to suggest what the council considers prime evidence:

All three of the following components must be adequate for the program and its clientele.

Books and Related Materials: The nature and extent of the educational social work resources held by the library should reflect the level of the social work program (master's degree or baccalaureate degree), the size of the faculty and student body, and the nature of the parent institution. Although library resources for social work students and faculty may include books, periodicals, films, cassette and video tapes, government documents, fugitive materials, computer services, and various nonprint materials, minimum holdings are necessary. There must be a reasonable quantity of periodicals and books, including duplicate copies of heavily used book titles, and the library materials must be relevant to the range and level of the curricula offered.

The library of the parent institution is expected to meet the standards promulgated for libraries by the regional accrediting association. Compliance with the regional accrediting body's criteria for libraries should be reviewed with the administration of the library or the institution or both....

The minimum holdings necessary for social work programs include books and periodicals necessary to support the social work curriculum. Students should have access within reasonable time to the books and periodicals cited in course bibliographies. It is suggested that reviewers check the availability of the bibliographic materials cited in at least two syllabi.

Although the accessibility of library materials may be enhanced through interlibrary loan or other exchange arrangements or through student use of neighboring library centers, if off-campus, extended degree, or branch programs exist, specific written provisions must be made to ensure the availability of needed instructional and research social work and social work–related materials during the time periods that are compatible with students' schedules. Some off-campus programs may need to meet this requirement by providing students with photocopied instructional materials.

Acquisition procedures are to include the selection and evaluation of social work library resources through the cooperative efforts of the teaching faculty and library staff. The specialized expertise of social work faculty should be used to advise the library concerning the nature and scope of the resources that will support the curriculum. Budgetary allocations for purchase of library materials must be available on an annual basis and must be sufficient to permit annual growth rates consistent with teaching and learning needs—generally around a five percent growth in the collection per year; the introduction of new courses or concentrations would be expected to create additional requirements for library resources.

The physical condition of the collection must be adequate to ensure availability for the next generation of students. Reference works, indexes, bibliographies, primary sources, and journals should be strongly bound or appropriately preserved. Library procedures should ensure a minimum of pilferage and abuse to library materials, and appropriate measures must be taken to restore damaged materials.

Evaluators should be familiar with the basic social work periodicals and with current books in the field. In evaluating the collections in libraries used by social work programs, the evaluator may need to refer to selected lists of social work and social science publications to determine the adequacy of the library holdings for their courses. Students should be asked about their ability to obtain needed library resources.

Library Physical Facilities: The location of the library on campus must be convenient so that trips from classrooms, dormitories, or parking areas do not discourage library use. When educational offerings or programs are conducted off campus, library resources must also be provided in a location that is convenient to the off-campus site and that encourages student use. Library hours must be arranged to adequately meet the needs of social work students, which vary as a result of field instruction assignments, evening classes, and other responsibilities.

There must be adequate space for student and faculty use of library resources for study and research. Lighting, ventilation, and sound control must be conducive to functional, distraction-free use of library facilities. Photocopying facilities should be available to students at reasonable cost. Library facilities must be accessible to physically disabled students, or the library must make suitable alternative provisions.

Programs offering off-campus and extension programs must assume responsibility for the library needs of their students. Various arrangements may satisfy such needs, and these may include the establishment of a branch library, a contractual agreement with another library, and an arrangement with the course instructor to transport the necessary resources to the educational site.

Professional Staff and Staff Services: Since no library can be better than those who create and operate it, evaluation should be made of the quality and quantity of staff. Librarians (persons with graduate degrees from programs accredited by the American Library Association) should be on staff and should be assisted in their tasks by an adequate nonprofessional support staff. Qualified professional reference direction or guidance should be easily and constantly available nearly all hours the library is open.

Library materials should be circulated under equitable policies and for as long a period as possible without jeopardizing their availability. Books should be easily found on library shelves and clear records maintained of books not in regular shelf order. Loan policies should aid, not hamper, easy access to the collections.

Evaluation should include talking with a sampling of social work students and faculty to gain insight into their satisfaction with services. Talking with library staff at major service points would provide a sense of the service readiness of library staff.

To assess off-campus or extension programs, the evaluator should determine the nature and extent of the cooperative planning between social work faculty and library staff that preceded the initiation of credit social work courses at such locations. Evaluations should be made of the social work program's ongoing utilization of library staff to provide a plan for the library service needs of students in off-campus locations. (119–21)

Secondary evidence is also considered as the council looks at programs. Secondary evidence is viewed as:

Use: The use students make of the library is the ultimate test of its effectiveness and is the result of various library conditions and of the faculty's teaching methods. Significance may be found in the extent to which students use reading spaces, in the quantity of reference services asked of librarians, and in the annual circulation volume of the reserve and general collections.

Budget: Significant figures are the percentages of the institution's instructional and research expenditures that go into the library over a period of years. Another useful set of figures is the percentage of the library budget that goes to each of the categories of personnel, books, binding, and miscellaneous expenses. Changes in these categories could reveal trends and persistent weaknesses.

Minutes of the Faculty's Library Committee: The record of discussions and decisions, even though brief, may reveal administrative emphases, major concerns, long-range goals, and even special reasons for the particular treatment of book funds. (121)

The council's specific baccalaureate evaluative standard is found under Baccalaureate Evaluative Standard 14: Resources: "The administration of the institution and the program shall provide the library holdings necessary for the attainment of the program's objectives" (122).

The council's specific master's evaluative standard is found under Master's Evaluative Standard 14: Resources and is stated in the same words as the baccalaureate evaluative standard.

American Physical Therapy Association

Education for the physical therapist has been recognized in some fashion since 1928. In that year the American Physical Therapy Association published its first list of approved educational programs. Since 1983 the Commission on Accreditation in Education/American Physical Therapy Association has been the accrediting agency for entry-level programs for the physical therapist and the physical therapist assistant (American Physical Therapy Association 1992, i–ii).

The association's concern with libraries and other academic support services is found in the following statement in its 1992 Draft evaluative criteria: "There are adequate and accessible library facilities. Instructional materials are current and sufficient in number and breadth to support the content of the curriculum and to meet the needs of the program" (9).

In its *Self-Study Report* document, the association notes that "interpretive comments and guidelines are included" for the criteria whenever it is "deemed necessary to provide further clarification of the criteria or to show the relation of criteria to a standard" (American Physical Therapy Association 1991, ii). The interpretative comment under the draft criteria is stated as follows:

The institution's library resources should be reasonably accessible to the physical therapy educational program. The library hours should provide for accessibility by the students and faculty during non-class hours. Library holdings represent a wide range of books, periodicals, and other instructional materials, including audio-visuals, relevant to the profession and the content of the curriculum. These materials are available in sufficient quantity to meet the needs of the program.

If the educational program has its own facility for books, for periodicals, instructional, audio-visual materials, this facility should be close to the classroom and laboratory facilities of the program and be accessible to students and faculty on evenings and weekends. Any and all of such facilities and materials are in an environment that is conducive to their intended purpose and use. A program's reliance on an individual's personal resources and/or heavy reliance on hospital or other external holdings is not adequate. Instructional materials are available to the students for independent study. (9)

American Speech-Language-Hearing Association

The American Speech-Language-Hearing Association was founded in 1925 as the American Academy of Speech Correction. Among the association's purposes are the encouragement of the scientific study of the processes of individual human communication, with a special focus on speech, language, and hearing and the promotion of appropriate academic and clinical preparation for those entering the discipline of human communication sciences and disorders (American Speech-Language-Hearing Association 1992, 3). The association's guidelines for self-study reveal the following statement on libraries under the area of facilities: "Are the library holdings adequate both within the professional disciplines of the program and related disciplines? Is the budget sufficient to ensure that holdings are current?" (28).

The association's standard for libraries and other instructional resources is found under Section 1.3 of the 1992 standards for accreditation:

The program must have physical facilities (classrooms, offices, clinic rooms, research laboratories), instructional materials, equipment, library holdings, and support services that are appropriate and sufficient to meet its present needs and its projected needs during the accreditation period.

The program's facilities should reflect contemporary standards of ready and reasonable access and use. Provision should be made to accommodate the needs of persons with disabilities.

The program's instructional materials, equipment, library holdings, and support services must be appropriate and adequate. (14)

American Library Association

The Council of the American Library Association has given the Committee on Accreditation responsibility to develop and formulate standards for graduate programs in library and information studies that lead to the master's degree (American Library Association 1992, 2). The association, through the Committee on Accreditation, describes the "essential features of the programs of education that prepare library and information professionals" (2).

The concern with library resources, information technologies, and academic computing is found in the association's 1992 standards under VI: Physical Resources and Facilities:

Instructional and research facilities and services for meeting the needs of students and faculty include access to library and multimedia resources and services, computer and other information technologies, accommodations for independent study, and media production facilities.

The staff and the services provided for a program by libraries, media centers, and information technology facilities, as well as all other support facilities, are sufficient for the level of use required and specialized to the degree needed. These facilities are appropriately staffed, convenient, accessible to the disabled, and available when needed, regardless of forms or locations of delivery of the school's program. (21)

In a later section of the 1992 *Standards*, it is noted: "The Standards make it explicit that the location of the offering of a program or its components, and the means by which a program or its components are delivered, e.g., satellite, closed circuit television, are relevant to the accreditation process simply as one aspect of a total program. The Standards neither extol nor caution against distance education. For accreditation purposes, programs are evaluated in the same way regardless of locations or forms of delivery of a program" (24).

LAW

American Bar Association

Since its inception in 1878 the American Bar Association has been concerned with the improvement of legal education in the United States. As early as the late 1880s, it was believed that an objective method needed to be developed that would begin to ensure the quality of education for the prospective attorney. In 1921 the association adopted a statement of minimum standards for legal education and subsequently published a list of law schools that complied with those standards (American Bar Association 1989a, 1).

The executive head of the American Bar Association's accreditation program, called the consultant, is responsible for all law school accreditation activities of the association and works in cooperation with the executive director of the Association of American Law Schools and the president of the Law School Admission Council. Thus, the consultant provides liaison among the three principal organizations that deal with legal education (American Bar Association 1991b, 1).

Library standards are found under Standards 601, 602, 603, 604, and 605 of the 1991 list of standards (American Bar Association 1991a). Standard 601 reads as follows:

The law school shall maintain and administer a library adequate for its program.

a. In order to inform applicants for accreditation of procedures and important facets of law library operations relating to adequacy, the Consultant may prepare appropriate memoranda.
b. The Dean and the Law Librarian shall maintain a current written plan for implementation of law library support for the law school program as developed in its self-study. (S601)

Following the standard, the association states the interpretations for this standard:

Interpretation 1 of 601: Scantiness of a library collection, the nature of its arrangement, deficiencies in shelf and seating space, the relative physical isolation from students and faculty, the hours of operation, the low salary levels of current library staff, the minimal size of the staff and a totally inadequate library budget violates Standard 601.

Interpretation 2 of 601: A weakness of a law library collection must be addressed with the degree of financial support commensurate with the need, as required by Standard 601.

Interpretation 3 of 601: Where a law school library collection is inadequate in terms of total volumes and the depth and breadth of the collection, Standard 601 cannot be satisfied by stating that the students have access to other law libraries within the region. (S601)

Standard 602 of the association reads as follows:

a. The law school shall contain the Core Collection Library Schedule, attached as Annex II.

b. The law school library shall contain or provide appropriate access to additional publications and information services reasonably necessary for the proper conduct of the school's educational and research programs. Any arrangements for sharing of these publications and information services shall be in writing and adequate to ensure ease of access and availability of materials when and where needed.

c. The Council is delegated the authority to revise the Library Schedules from time to time. (S602)

Standard 603 reads as follows:

a. All sets of materials necessary to the programs of the law school shall be complete and current except when volumes of a set are either unavailable or are available only at an excessive price. A set is not complete unless it includes supporting materials required for its use, such as indices, desk books, digests, finding tools, and citators published as part of the set or generally available for use with the set.

b. All printed materials of long term value shall be permanently bound or converted to permanent non-print format as soon as reasonable.

c. The library shall provide adequate access to commonly used materials by additional copies or on-print means for use by the faculty and students.

d. If the library contains any materials in microform, tape, or similar form, it shall provide the necessary viewing and listening equipment in an area suitable for its use. If items in Annex II are held exclusively in microform, adequate equipment shall be provided to make hard-copy printouts readily available. (S603)

One interpretation follows Standard 603: "Interpretation of Standard 603(b): This Standard applies only to material that is in printed form. It does not address the issue of which materials should be kept in printed form" (S603).

Standard 604 reads as follows:

The law school library must be a responsive and active force within the educational life of the law school. Its effective support of the schools's teaching and research programs requires a direct, continuing and informed relationship with the faculty and administration of the law school. The law school library shall have sufficient administrative autonomy to direct its growth, development and utilization to afford the best possible service to the law school.

a. The dean, law librarian, and faculty of the law school shall be responsible for determining library policy, including the selection and retention of personnel, the selection of acquisitions, arrangements of materials and provision of reader services.
b. The budget for the law library shall be determined as part of, and administered in the same manner as, the law school budget.
c. The selection and retention of the law librarian shall be by the dean and faculty of the law school. (S604)

There are a number of interpretations for Standard 604:

Interpretation 1 of 604: The intent of this Standard is to recognize that substantial operating autonomy rests with the dean and faculty of a school of law with regard to the operation of the law school library. The accreditation standards do not preclude administration of the law library as part of the university library system. Rather, the Standards require that decisions with regard to the law library be enlightened by the interests and demands of the law school educational program and not simply made on the basis of rules governing uniform administration of the university library. While the preferred structure for administration of a law school library is one of law school administration, the law school library may be administered as part of a general university library system if the dean, law librarian and faculty are responsible for the determination of basic law library policies.

Interpretation 2 of 604: Inefficiencies created by centralized university library supervision of the law school library may place law school in violation of Standard 604.

Interpretation 3 of 604: A law school in which the dean of the law school and the law librarian are not granted adequate administrative autonomy from the university library system, particularly with respect to budgeting, salaries, acquisitions and the employment of library personnel, is in violation of Standard 604.

Interpretation 4 of 604: A law library must have adequate staffing and physical housing of all the collections of the library to permit its continued development and conformity with Standard 604.

Interpretation of 604(c): Appointment of a law librarian is to be "by the dean and faculty of the law school." (emphasis added). This Standard contemplates that faculty participation includes formal faculty approval of appointment of a law librarian. (S604)

Standard 605, and the last standard applicable to libraries, reads as follows:

The law library shall be administered by a full-time law librarian whose principal activities are the development and maintenance of the library and the furnishing of library assistance to faculty and students, and may include teaching courses in the law school.

a. The law librarian should have a degree in law or library science and shall have a sound knowledge of library administration and of the particular problems of a law library.
b. The law library shall have a competent staff, adequate to maintain library services, under the supervision of the law librarian. (605)

Association of American Law Schools

Having its beginnings in 1900, the Association of American Law Schools seeks the improvement of the legal profession through legal education. The association is composed of law schools and serves as the learned society for law faculty (Association of American Law Schools 1992, 1). The association also is the legal profession's major representative with the federal government and with other higher education associations and learned societies (1).

In its Bylaws, Section 6–10, the association makes the following statements relative to law libraries:

a. A member school shall maintain a library adequate to support and encourage the instructing and research of its faculty and students. A law library of a member school shall possess or have ready access to a physical collection and other information resources that substantially:
(i) Meet the research needs of its students, satisfy the demands of its curricular offerings, particularly in those respects in which student research is expected, and allows for the training of its students in the use of various research methodologies;
(ii) Support the individual research interests of its faculty members;
(iii) Serve any special research and educational objectives expressed by the school or implicit in its chosen role in legal education.
b. The library shall be organized and administered to perform its educational function as an integral part of the law school. The law library shall have sufficient autonomy within the university in matters of administration, including budget and personnel, to assure a high standard of service.
c. A member school shall have a full-time librarian and a staff of sufficient number and with sufficient training to develop and maintain a high level of service to the program. A director of the library should be a full participating member of the faculty. (26)

Under the association's Executive Committee Regulations, chapter 8, Library, the following is stated:

Library Governance. As an integral part of the law school, the library shall formulate its policies with faculty participation....

Staffing of the Library.

a. The director of the library should have both legal and library education.
b. A member school shall have at least one professional librarian in attendance at all times when there is a substantial use of the library.
c. The law library shall be designed, organized, and equipped to enable its staff to carry out their research, teaching, and administrative responsibilities.

Conditions conducive to Library Use. The law library shall be designed, organized, equipped and operated to contribute to efficient, comfortable, and productive use by its patrons. This requirement envisions that a member school shall provide sufficient space to enable its students and faculty to carry out their research responsibilities, including ready availability of, and access to, appropriate research technology. Seating accommodations, with generous table or desk space, should be available at any one time for 65 per cent of the student body (or of the more numerous of its divisions, if it maintains separate sessions for full-time and part-time students).

Maintaining Physical Condition of Collection. The law library shall assure the preservation of its collection, including binding, restoring, and microforming. It shall also have a preservation program to maintain any unique hard copy materials it possesses.

Access to Information Resources. Availability of information resources includes ready access to central collections, databases, jointly held special collections, numerous supportive interdisciplinary materials, and any other type of off-site auxiliary resources that may enhance the member school's ability to meet, and especially exceed, the objectives stated in Bylaw 6–1. This requirement also envisions that the library will provide resources sufficient to ensure reasonable availability by faculty and students, which may require duplication of certain materials. "Ready access" means reasonable access in terms of time and form based upon the type of material and nature of the teaching and research being performed.

Planning. A member school, with the participation of the librarian and faculty, shall prepare, periodically review, and implement a written plan of library development, identifying in detail steps appropriate and resources sufficient to achieve its objectives, including appropriate growth of the collection, sufficient personnel to provide services, suitable physical facilities, and an effective system for facilitating access to materials. (38–39)

ENGINEERING AND CONSTRUCTION

American Council for Construction Education

This is the national accrediting agency for four-year baccalaureate programs in construction, construction science, construction management, and construction technology. It also accredits two-year associate degree programs in construction. The council was founded in 1974 (American Council for Construction Education 1992a, 1).

Library, computer, and media service expectations are found under Standard VI: Facilities and Services and are stated as follows:

A. Physical Facilities. Physical facilities should be well maintained and organized to accommodate academic activities such as lectures, discussions, seminars, conferences, laboratory work, and research. The nature of construction programs imposes a need for special types of space and equipment to introduce the student to realistic construction methods and procedures. It is important that the facilities be arranged to encourage student and faculty interaction.

B. Library. The library is a critical resource of any educational system. Adequacy of the library facilities must be shown in the scope and depth of library holdings as related to the general and professional components in the field of construction. Adequacy should also be reflected in the acquisition of current publications relative to construction. There should be evidence of both adequacy and use in the selection of library materials, and of responsibility for their effective use.

C. Other Services. Appropriate services on campus should be effectively used in the construction education unit. These include the computer center, audiovisual, placement and student services, and financial aides. (8–9)

National Association of Industrial Technology

The National Association of Industrial Technology has as one of its major purposes the recognition of the attainment of certain professional standards for the field of industrial technology. The association defines *industrial technology* to include any field of study designed to "prepare technical and/or technical management–oriented professionals for employment in business, industry, and government" (National Association of Industrial Technology 1990, 1). Baccalaureate degree programs in this field include manufacturing/production technology, communication technology, computer-aided design technology, electronics technology, computer technology, construction technology, computer integrated manufacturing technology, and aerospace technology, among others. Associate degree programs typically include such areas as production technology, industrial safety technology, design technology, computer-aided manufacturing technology, and robotics technology, among others (2).

Baccalaureate degree–level standards for computer systems and library services are stated as follows:

Computer Systems.

1. Availability of Computer Systems: Appropriate computer systems shall be available to students and faculty to cover appropriate functions and applications for each program area. These systems may be on or off-site or centralized or decentralized as long as the systems are accessible to the students and faculty by means of remote terminals and/or input/output devices.

2. Utilization of Computer Systems: Evidence shall be available which indicates students and faculty are making adequate and appropriate use of computer systems.

Library Services.

1. Library Resources: The administrative unit containing the Industrial Technology pro-

gram(s) and/or the institutional library shall maintain a collection of Industrial Technology literature and reference materials adequate to meet the curriculum and research needs of students and faculty.

2. Utilization of Library Resources: Evidence shall be available which indicates that students and faculty are making adequate and appropriate use of library resources. (32–33)

The association's expectations for computing and libraries in associate degree programs are identical to those expectations for baccalaureate degree programs (24).

Accrediting Board for Engineering and Technology

In the 1920s the American Association of Engineers created the Committee on Accredited Schools and sought more comprehensive and discriminating standards from which to evaluate schools of engineering. It has as one of its major purposes the promotion and advancement of engineering education (Accrediting Board for Engineering and Technology 1992a, 101). The board is the leading organization responsible for the establishment of standards in engineering, engineering technology, and engineering-related education. The board's expectations for libraries, information technologies, and computer centers may be found in its *Criteria for Accrediting Programs in Engineering in the United States* (1992a). These expectations are found under Criteria IV.C.6 and IV.C.7, Institutional Facilities and Institutional Commitment, respectively. What follows are the comments made under IV.C.6, Institutional Facilities:

An engineering program must be supported by adequate physical facilities, including office and classroom space, laboratories, and shop facilities suitable for the scope of the program's activities.

The libraries in support of the engineering unit must be both technical and nontechnical, to include books, journals, and other reference material for collateral reading in connection with the instructional and research programs and professional work. The library collection should reflect the existence of an active acquisition policy; this policy should include specific acquisitions on the request and recommendation of the faculty of the engineering unit. While the library collection should be reasonably complete and should go well beyond the minimum collection required for use by students in specialized programs, there should be in existence such arrangements as are necessary for computer-accessible information centers and inter-library loan services for both books and journals. The library collections, whether centralized or decentralized, should be readily available for use with the assistance of a trained library staff, or through an open-stack arrangement, or both. The ultimate test of a library is the use made of it by the students and faculty. Use of the library depends on many factors including opening and closing hours, reading room space, availability and helpfulness to the staff, and accessibility of material.

The computer facilities available to the engineering students and faculty must be adequate to encourage the use of computers as part of the engineering educational experience. These facilities must be appropriate for engineering applications such as engineering computation, modeling and simulation, computer-assisted design, and laboratory applications. Students and faculty should have ready access to computational facilities. These facilities should have reasonable turnaround and response time and a competent support staff. The ultimate test of the computer facilities is the use made of them by the students and the faculty.

The laboratory facilities must reflect the requirements of the offered educational program. The laboratories must be equipped with instruments and equipment of kind and quality to ensure the effective functioning of the laboratory.

Each curriculum must have a carefully constructed and functioning plan for the continued replacement, modernization, maintenance, and support of laboratory equipment and related facilities. This plan is an essential part of these criteria and must be carefully presented, monitored, and implemented. (9)

Following are the board's comments under IV.C.7, Institutional Commitment:

This section of the criteria relates to the commitment of the institution, both financially and philosophically, to the program in engineering. This commitment may be evidenced by the relationship of the engineering unit to the institution as a whole, by the fiscal policy toward and the financial resources available to the engineering unit, and by the suitability of facilities including laboratories, libraries, and computer facilities.

The organizational structure of a university should be designed to bring together and to correlate its resources effectively. ABET is specifically interested in the general status of the engineering unit and its programs in the institution, and in the overall administration as it relates to the engineering unit and the achievement of its educational objectives.

A sound fiscal policy must ensure the provision of sufficient funds for the acquisition and retention of a well-qualified faculty; the acquisition, maintenance, and operation of office and laboratory facilities, equipment, and instrumentation; the creation and maintenance of a library, both technical and non-technical; and the creation, maintenance, and operation of computer facilities appropriate to the needs and requirements of the engineering unit. A sound fiscal policy must ensure the provision of sufficient funds for the acquisition, retention, and continued professional development of a well-qualified faculty.

The institution must provide facilities adequate for the support of the engineering programs offered, as defined in section IV.C.6a. (8–9)

The board also provides a self-study questionnaire used in the review of engineering programs. The questionnaire, to be completed by local institutional self-study committees as part of their work, includes a range of questions related to libraries, information technologies, and computing facilities. As with many disciplinary and professional accrediting groups, this questionnaire includes provision for listing the number of acquisitions made to the library over the previous three years and funds spent on library acquisitions (Accrediting Board for Engineering and Technology 1992b, I–5, I–6).

THEOLOGICAL

American Association of Bible Colleges

Bible colleges were established in the late 1880s to prepare lay and semiprofessionals workers for ministry. Among the first leaders in the Bible college movement was Dwight L. Moody, founder of the Moody Bible Institute in 1886. Colleges founded within this movement set a "pattern for a new expression in higher education" (American Association of Bible Colleges 1992, 3). Today, Bible colleges offer students coursework in three areas: biblical/theological, general, and professional. Most such programs are four years in length; however, one-, two-, three-, and five-year programs exist (3).

The American Association of Bible Colleges serves as the accreditation agency for these institutions, and its current standards are found in the *Manual* (1992). Criteria relative to libraries/learning resources may be found under section C.2.0 of the *Manual*. They read as follows:

Library/learning resources: A college must demonstrate that principles of good practice are followed with respect to the college library.

Library objectives: A college must demonstrate that its library is achieving the explicitly stated library objectives that are in accord with institutional goals.

The library collection: The library must have a written development policy to assure that proper attention is given to the various factors affecting collection management and growth.

Library's support of the curriculum: A college must demonstrate that the collection appropriately supports the entire curriculum. If a college depends on adjacent library collections, it must demonstrate the rate of actual use by its students of such collections.

Library staff: A college must demonstrate that its library staff is of adequate size and quality. Their task is to assure that the collection is organized according to professionally accepted conventions and arranged for efficient retrieval and maximum accessibility. Librarians must have a graduate degree in library science and should have additional course work in biblical and theological studies. The professional librarians should have faculty or administrative status.

Library services: The library must maintain a range and quality of services that promote the academic program of the college and encourage optimal library use. Hours of access to the library should be consistent with reasonable demand. Reference services must be available for the number of hours necessary to ensure that users are not inconvenienced. A library handbook must be available to explain the use of the library. An exemplary library will enhance its collection by participation in the interlibrary loan program either directly or by cooperative arrangement. Services should include learning resources, such as computers, audio-visuals, and other media.

Library services at off-campus sites: When academic programs are offered at off-campus sites, appropriate library services must be provided.

Library facilities: The library building must provide secure and adequate housing for the collection. Ample, well-planned space should be available for the staff and for users.

Library administration: The college must demonstrate that the policies and procedures governing internal library operation are being followed and that a systematic and continuing library evaluation program is in place and functioning.

Library advisory committee: A college should demonstrate that a standing committee on library policy, composed of the librarian and faculty, administrative, and student representatives, is actively promoting library use and development.

Library budget: A college should demonstrate that 6 percent of the institutional budget for education and general expenditure (besides facility maintenance) is allocated to the library. This appropriation is to be augmented above 6 percent to correct deficiencies if the library bears responsibility for acquiring, processing, and servicing audio-visual materials, microcomputer resources, and other library equipment.

Librarian's authority: The head librarian should be responsible for recommending, justifying, and administering the library budget according to agreed-upon objectives. In addition, the librarian should have authority to apportion funds and initiate expenditures within the library budget in accord with institutional policy. The librarian should maintain internal accounts for approving invoices for payment, monitoring encumbrances, and evaluating the flow of expenditures. (28–30)

Association of Theological Schools in the United States and Canada

The association, founded in 1918, was during its early years largely Protestant in character; however, since 1966 the association has received into membership the two major Eastern Orthodox seminaries and nearly all Roman Catholic seminaries. A broad range of theological positions may be found among the Protestant membership (Association of Theological Schools in the United States and Canada 1992, 3).

Standards relative to library and other learning resources are found in *Bulletin 40*, published by the association.

Library and other learning resources, including classrooms, offices, and other facilities necessary to support programs being offered, shall be available in such number and quality as appropriate to the stated purpose. The school must demonstrate it has access to library resources appropriate to its programs. If it is expected that libraries of other institutions will be used, the member seminary must have a written agreement with the school and demonstrate both the functional availability and adequacy of the claimed resources as well as their actual use. Library reserve lists, required readings, and course bibliographies should be available to students at all times. (77)

The association, in addition, makes a statement relative to institutional responsibilities and off-campus educational programs: "In instances where off-campus programs are designed to use faculties or resources of local institutions, including library, faculty, or staff resources, the initiating school is obligated to negotiate with the local institution all aspects of the shared resources including suitable compensation for such use. These negotiations should be carried out according to the spirit of mutuality, cooperation, sound business principles and practices, and should result in formal agreements executed by chief administrative officers of contracting schools or their delegated representatives'' (25).

Finally, the association's *Handbook of Accreditation* (1990) lists seven specific questions that theological libraries should address:

1. What procedures exist to insure that the library is indeed a primary information resource for educational and research programs? Is library usage consistent with the range of degree programs? What is the library development policy?

2. How has the library development policy been determined and how is it monitored?

3. What is the role of the library director in relation to the faculty?

4. How has the role of the library changed in recent years, especially in relation to learning?

5. What are the ongoing evaluative procedures utilized to determine the adequacy of the library's holdings for support of programs offered by the school?

6. How is the adequacy of library staff in relation to the school's mission and constituencies determined and monitored?

7. What is the history in recent years of library use by faculty and students? (24)

Association of Advanced Rabbinical and Talmudic Schools

Founded in 1944, the Association of Advanced Rabbinical and Talmudic Schools accredits schools that educate rabbis, teachers, and scholars within the Orthodox Jewish community (Association of Advanced Rabbinical and Talmudic Schools 1991, 1). At present there are approximately sixty-five schools in the United States that offer programs of study centered on the Talmud but also offering coursework in philosophy, law, language, and ethics (2). Graduates of these schools serve in a wide variety of fields including service as chaplains, youth directors, rabbis, community professionals, writers and editors, and administrators of campus, schools, congregations, and family agencies (5).

The association's standards for libraries may be found in its *Handbook* (1992).

The Library is an important component in the educational program and the collection should be consistent with the institutional mission. The number of volumes is one indication of quality; the extent to which the holdings are representative is another. Accessibility and student use are, however, far more important indicators of adequate library facilities. The self-study should indicate the mechanism whereby book collections are ordered; the availability of professional help for students and faculty; the hours it is open; the percentage of regular users among the student body; and the availability of significant collections in every area of school concentration.

Aspects discussed earlier such as budget and physical plant should have devoted special mention to the library. If not, the study should include these considerations at this point. (28)

Three questions are asked of schools and are related to the above standards:

1. Is the collection of books and other resource material large enough and broad enough to serve as an effective adjunct to the educational process? Are the resources accessible to the students? Is there evidence of extensive student use?
2. What is the situation regarding accessibility of the library? Is the staff helpful? Are the hours convenient? Is there adequate room for quiet study?
3. How are books ordered? What role do students and faculty play? Is the library budget large enough to keep the collection current? Are any important changes planned? (39)

MEDICAL AND MEDICAL-RELATED

American Dental Association

Accreditation for dental education was initiated in 1906, functioning under the Dental Educational Council of America. That organization had the responsibility of classifying dental schools until 1937, when the responsibility for classification fell to the newly created Council on Dental Education of the American Dental Association. Accrediting functions continued through 1974, and in 1975, the Commission on Accreditation of Dental and Dental Auxiliary Educational Programs were created. Finally, in 1979 the name of the accrediting commission under the American Dental Association was changed to the Commission on Dental Accreditation (Santangelo 1981, 513–14). Accreditation standards for dentistry are noted here in the following areas: General Dentistry, Dental Hygiene Education, Dental Assisting, and General Practice Residency.

Concern for library and learning resources in D.D.S. programs may be found in the association's *Accreditation Standards for Dental Education Programs* (1991a).

Resources of the library and related learning centers must be adequate to meet the educational and research goals of the institution.

The library must maintain holdings in the fields of dentistry, biomedical sciences and related areas that are highly diversified and of high quality. The holdings must be current with a mechanism for faculty to review and select current titles and periodicals for acquisition. Space and materials for alternative instruction modes should be available to faculty and students. (3)

The association holds expectations for library resources within its advanced education programs in general practice residency as follows: "Library Resources: Residents must have ready access to adequate library resources, including a diversified collection of current dental, medical and other pertinent reference books and/or audiovisual materials. Dental holdings must, at a minimum, include texts in each discipline of dentistry. Appropriate current and back issues of major dental journals land a dental literature index must be readily accessible'' (American Dental Association 1991b, 8).

Dental assisting programs require the following:

Standard 9: Learning Resources

A wide range of printed materials and instructional aids and equipment must be available for utilization by students and faculty.

9.1 Library: A diversified collection of current references on dentistry, dental assisting and related subjects must be accessible.

The adequacy of the library holdings in dental assisting and related areas is based on their diversity and quality.

Current, specialized reference texts should be accessible in the following areas: anatomy and physiology, anesthesia and pain control, applied psychology, current concepts of dental auxiliary utilization, dental and oral anatomy, dental materials, diet and nutrition, emergencies, endodontics, ethics and jurisprudence, history of dentistry, microbiology, operative dentistry, oral health education, oral histology, oral pathology, oral and maxillofacial surgery, orthodontics, pathology, pediatric dentistry, pharmacology, practice management, preventive dentistry, prosthodontics, public health, radiology and radiation safety, sterilization and asepsis, and tool morphology. In addition, references on educational methodology and medical and dental dictionaries and indices should be available. New editions and titles should be acquired as content warrants. There must be a mechanism for faculty to periodically review and select current titles for acquisition.

Current and back issues of major scientific and professional journals related to dental assisting and general dentistry must be accessible for student and faculty reference. Current journals related to the dental specialties should also be available.

Facilities, hours and policies of the library should be conducive to use by faculty and students.

9.2 Instructional Resources: Instructional Aids and Equipment must be available to support instruction.

Audiovisual materials and equipment must be available for use in instruction. As appropriate self-instructional materials become available, they should be provided for the student's use. (American Dental Association 1992a, 21–22)

Expectations for dental hygiene education programs are noted as follows:

Standard 9: Learning Resources

A wide range of printed materials and instructional aids and equipment must be available for utilization by students and faculty.

9.1 Library: Institutional library holdings must include or provide access to a diversified collection of current dental, dental hygiene and multidisciplinary literature and references necessary to support teaching, student learning needs service, research and development.

Current and back issues of major scientific and professional journals related to dentistry and dental hygiene must be available for student and faculty reference. Back issues of major scientific and professional journals covering at least the past five years is considered sufficient to providing a review of current dental literature.

Current, specialized reference texts must be available. There must be a mechanism for dental hygiene faculty to periodically review and select current titles for acquisition.

Facilities, hours and policies should be conducive to faculty and student use of the library. Budget provisions should be made to ensure the currency of learning resources.

9.2 Instructional Resources: Instructional aids and equipment must be available to support student learning needs. (American Dental Association 1992b, 20)

Committee on Allied Health Education and Accreditation

In the early 1930s several organizations requested the assistance of the American Medical Association in establishing accreditation for educational programs in such areas as occupational therapy, medical technology, physical therapy, and medical records librarianship. Such early efforts established a pattern for collaboration by the American Medical Association with other national organizations that accredited allied health field programs (Committee on Allied Health Education and Accreditation 1991, viii).

The Committee on Allied Health Education and Accreditation is composed of fourteen members who include individuals whose major interest is in educating allied health professionals. Standards for libraries and other instructional support services are found under Standard 3:

Physical Resources:

a. Facilities
   Adequate classrooms, laboratories, clinical and other facilities, and administrative offices shall be provided for students, program staff, and faculty.

b. Equipment and Supplies
   Appropriate and sufficient equipment, supplies, and storage space shall be provided for student use and for teaching the didactic and supervised clinical practice components of the curriculum. Instructional aids, such as clinical specimens, documents and related materials, reference materials, equipment, and demonstration aids, must be provided when required by the types of learning experiences delineated for either the didactic or supervised clinical education components of the curriculum.

c. Learning Resources
   Library. Students shall have ready access in time and location to an adequate supply of current books, journals, periodicals and other reference materials related to the curriculum.
   Instructional aids. Clinical subjects, specimens, records and related reference materials, computer hardware and software, and audio and visual resources shall be available in sufficient number and quality to enhance student learning. (5)

National League for Nursing

The National League for Nursing is the single designated accrediting agency for nursing education. The accreditation program "is founded on the belief that specialized accreditation provides for the maintenance and enhancement of educational quality, provides a basic assurance of program improvement, and contributes to the improvement of nursing practice" (National League for Nursing 1992, 1). The criterion noted here is only for four-year, baccalaureate nursing programs and is found in the league's *Criteria and Guidelines for the Evaluation of Baccalaureate Nursing Programs* (1992).

Criterion 44. Library resources provide comprehensive appropriate reference materials, current books, periodicals, and audiovisuals which are readily available to faculty and students.

I. Documentation for Self-Study Report:

A. Suggested Questions for Documentation:

1. Are library holdings sufficiently current and comprehensive to meet program goals? Explain.

2. What is the extent of faculty and student use of library resources?

3. Are audiovisual materials current and of sufficient breadth to support program goals? Explain.

B. Suggested Evidence for Self-Study Report: Table showing budgetary allocation for library and other learning resources for previous three years.

II. Evidence for Program Evaluators:

A. Tour of library, computer center, study skills center, learning laboratories and other pertinent learning resource facilities.

B. Library schedules and other learning center schedules.

C. Interview with students, faculty, and personnel in student services and in the library.

D. List of the nursing periodicals.

E. List of publishers for which the library maintains blanket orders.

III. Definitions:

A. Data bases. (38)

American Osteopathic Association

In 1892, Dr. Andrew Taylor Still established the first school of osteopathic medicine in Kirksville, Missouri. The governing board of the American School of Osteopathy chose to award the degree of Doctor of Osteopathy. By 1898 a number of additional schools of osteopathic medicine had been established, and because of the lack of uniformity in both admission and graduate requirements, osteopathic educators chose to crate an organization that would help maintain high standards in osteopathic medicine (American Osteopathic Association 1991, 3).

Expectations for libraries and learning resources are found under Standard VI: Standards for Facilities:

A College of Osteopathic Medicine (COM) must have available sufficient and appropriate facilities that enable students and faculty to successfully pursue the educational goals and curriculum of the COM.

The COM must provide access to appropriate learning resources necessary for the delivery of the curriculum.

The learning resources centers of all campuses and affiliated teaching sites must be monitored by the COM. (11)

In developing their self-studies, Schools of Osteopathic Medicine are asked by the American Osteopathic Association to provide evidence to support the above standard within the following areas:

Library holdings

Library use

Instructional materials

Multimedia staff

Accrediting Commission on Education for Health Services Administration

Organized in 1968, the Accrediting Commission on Education for Health Services Administration currently accredits sixty-two graduate programs. Accreditation is offered to academic programs leading to master's degrees in health services administration (Accrediting Commission on Education for Health Services Administration 1991, 23). Health services administration includes the administration of a broad spectrum of programs and institutions having a primary focus on health services. These services include hospital administration, health services management, and other related medical services management (Accrediting Commission on Education for Health Services Administration 1992, 2).

Concern with library and related services is subsumed under Criterion VI: Resources and Academic Relationships: "There will be demonstrated adequacy, stability and continuity of support provided to the Program by the University. Both educational policy and administrative practices within the University will give the Program access to these resources and the Program will demonstrate effective utilization of them" (1991, 75).

Under this criterion, and elsewhere in its *Self-Study for Graduate Programs in Health Services Administration* document, the Accrediting Commission states the following with respect to libraries and computer resources:

Describe library facilities available to students and faculty of the program. Indicate whether a special library is maintained for the use of the Program. Indicate the number of volumes maintained in the library, and whether there is a professional librarian in attendance. Indicate the costs of maintaining the collection, as carried in the departmental/ Program budget, the budget of a general or other special library, and other administrative budget centers.

Describe the collection of the most pertinent books and periodicals in other special libraries (e.g., medicine, business, public health). Name the libraries and indicate their location (e.g., health sciences campus, other University campus, off-campus). Indicate the proportion of health administration volumes with respect to the total library holdings of each library where health administration volumes are maintained. Indicate funds contributed by the Program to those libraries.

If pertinent books and periodicals are available in the general collection of the University library, describe the nature of the collection.

Describe any other arrangements for library facilities, including if the library serving the Program is part of an established network or consortium.

Indicate whether student theses are available in the library, and whether these are regularly submitted to any abstracting service (specify name of service).

Describe any limits placed on students and/or faculty in utilizing library resources, including barriers to access (physical, hours, etc.).

Describe the library orientation for incoming students, and the relevance of this orientation to health services administration students. Describe the procedures used to select health administration and other relevant titles for acquisition by the University library. Indicate how these decisions are made: by a professional librarian with subject expertise, by the library's collection staff in consultation with Program faculty, in response to specific requests by Program faculty, etc.

Indicate in Volume II [of the self-study] the completed "Library Holdings" list, indicating availability of periodicals and their location. Add titles the Program considers particularly useful. [The Accrediting Commission includes in its self-study guide a check sheet of approximately seventy periodical titles.]

Describe the computational facilities available to the faculty, including access to personal computes, clustered networks and mainframe, as well as computing capability of available resources. Also describe available software packages and systems (e.g., SAS, SPSS, MIDAS, MERIT, etc.) and expert support available to faculty. Faculty access to computer networks (Internet, Bitnet, etc.) should be described as well.

Describe the computational facilities available to students, including available hardware (number of personal computer labs, computer terminals, printers, etc.). Identify any barriers to utilization, such as scheduling, location, etc. Availability of expert assistance in using the computational facilities and systems should be described as well. Indicate the number of hours of student use of computational resources required per session (e.g., semester) and courses requiring this use; include the number of hours of actual student use per session. (76)

Liaison Committee on Medical Education

Accreditation of medical education leading to the M.D. degree is the responsibility of the Liaison Committee on Medical Education. Its primary responsibility "is to attest to the educational quality of accredited programs, directly serving the interests of the general public and of the students enrolled" (Liaison Committee on Medical Education 1991, 5).

Noted under "Resources for the Educational Program" are expectations for libraries in medical schools:

The medical school must have a well-maintained and catalogued library, sufficient in size and breadth to support the educational programs offered by the institution. The library should receive the leading biomedical and clinical periodicals, the current numbers of which should be readily accessible. The library and any other learning resources should be equipped to allow students to learn new methods of retrieving and managing information, as well as to use self-instructional materials. A professional library staff should supervise the library and provide instruction in its use.

If the library serving the medical school is part of a medical center or of a university library system, the professional library staff must be responsive to the needs of the medical school, its teaching hospitals and the faculty, resident staff and students who may require extended access to the journals and reference book collections. The librarian should be familiar with the methods for maintaining relationships between the library and national library systems and resources, and with the current technology available to provide services in non-print materials. If the faculty and students served by the library are dispersed, the utilization of departmental and branch libraries should be facilitated by the librarian and by the administration and faculty of the school.

The library should also be a community resource in support of continuing medical education. (17)

American Optometric Association

The Council on Optometric Education of the American Optometric Association has as its major role the accreditation of professional optometric, paraoptometric educational, and optometric residency programs. It was established in 1934 (American Optometric Association 1985, 1).

For professional optometric degree programs, Under Standard E: Library found in the 1983 *Accreditation Manual*, the accrediting body notes:

The Council regards adequate library facilities as essential in a program of optometric education. The expanding content of the curriculum, the encouragement of independent study, and the demands of research create a continuous need for the accumulation and intelligent use of all library resources of optometry and its related sciences. Such resources should be broad enough to meet the teaching and research needs of the institution.

The optometric library, whether established separately or as a section of a combined library, should be well housed, conveniently located, and open for the use of students and faculty at all reasonable hours. It should be administered by a professionally qualified staff and should have an adequate budget.

The Council encourages efforts to improve and expand the functions and effectiveness of the library, thus promoting improved teaching, learning, and research. The library should be sensitive and responsive to the needs of the teaching and research activities of the optometric educational program and should foster liaison and communication with the faculty to promote an effective teaching and learning environment.

The library should be a learning center and should provide substantial collections of reference materials, periodicals, audio-visual aids, and information retrieval systems. The Council encourages the expanded development and use of modern techniques of information retrieval and encourages libraries to become an active force in promoting student, faculty and staff understanding of the information available for their use. Demonstration of an effective interlibrary loan system is considered an essential aspect of good library service. (American Optometric Association 1983, 23)

For library and audiovisual resources to be found within optometric residency programs, the Council notes: "Library resources should be adequate to meet the instructional needs of the program, including library holdings in the optometric specialty. Suitable audio-visual equipment should be available for use by the individual residents and for use in the lecture rooms and clinics. Appropriate clinical reference works should be readily available for day-to-day use" (American Optometric Association 1983, 10).

In 1992 the council was reviewing a second draft of resource standards for optometric technical programs. The draft standards at that time were:

The optometric technician program must have available resources in sufficient quantity and quality to enable it to accomplish its objectives and to ensure the program's stability and continued viability. These resources include facilities, supplies, equipment, library, finances, faculty, staff, and an advisory committee.

Library: The institution must provide students and faculty reasonable access to a library containing appropriate books, periodicals, and resource materials, related to the profession and paraoptometric education.

The library holdings must represent a diversified collection of relevant materials which are maintained by qualified personnel. The location, space, hours, budget and staff of the library must be adequate to meet the needs of the curriculum, students, and faculty. The director and faculty members should be responsible for communicating those needs to the library administration.

Records of library usage must be maintained and periodically evaluated. (American Optometric Association 1992, 6–7)

American Veterinary Medical Association

Founded in 1863, the American Veterinary Medical Association established a Committee on Intelligence and Education in 1890. Subsequently in 1906 the committee initiated a college evaluation program. In 1946 the entire structure of the association was reorganized, and a Council on Education was formed to replace the older evaluation and accreditation committee (American Veterinary Medical Association 1992, 3).

The Council on Education evaluates each college of veterinary medicine in the United States and Canada with respect to the degree with which it meets its own objectives as well as the established criteria of the association (14). The association states its library and learning resources expectations within its "Essential Requirements" under Physical Facilities and Equipment:

All aspects of the physical facilities must provide an appropriate learning environment. Classrooms, teaching laboratories, seminar rooms, and other teaching spaces shall be clean, maintained in good repair, and adequate in number, size, and equipment for the instructional purposes intended and the number of students enrolled. Adequate lighting and ventilation shall be provided.

Administrative and faculty offices, library facilities, research laboratories, and storage space must be sufficient for the needs of the faculty and staff. (16)

The Association notes specifically, however, that: The Council does not plan to establish any standards for libraries in colleges of veterinary medicine beyond those listed in the "Essential Requirements."

The Council does not plan to develop a list of recommended publications or books for veterinary college libraries, since such a list tends to become a maximum as well as a minimum requirement, thereby serving to reduce rather than expand the acquisition of new information. (67)

REFERENCES

Accrediting Board for Engineering and Technology. 1992a. *Criteria for Accrediting Programs in Engineering in the United States.* New York: Accrediting Board for Engineering and Technology.

———. 1992b. *Self-Study Questionnaire for Review of Engineering Programs.* New York: Accrediting Board for Engineering and Technology.

Accrediting Commission on Education for Health Services Administration. 1991. *Self-Study for Graduate Programs in Health Services Administration.* Arlington, Va.: Accrediting Commission on Education for Health Services Administration.

———. 1992. *Criteria for Accreditation.* Arlington, Va.: Accrediting Commission on Education for Health Services Administration.

Accrediting Council on Education in Journalism and Mass Communications. 1992. *Accredited Journalism and Mass Communications Education 1992–93.* Lawrence, Kans.: Accrediting Council on Education in Journalism and Mass Communications.

American Assembly of Collegiate Schools of Business. 1992. *Achieving Quality and Continuous Improvement Through Self-Study and Peer Evaluation: Standards for Business and Accounting Programs.* St. Louis, Mo.: American Assembly of Collegiate Schools of Business.

American Association of Bible Colleges. 1991. *Guidelines for Bible College Libraries.* Fayetteville, Ark.: American Association of Bible Colleges.

———. 1992. *Manual: Criteria, Policies and Procedures, Constitution and Bylaws.* Fayetteville, Ark.: American Association of Bible Colleges.

American Bar Association. 1989a. *The American Bar Association's Role in the Law School Accreditation Process.* Indianapolis: American Bar Association.

———. 1989b. *Standards for Approval of Law Schools and Interpretations.* Indianapolis: American Bar Association.

————. 1991a. *American Bar Association Standards for Approval of Law Schools and Interpretations.* Indianapolis: American Bar Association.

————. 1991b. *Annual Report of the Consultant on Legal Education to the American Bar Association 1990–91.* Indianapolis: American Bar Association.

American Council for Construction Education. 1992a. *Standards and Criteria for Associate Degree Programs.* Monroe, La.: American Council for Construction Education.

————. 1992b. *Standards and Criteria for Baccalaureate Programs.* Monroe, La.: American Council for Construction Education.

American Dental Association. 1991a. *Accreditation Standards for Dental Education Programs.* Chicago: American Dental Association.

————. 1991b. *Standards for Advanced Education Programs in General Practice Residency.* Chicago: American Dental Association.

————. 1992a. *Accreditation Standards for Dental Assisting Education Programs.* Chicago: American Dental Association.

————. 1992b. *Accreditation Standards for Dental Hygiene Education Programs.* Chicago: American Dental Association.

American Dietetic Association. 1991. *Accreditation/Approval Manual for Dietetic Education Programs.* 2d ed. Chicago: American Dietetic Association.

American Home Economics Association, 1990. *Accreditation Documents for Undergraduate Programs in Home Economics.* Alexandria, Va.: American Home Economics Association.

American Library Association, 1992. *Standards for Accreditation of Master's Programs in Library and Information Science.* Chicago: American Library Association.

American Optometric Association, 1983. *Accreditation Manual: Professional Optometric Degree Programs.* St. Louis, Mo.: American Optometric Association.

————. 1985. *Accreditation Manual: Optometric Residency Programs.* St. Louis, Mo.: American Optometric Association.

————. 1992. *Bulletin No. 65 from the Council on Optometric Education.* St. Louis, Mo.: American Optometric Association.

American Osteopathic Association, 1991. *Administrative Handbook for the Accreditation of COMs.* Chicago: American Osteopathic Association.

American Physical Therapy Association. 1991. *Self-Study Report.* Alexandria, Va.: American Physical therapy Association.

————. 1992. *Evaluative Criteria for Accreditation of Education Programs for the Preparation of Physical Therapist Assistants with Interpretive Comments and Guidelines (Graft).* Alexandria, Va.: American Physical Therapy Association.

American Psychological Association. 1986. *Accreditation Handbook.* New York: American Psychological Association.

American Speech-Language-Hearing Association. 1992. *Accreditation Manual.* Rockville, Md.: American Speech-Language-Hearing Association.

American Veterinary Medical Association. 1992. *Council on Education Accreditation Policies and Procedures.* Schaumburg, Ill.: American Veterinary Medical Association.

Association of Advanced Rabbinical and Talmudic Schools. 1991. *A Brief Outline to Rabbinical and Talmudic Education.* New York: Association of Advanced Rabbinical and Talmudic Schools.

————. 1992. *Handbook of the Accreditation Commission.* New York: Association of Advanced Rabbinical and Talmudic Schools.

Association of American Law Schools. 1992. *Handbook.* Washington, D.C.: Association of American Law Schools.

Association of Theological Schools in the United States and Canada. 1990. *Handbook of Accreditation.* Pittsburg, Pa.: Association of Theological Schools in the United States and Canada.

————. 1992. *Bulletin 40: Part 3, Procedures, Standards and Criteria for Membership.* Pittsburg, Pa.: Association of Theological Schools in the United States and Canada.

Commission on Accreditation for Marriage and Family Therapy Education. 1991. *Manual on Accreditation.* Washington, D.C.: Commission on Accreditation for Marriage and Family Therapy Education.

Commission on Accreditation in Physical Therapy Education. 1991. *Accreditation Handbook.* Alexandria, Va.: Commission on Accreditation in Physical Therapy Education.

————. 1992. *Evaluative Criteria for Accreditation of Education Programs for the Preparation of Physical Therapist Assistants with Interpretive Comments and Guidelines, 3rd Draft.* Alexandria, Va.: Commission on Accreditation in Physical Therapy Education.

Committee on Allied Health Education and Accreditation. 1991. *Accreditation Manual.* Chicago: Committee on Allied Health Education and Accreditation.

Computing Sciences Accreditation Board. 1992. *Annual Report for the Year Ending September 30, 1992.* New York: Computing Sciences Accreditation Board.

Council for Accreditation of Counseling and Related Educational Programs. 1991. *Accreditation Procedures Manual and Application.* Alexandria, Va.: Council for Accreditation of Counseling and Related Educational Programs.

Council on Rehabilitation Education. 1991. *Accreditation Manual for Rehabilitation Counselor Education Programs.* Washington, D.C.: Council on Rehabilitation Education.

Council on Social Work Education. 1991. *Handbook of Accreditation Standards and Procedures.* Alexandria, Va.: Council on Social Work Education.

Foundation for Interior Design Education Research. 1988. *FIDER Standards and Guidelines for the Accreditation of First Professional Degree Level Programs in Interior Design.* Grand Rapids, Mich.: Foundation for Interior Design Education Research.

Landscape Architectural Accreditation Board. 1990. *Accreditation Standards and Procedures for Programs Leading to First Professional Degrees in Landscape Architecture.* Washington, D.C.: Landscape Architectural Accreditation Board.

Liaison Committee on Medical Education. 1991. *Standards for Accreditation of Medical Education Programs Leading to the M.D. Degree.* Washington, D.C.: Association of American Medical Colleges.

National Architectural Accrediting Board. 1991. *1991 Conditions and Procedures.* Washington, D.C.: National Architectural Accrediting Board.

National Association of Industrial Technology. 1990. *Accreditation Handbook.* Ann Arbor, Mich.: National Association of Industrial Technology.

National Association of Schools of Art and Design. 1991. *Handbook.* Reston, Va.: National Association of Schools of Art and Design.

National Association of Schools of Dance. 1991. *Handbook.* Reston, Va.: National Association of Schools of Dance.

National Association of Schools of Music. 1991. *Handbook.* Reston, Va.: National Association of Schools of Music.

———. 1992. *Preliminary Report on Music Libraries.* Reston, Va.: National Association of Schools of Music.

National Association of Schools of Public Affairs and Administration. 1990. *On-Site Manual.* Washington, D.C.: National Association of Schools of Public Affairs and Administration.

———. 1991. *Policies and Procedures for Peer Review and Accreditation.* Washington, D.C.: National Association of Schools of Public Affairs and Administration.

National Association of Schools of Theatre. 1991. *Handbook.* Reston, Va.: National Association of Schools of Theatre.

National Council for Accreditation of Teacher Education. 1992a. *Standards, Procedures, and Policies of the Accreditation of Professional Education Units.* Washington, D.C.: National Council for Accreditation of Teacher Education.

———. 1992b. *Board of Examiners Draft.* Washington, D.C.: National Council for Accreditation of Teacher Education.

National League for Nursing. 1992. *Criteria and Guidelines for the Evaluation of Baccalaureate Nursing Programs.* New York: National League for Nursing.

National Recreation and Park Association. 1992. *Handbook of the NRPA/AALR Accreditation Process.* Arlington, Va.: National Recreation and Park Association.

Planning Accreditation Board. 1992. *The Accreditation Document: Criteria and Procedures of the Planning Accreditation Program.* Ames, Iowa: Planning Accreditation Board.

Santangelo, M. V. 1981. "The Dental Accrediting Process." *Journal of Dental Education* 45(8): 513–14.

Society of American Foresters. 1990. *Accreditation Handbook.* Bethesda, Md.: Society of American Foresters.

16

Highlighting Regional Commission Standards for Libraries and Information Technologies by Selected Categories

Edward D. Garten

There are twelve categories of standards and expectations set forth by the six regional commissions that accredit senior colleges and universities. Those categories are:

Access to resources
Adequacy and appropriateness of staff
Audiovisual media
Computing
Evaluation and outcomes assessment
Facilities
Formal agreements with external libraries
Information literacy and bibliographic instruction
Linkages across support units
Off-campus library services
Resource selection/collection management
Sufficiency of resources for curricular support

These categories, highlighted in Tables 16.1 through 16.12, were formulated since they generally appear to be areas of concern that run across most of the commissions. As was noted in the chapter detailing the standards, the North Central Association of Colleges and Schools takes a different approach to the manner in which academic support units are assessed. Thus, these illustrations highlight, generally, statements that appear in the documents of the other five commissions.

It is clear from a review of these highlighted statements that those areas that appear to be of some substantial concern are the areas related to sufficiency of resources for curricular support, the concern for access to resources, formal agreements with external libraries, bibliographic instruction and information literacy, off-campus library services, adequacy and appropriateness of staff, and computing services.

Only two associations make any statement with respect to the desirability of linkages across campus units, with the Northwest Association making the most explicit statements in this area. However, the concern with assessment and effectiveness is becoming more explicit within several of the commissions, following from the broader expectation that institutions be concerned with this issue. While five of the commissions have explicit statements on computing, surprisingly only two of the commissions have explicit statements with respect to audiovisual media, although this area is frequently noted at other points in the commission statements as part of an array of academic support services that are expected to be in evidence. Finally, it is noted that none of the commissions yet make concrete statements about the scholarly networks, for example, Internet and Bitnet.

Table 16.1
Access to Resources

Resources in libraries, computer labs, media centers, and other instructional information locations are readily available to students, faculty, and staff. Computing and data communications services are used to extend the boundaries in obtaining information from other sources, including regional, national, and international databases. (Northwest)

Learning resources are readily accessible to all students and faculty. Special equipment, software, or telecommunications necessary for access to learning resources are regularly available to students and faculty in appropriate type, number, and quality. (Western)

The collections and other resource materials must be readily accessible at convenient hours and housed in a building designed to facilitate such access for all library users. (Middle)

While such broad access to the world of information resources should be available, it is still the obligation of each institution to provide critical reference and specialized program resources at or within easy reach of each instructional location. (Middle)

Resources in libraries, computer labs, media centers, and other instructional information locations are readily available to students, faculty, and staff. (Northwest)

Table 16.2
Adequacy and Appropriateness of Staff

The library must be adequately staffed by trained professionals who hold graduate degrees in library science or learning resources. In exceptional cases, outstanding professional experience and demonstrated competency may substitute for this academic preparation. Such exceptions must be justified by the institution on an individual basis. Because professional or technical training in specialized areas is increasingly important in meeting user needs, professionals with specialized non-library degrees may be employed, where appropriate, to supervise these areas. (Southern)

Professional staffs with appropriate expertise are available to assist users of the library, computer center, and other learning resources. (Western)

Personnel include qualifed professional and technical support staff, who demonstrate required competencies. Staff responsibilities are clearly defined and current job descriptions are maintained. The institution provides appropriate opportunities for the professional development of staff, including continuing education for professional staff and training for support staff. Like faculty, information resources staff play an active role in planning and governance and are involved in the life of the campus community. (Northwest)

Librarians and other resource center staff must demonstrate their professional competence on the basis of criteria comparable to those for other faculty and staff. Status should be commensurate with the significance and responsibilities of their positions. (Middle States)

The Commission looks for each of the various human resources at the institution to determine whether they are appropriate to the institution's purposes. (Southern)

Professionally qualified and numerically adequate staff administer the institution's library and information resources. (New England)

Table 16.2 (continued)

The library support staff must be adequate to carry out the responsibilities of a technical nature. Qualifications or skills needed for these support positions should be defined by the institution. (Southern)

Competent library personnel must be assigned duties in planning and providing library resources and services and in ascertaining their continued adequacy. (Southern)

Library and information resources personnel are adequate in number and in areas of expertise to manage and provide assistance in the use of these services by students and faculty. Instructional support services (such as bibliographic instruction, research assistance, technical consultation, curriculum development, etc.) are provided to faculty and to students to meet their curricular and educational program needs. Information resources personnel exercise initiative to inform faculty about new and changing developments in teaching and learning technologies. (Northwest)

Professionally qualified and numerically adequate staff administer the institution's library and information resources. The institution provides appropriate orientation and training for use of these resources. Clear and disseminated policies govern access, usage, and maintenance of library and information resources. (Northwest)

Table 16.3
Audiovisual Media

To support its curriculum, each institution must provide a variety of facilities and
instructional support services (e.g., educational equipment and specialized facilities
such as laboratories, audiovisual and duplicating services, and learning skills
centers). These services should be organized and administered so as to provide easy
access to faculty and student users, should be adequate to allow the fulfillment of
institutional purpose to support the educational process, and should contribute to
the effectiveness of learning and to the wise and efficient use of resources. This
requirement applies to all programs wherever they are located and however they are
delivered. (Southern)

Instructional techniques and delivery systems are compatible with and serve to
further the mission and purposes of the institution as well as the objectives of
individual courses. Methods of instruction are appropriate to the students'
capabilities and learning needs. (New England)

Table 16.4
Computing

Computing services are essential to many educational programs and should be available to support the institution's management and administrative functions. Policies for the allocation of computing resources and the assignment of priorities for computer use must be clearly stated and consistent with an institution's purposes and goals. These policies should be evaluated regularly to ensure that academic and administrative needs are adequately served. Since the range of available computing services often requires a compromise between the needs of the various users and what is realistically affordable, the administration must establish priorities for computer usage and must balance the services provided among the user groups. Records should be kept to determine an accurate profile of computer resources use. These requirements apply to all programs wherever they are located or however they are delivered. Although the diversity of educational programs and goals will be a determining factor in the type and size of computer resources selected by an institution, all students should be encouraged to make some practical use of these available resources. (Southern)

The appropriate software and databases are available to support curricular needs of disciplines. The computing and data communication services adequately ensure security and privacy of records and data developed by faculty and students. (Southern)

Computing and data communication services are provided as learning resources to the academic community in sufficient quantity and quality to support the academic offerings of the institution. (Western)

Table 16.4 (continued)

A variety of computing resources (e.g., professional support staff, hardware, software, and, as appropriate, network access on- and off-campus to databases and computing resources) support the instructional and research needs of students and faculty. Access to computing resources is convenient for faculty and students. The institution provides adequate computer support services (including consulting, documentation, and software) to meet academic needs. (Western)

Access to external as well as internal information resources is essential for students and faculty. Computer and other technological systems, including voice/data/facsimile transmission, can assist in providing convenient access. (Middle States)

Library and information resources may include the holdings and necessary services and equipment of libraries, media centers, computer centers, language laboratories, museums, and any other repositories of information required for the support of institutional offerings. (New England)

Information reosurces include the holdings, equipment, and staff expertise of libraries, media and production centers, computer centers, telecommunication centers, and other repositories of information significant to the accomplishment of the institution's educational mission. (Northwest)

Table 16.5
Evaluation and Outcomes Assessment

The institution regularly and systematically evaluates the adequacy and utilization of its information resources, including those provided through cooperative arrangements, and at all locations where courses, programs or degrees are offered, and uses the results of the evaluation to improve and increase the effectiveness of those resources. (Northwest)

The institution regularly and systematically evaluates the adequacy and utilization of its library and information resources, and uses the results of the data to improve and research the effectiveness of these services. (New England)

Careful evaluation of all learning resources available to the institution's educational program, including on-site collections and services, should be an ongoing process. Therefore, a system for assessing the effectiveness of library and learning resources, including utilization, accessibility and availability of materials; quality and relevance of the collections; and effectiveness of reference and referral services must be an integral part of the library/learning resources center's self-assessment program. Ultimately, the most important measure will be how effectively students are prepared to become independent, self-directed learners. (Middle States)

The institution can continue to accomplish its purposes and strengthen its educational effectiveness. [Pattern of Evidence Example: Structured assessment processes that are continuous, that involve a variety of institutional constituencies, and that provide meaningful and useful information to the planning processes as well as to students, faculty, and administration.] (North Central)

Table 16.6
Facilities

The institution has effectively organized the human, financial, and physical resources necessary to accomplish its purposes. [Pattern of Evidence Example: Academic resources and equipment (e.g., libraries, electronic services and products, learning resource centers, laboratories and studios, computers) adequate to support the institution's purposes.] (North Central)

The institution provides facilities adequate to house and use information resources and equipment which foster an atmosphere conducive to inquiry, study, and research among students, faculty, and staff. (Northwest)

The library must have adequate physical facilities to house, service and make the library collections easily available. (Southern)

The size of the central library structure and other decentralized units, as required, is adequate and appropriate to the nature of academic programs, student enrollment, the size and character of the collections, the specialized equipment, and the size of the staff. (Western)

The library facilities accommodate the collections, readers, and staff so as to foster an atmosphere of inquiry, study, and learning. (Western)

The institution provides facilities adequate to house the collections and equipment so as to foster an atmosphere conducive to inquiry, study, and learning among students, faculty, and staff. (New England)

Table 16.7
Formal Agreements with External Libraries

Institutions having formalized agreements to supplement their own collections with those of other institutions have mutually agreed upon arrangements with those other institutions and contribute appropriately to the maintenance of those resources. (Western)

Cooperative relationships and links with other institutions and agencies are encouraged in order to increase the ability of the institution to provide the resources and services needed by users. In cases of cooperative arrangements with other libraries, formal agreements are established. However, these cooperative relationships and external information services are not a substitute for an institution's responsibility to provide its own adequate and accessible core collection and services. (Northwest)

An institution's library/learning resources center can augment its existing learning resources and draw upon collaboration and resource-sharing through formal networks and cooperative agreements. Access external as well as internal information resources is essential for students and faculty. (Middle States)

Cooperative relationships with other libraries and agencies should be considered in order to increase the ability of the library to provide the resources and services needed by its users. However, these cooperative relationships must not be used by institutions to avoid responsibility for providing their own adequate and accessible library resources and services. In all cases of cooperative arrangements, formal agreements must be established, thereby safeguarding the integrity of library resources and services. The effectiveness of such cooperative arrangements must be evaluated regularly. (Southern)

Table 16.8
Information Literacy and Bibliographic Instruction

Basic library services must include an orientation program designed to teach new users how to obtain individual assistance, access to bibliographic information and access to materials. Any one of a variety of methods, or a combination of them, may be used for this purpose: formal instruction, lectures, library guides and user aids, self paced instruction and computer assisted instruction. (Southern)

The library must provide students with opportunities to learn how to access information in a variety of formats so that they can continue life-long learning. Librarians must work cooperatively with the teaching faculty in assisting students to use resource materials effectively. (Southern)

The library and related information resources and services are critically important to students, faculty, and staff toward the development and the achievement of information literacy. Types, formats, and location of information resource materials will depend on the nature of the institution and its educational programs. (Northwest)

Each institution should facilitate optimal use of its learning resources through a variety of strategies designed to help students develop information literacy -- the ability to locate, evaluate, and use information and to become independent learners. It should encourage the use of a wide range of non-classroom resources for teaching and learning. It is essential to have an active and continuing program of library orientation and bibliographic instruction, developed collaboratively by teaching faculty, librarians, academic deans, and information providers. (Middle States)

Table 16.9
Linkages Across Support Units

The institution, in its planning and organization, provides for cooperation, efficient management and coordination of resources among various information resource areas (libraries, academic computing resources, media production resources, resource programs, and telecommunications/network services). (Northwest)

Institutional planning recognizes the need for service linkages among complementary resource bases (e.g., libraries, computer centers, learning resource centers). (Western)

While each institution is organized in such a way to accomplish its unique mission and objectives, the responsibility to provide for appropriate cooperation, collaboration, and communication among institutional library and information resource entities remains a critical priority. The institution's organizational structure facilitates and fosters innovation and integration of information resources and services in the teaching/learning environment. (Northwest)

Table 16.10
Off-Campus Library Services

At any off-campus location where credit courses are offered, an institution must ensure the provision of, and access to, adequate learning resources and services required to support the courses, programs and degrees offered. The institution must own the learning resources or provide them through formal agreements. (Southern)

Where off-campus programs exist, students are provided ready access to basic collections held by the institution. (Western)

The institution provides services and holds readily available basic collections at all program sites not serviced by the main library. Interlibrary loan or contractual use arrangements may be used to supplement basic holdings, but are not used as the main source of learning resources. (Western)

Collections are readily available for use by the institution's academic community on-campus and where, by virtue of program or distance from the main campus, they are needed off-campus. (Western)

Table 16.10 (continued)

Through the institution's ownership or guaranteed access, sufficient collections, equipment, and services are available to students wherever programs are located or however they are delivered. These collections and services are sufficient in quality, level, scope, quantity, and accuracy to meet the needs of the institution's educational program. (Northwest)

Multi-campus institutions and those with off-campus programs should design special procedures or systems to provide sufficient on-site access to learning resources and services. (Middle States)

Students and faculty, and other users, should have access to the broadest range of information resources and services wherever they might be and in whatever form, both at the primary and off-campus instructional sites and through other means. While access to these resources is customarily gained through a library or learning resources center, access is not limited to a single place. Whatever the source, learning resources support the educational program, and facilitate the learning and research of students, faculty, and other constituents. (Middle States)

Through the institution's ownership of guaranteed access, sufficient collections and services are readily accessible to students wherever programs are located or however they are delivered. These collections and services are sufficient in quality, level, diversity, quantity, and currency to support and enrich the institution's academic offerings. (New England)

Table 16.11
Resource Selection/Collection Management

Teaching faculty, librarians, and other information providers should collaborate on the selection of materials chosen for intellectual depth as well as breadth. They should work together to plan for collection development and evaluation and for the utilization of resources. (Middle States)

Written collection development and weeding policies are documented, updated, communicated to the faculty, and implemented. These policies include the bases for accepting gifts. (Western)

Faculty participate in the selection and evaluation of resources. (Western)

Librarians, teaching faculty and researchers must share in the development of collections and the institution must establish policies defining their involvement. (Southern)

Table 16.12
Sufficiency of Resources for Curricular Support

The curriculum is supported by appropriate learning resources. (Western)

Information resources include the holdings, equipment, and staff expertise of libraries, media and production centers, computer centers, telecommunication centers, and other repositories of information significant to the accomplishment of the institution's educational mission. The goals and objectives of these information resources and services are compatible with, and supportive of, the institutional mission and objectives. These information resources are sufficient to support the curriculum, faculty, and student scholarship to the level of degrees offered, and the intellectual, cultural, and technical development of students, faculty, and staff. (Northwest)

The purpose of the library and information resources and services is to support and improve instruction and learning in ways consistent with the philosophy and evolving curricular programs of the institution. The institution ensures that all students, faculty, and staff have access to adequate information resources and services needed to support their efforts in learning, instruction, and research. (Northwest)

The scope of library/learning resources holdings, the nature of services provided, and the form of access must be in reasonable proportion to the needs to be served, but numbers alone are no assurance of excellence. Of more importance are the quality, accessibility, and availability of the services and holdings on site and elsewhere; their relevance to the institution's current educational programs; the means by which an institution enhances use of library/learning resources; and the degree to which resources are actually used. (Middle States)

Each institution must ensure that all students and faculty have access to adequate learning resources and services needed to support its purposes and programs. Because these resources and services are an integral part of the learning experience of students, they must be available to all students enrolled in programs wherever they are located or however they are delivered. (Southern)

Information and learning resources, including the holdings and any equipment needed to access the holdings of libraries, media centers, computer centers and any other repositories, are sufficient to support institutional offerings at appropriate levels. (Western)

17

Observations on the Expectations for Libraries, Academic Computing, and Other Information Technologies as Found in the Professional and Disciplinary Standards

Edward D. Garten

As with the earlier analysis of the regional accreditation association standards with respect to libraries, academic computing, and other information technologies, numerous and varied observations might be offered relative to the manner in which these academic support areas are treated by the forty-one professional and disciplinary accreditation associations discussed in the previous chapter. Even a casual reading of that chapter would suggest that the professional and disciplinary associations vary widely in their treatment of these areas. Some associations note extensive and detailed standards, requirements, and associated guidelines. A few require that college and university libraries hold specific resources. Other associations would appear to offer broad statements with respect to these areas and made few explicit requirements.

This chapter will not attempt to offer an extensive analysis of the standards and guidelines promulgated by the forty-one associations; rather, it will offer a more limited analysis in two areas. First, summary comments on larger accreditation issues as well as more specific concerns with respect to library and information technology issues will be presented. Nearly half of forty-one executive directors associated with these professional and disciplinary accreditation associations responded to a survey that asked them to indicate what they viewed as the one major issue facing accreditation in general. Comments were summarized into the eleven statements found in Table 17.1 at the end of the chapter. A number of executive directors offered similar comments, only worded slightly differently. Likewise, these executive directors were asked to indicate the two most important issues currently being faced by their particular disciplinary or professional body. While many of the comments were similar and overlapped, fourteen summary comments are noted in Table 17.2. These executive directors were asked to note one issue that most concerns them when they considered the rapid changes in libraries, academic computing, and other information technologies. These responses are noted in Table 17.3.

Second, twenty-six areas of concern or issues were viewed in the context of the standards set forth by the forty-one professional and disciplinary accreditation associations. To be identified as an association expectation, the concern or issue had to appear in the association standards as an explicit statement and not one that could be inferred. Table 17.4 lists eleven concerns or issues that were most frequently noted within the collective standards and guidelines. Table 17.5 lists fifteen concerns or issues that were less frequently noted within the collective standards.

Perhaps not surprisingly, thirty-two of the disciplinary and professional associations, or 78 percent of them, noted a concern for the sufficiency of resources that are available for program and curricular support. Clearly, the majority of these associations wish to ensure that the programs they accredit are being adequately supported by library and other information technology resources. Access to resources was construed to include an association's concern for adequate access to the collections via catalogs; access to collections through demonstration that the collections were largely available in open stacks; reasonable circulation and loan policies; and access to collections held in other campus locations in off-campus locations. However, an association might make reference to only one or two of these in its definition of "access to resources." No association made access via an on-line catalog an explicit expectation.

Only slightly more than half of the associations make any explicit reference to audiovisual, media, or related instructional resources and equipment. Following this concern, the other most frequently cited concerns fall to less than 50 percent of the associations. Only the concern for adequacy and appropriateness of the library or information technology professional or support staff, the concern for academic computing, and the concern for facilities to house these areas were explicitly cited by over 40 percent of the forty-one associations. Given the pervasiveness of academic computing and its subsequent integration within the curriculum of many academic disciplines, it is noteworthy that only seventeen of the forty-one associations cited a concern with this area.

Concerns cited by 34 to 39 percent of the forty-one associations were the concern that the college or university provide adequate budgetary support for the various academic support units; the concern that libraries and other information support units be open reasonable hours; the concern that the collections in the library be current; the concern that evidence be available to support the belief that libraries and other academic support units are being used by students and faculty; and the concern that the library have an explicit resource selection model or that the department and library in tandem have certain collection development expectations.

Following these eleven most commonly cited expectation areas, other concerns held in common fall off rapidly. Only the expectation for a program of information literacy or bibliographic instruction could be found in 20 percent of the disciplinary and professional associations studied. A concern with how the library reported within the total college or university structure was noted by seven, or 17 percent, of the associations, while the concern with how a college or university library approached the provision of services to off-campus instructional sites was explicitly noted by six, or fifteen percent, of the associations. Whether academic support units were provided linkages among themselves on a campus and the concern with the preservation, conservation, and security of library and information technology resources both garnered the support, as well, of 15 percent of the associations.

Only five of the forty-one associations noted within their standards a concern for evidence of formal agreements for the use of external libraries; a concern that the library supporting the program demonstrate that specific, mandated holdings were available to students and faculty; and the concern that departmental faculty were involved on library committees or other advisory bodies. Subsequently, only four of the associations had any concern that the library have multiple or duplicate copies of resources available to students studying in the academic programs they accredit. Given the present trend toward a stronger emphasis on outcomes assessment, it must be noted that only three of the associations noted any concern with this issue within their library and information technology standards.

Finally, only two or three of the disciplinary and professional associations noted any concern that academic support facilities be accessible to the handicapped, evidence of planning within academic support units, access to scholarly networks like the Internet, or that a high-quality and current reference collection be available. Only three of the associations made any reference to other standards promulgated by other associations, for example, the Association for College and Research Libraries.

A FEW CONCLUSIONS

None of the disciplinary and professional associations saw the rapid changes taking place within libraries, academic computing, and related information technologies as being a major issue to their accrediting group. As these groups looked at their own standards in these areas, many were concerned that their standards begin to reflect the changes taking place in these areas, although many of these same associations were planning no changes over the next few years in their expectations in these areas. Other associations were concerned that their disciplines begin to harness the instructional support capabilities provided by the new multimedia technology, the advances in video and audio technology, and other information and instructional technologies.

When specific concerns and expectations were identified within the forty-one associations, only nine of the associations, or less than a fourth, had standards in the areas under investigation that included reference to a third or more of the twenty-six concerns highlighted. These associations were the American Bar Association, the American Association of Bible Colleges, the National Association of Schools of Music, the National Association of Schools of Dance, the Council on Social Work Education, the National Association of Schools of Art and Design, the Society of American Foresters, the Accrediting Commission on Education for Health Services Administration, and the National Architectural Accrediting Board.

Given the importance of academic computing in the support of most disciplinary and professional programs today, it again should be noted that less than half of the forty-one accrediting associations even mention this area within their standards. Only around a third have any statement relative to the use of libraries or computing services, while only around a third have any concern with the manner in which academic support resources are selected. Finally, only eight of the associations make any reference to a concern with information literacy, this in a time when many of the regional accreditation commissions as well as institutions of higher education themselves appear to be more concerned with this issue.

Collectively, these accrediting associations approach libraries, computing services, and information technologies in a range of ways. At present, only a few appear to have, at least as reflected in their standards, a broad appreciation for the many and far-reaching changes that are taking place in academic libraries, computing services, and other instructional support services.

Table 17.1
Perception of Major Issues Facing Accreditation in General

Public support for voluntary, nongovernmental accreditation appears to be lacking.

Identifying the nature and quality of education in the context of an educationally pluralistic world.

Outcomes measures of the effectiveness of accreditation efforts.

Societal acceptance of voluntary accreditation across all professions and retention of a nongovernmental process for the recognition of accrediting bodies.

Financial resources to support accreditation expectations in institutions of higher education, e.g., libraries, research, faculty, etc.

Cost of accreditation versus the value of accreditation.

Will there be a national accrediting body to replace the Council on Postsecondary Education and will our association choose to participate in it?

Lack of importance of accreditation as viewed by many higher education administrators.

Helping programs maintain educational quality.

Fear of programs that a negative review or major criticism could result in their program being eliminated by the university in difficult economic times.

Maintaining a focus on substantive issues in an era concerned with superficialities, overreliance on public relations, and political technique as well as fundamentalist approaches on many professional topics.

Table 17.2
Most Important Issues Facing Disciplinary and Professional Accrediting
Associations

Maintaining standards that reflect an emerging and dynamic body of knowledge.

Continued focus on issues of quality within a tightening economic environment.

Accommodating institutional program diversity of purpose and process without compromising the nonnegotiable tenets of graduate education in our discipline.

Determining strategies for outcomes assessment that are sensitive to the diverse programs we serve, yet also coherent with expectations of the profession.

Acceptance of voluntary accreditation by dental schools and the sponsoring institution.

Perception by the profession that the accreditation process is effective.

The existence of an organization to replace the Council on Postsecondary Education that will achieve a stature similar to that of the former agency.

The maintenance of accreditation in institutions of higher education representing the spectrum of research, teaching, and service.

Academic leader preparation to handle the multiple responsibilities, e.g., faculty development, outcomes measurement, financial needs in higher education.

Outcomes assessment and the preparation and implementation of survey instruments and using feedback to strengthen programs.

Rapid technological change: Technologically based disciplines are having a difficult time keeping up with rapid changes taking place in technology systems.

Extremely scarce resources from many universities to adequately support disciplines and programs.

Massive change happening in American higher education today.

Helping institutions and programs to maintain flexibility in an increasingly regulatory climate.

Table 17.3
Change in Information Technologies: What Concerns Disciplinary and
Professional Accreditation

Harnessing the capabilities of multimedia presentations (database searches,
hypermedia, video and audio, computers, etc.) without allowing the structures
imposed by these technologies to inappropriately influence the information search
or presentation.

It is likely that future standards will make more specific reference to information
technologies, computer literacy, and information management skills.

More and more current technological information is available on computer
databases that may be networked to personal computers within academic
departments. New standards are needed in this area.

The role of electronic networks and their adequacy to meet the learning
requirements of our students.

Teaching students to properly use library facilities and take full advantage of
resources available to them.

Concern with the relationship of technological advances to the substance of work in
and about the arts disciplines.

Fear, in a technologically driven environment, that libraries could excuse themselves
from good collection development because they think technology can do what it
might not be able to do for certain disciplines.

Table 17.4

Library and Information Technology Expectations and Concerns Cited Most Frequently Within Disciplinary and Professional Accreditation Standards, Based on Forty-one Accrediting Associations

Expectation/Concern	Number of Associations Having Explicit Statements in This Category and Percentage of All
Sufficiency of Resources for Curricular Support	32/78%
Access to Resources	27/66%
Audiovisual, Media, Related Instructional Resources and Equipment	21/51%
Adequacy and Appropriateness of Staff	19/46%
Academic Computing	17/41%
Facilities	16/39%
Institutional Budgetary Support for Libraries and Other Academic Support Services	16/39%
Hours of Operation of Libraries, Computer Services, and Other Academic Support Units	14/34%
Currency of Collections	14/34%
Evidence of Utilization of Libraries, Computing Services, and Other Academic Support Units	14/34%
Resource Selection Model/Collection Development Expectations	14/34%

Table 17.5
Library and Information Technology Expectations and Concerns Cited Less Frequently Within Disciplinary and Professional Accreditation Standards, Based on Forty-one Accrediting Associations

Expectation/Concern	Number of Associations Having Explicit Statements in This Category and Percentage of All
Information Literacy/Bibliographic Instruction	8/20%
Reporting Structure of Library	7/17%
Off-Campus Library Services	6/15%
Linkages Across Campus Academic Support Units	6/15%
Conservation/Preservation/Security of Collections and Resources	6/15%
Formal Agreements for the Use of External Libraries	5/12%
Specific Lists of Expected Library Resources	5/12%
Involvement of Departmental Faculty in Library Committees/Advisory Committees	5/12%
Duplicate/Multiple Copies of Library Resources	4/10%

Table 17.5 (continued)

Expectation/Concern	Number of Associations Having Explicit Statements in This Category and Percentage of All
Evaluation/Outcomes Assessment	3/7%
Reference Collection	3/7%
Reference to Other Standards Such as Those Promulgated by ACRL	3/7%
Access to Internet	2/5%
Evidence of Planning in Libraries and Other Academic Support Units	2/5%
Provision for Access by the Disabled	2/5%

PART V

Libraries and Accreditation: A Bibliographic Essay

18

Academic Libraries and the Literature of Accreditation

Delmus E. Williams and Phyllis O'Connor

Every so often, institutions of higher education and their libraries are asked to prepare themselves for a visit from an accrediting agency. Regional accreditors come once a decade, but specialized accreditation agencies are constantly visiting to evaluate programs like business, nursing, social work, and education. Accreditation is designed to certify quality programs and to help institutions improve their academic programs. But too often little effort is expended in making library administrators who have been charged with preparing for these evaluations and with using the results of these visits understand what they are about. This chapter is designed to present insights from the literature of accreditation in a package that can be used by library managers to get the most from accreditation.

The objective of this chapter is to examine the literature of accreditation as it applies to libraries. In order to truly understand the process, though, the reader will be required to range well beyond the literature relating to the application of accreditation in a library environment. Accreditation always considers the components of the university within the context of either the whole university or the specific program that is being studied. Therefore, the manager must understand how that process is applied to the whole of the organization if one is to understand how the library will be evaluated. And beyond that, much of accreditation is based on broader concepts of program evaluation and change management. A grounding in that literature is also required if one is to evaluate how accreditation might be used in the university or in its library.

For these reasons, the chapter that follows will begin with a discussion of the philosophy and history of accreditation, followed by a discussion of how accreditation is applied to American colleges and universities and their libraries.

It will then address the literature of organizational change from which much of the theory of accreditation has come. The chapter will discuss related evaluation processes used in libraries and in other not-for-profit organizations, concluding with a discussion of evaluability studies designed to prepare the institution for any comprehensive evaluation.

ACCREDITATION—AN OVERVIEW

As this discussion begins, it is useful to introduce works that can provide an overview of the accreditation process. The most important single work about accreditation is Kenneth Young's book *Understanding Accreditation* (Young, Chambers, and Kells 1983). Young has assembled a collection of essays that provides an overview of both regional and specialized accreditation, and even though Young was assembling the book at a time when accreditation was beginning a period of change, it is an important contribution that should be consulted by anyone working in the area. At about the same time, the *Journal of Higher Education* devoted its entire March-April 1979 issue to essays about accreditation written by those who were leading the effort to reform the process. While some of the essays are now dated, they lay a historical and philosophical foundation for current discussions of accreditation and should be consulted.

Readers should also consider Robert Miller's *The Assessment of College Performance* (1979) and Peter T. Ewell and Robert P. Lisensky's book *Assessing Institutional Effectiveness* (1988). Miller provides a step-by-step guide to the issues relating to the application of accreditation to various elements of the institutional program at the beginning of the debate on the effectiveness of accreditation. Ewell and Lisensky developed their book as a guide for effective use of accreditation by small colleges facing a visit from the North Central Association of Colleges and Schools. Their work provides a good summary of the theory of institutional effectiveness and a guide for applying it in academic situations that will be useful for large and small organizations. Both are worth considering.

The journal literature also offers much for those who are interested in accreditation. The *North Central Association Quarterly* is devoted entirely to issues relating to accreditation, and while it focuses primarily on the issues being confronted in that region, it also treats issues of more general interest. Of particular interest here is a series of articles run in volume 65 of this journal in which executive directors of the various regional accrediting associations discuss their approaches to the process (J. T. Rogers 1990; Mayhew and Simmons 1990; Thrash 1990; Wolff 1990). Patricia Thrash also published an excellent overview of the process in the same journal in 1991. For a foreign perspective on the process, the reader might consult Sigbrit Franke-Wikberg's 1990 article "Evaluating Education Quality on the Institutional Level," an article that tries to digest the issues of accreditation for a European audience.

For those who want a short discussion of accreditation, Mignon Adams's 1992 interview of Howard Stevens is useful, and for those interested in older literature relating to accreditation, there is the Council on Postsecondary Accreditation's 1984 *Bibliography on Postsecondary Accreditation. National Professional Accrediting Associations: How They Function* (1973) provides short summaries of the procedures used by all of the agencies charged with professional accreditation, and Kells and Parrish (1986) have published a study showing the relationship between regional and specialized accreditation.

For librarians, Julie Carroll Virgo and David Alan Yuro edited the proceedings of a conference held in1980 entitled *Libraries and Accreditation in Institutions of Higher Education* (1981). The book is not entirely successful in explaining the nuances of accreditation, and the volume became dated quickly as accrediting agencies radically changed the way they looked at institutions through the 1980s. Delmus E. Williams's article "Accreditation and the Process of Change in Academic Libraries" (1988) provides a good summary of thought relating to accreditation as used in the Southern Association, but it is limited in that its scope ends at about the time that the various associations began to focus on outcomes assessments and institutional effectiveness. Some effort was made to update this article in Williams's 1993 article "Accreditation and the Academic Library." Mary Casserly provides a similar analysis of the process in her 1986 article "Academic Library Regional Accreditation."

Recently, Patricia Ann Sacks and Sara Lou Whildin made an important contribution to the literature with their monograph *Preparing for Accreditation* (1993). This short book is designed to guide the librarian who is confronted with accreditation in much the way that Ewell and Lisensky (1988) tried to guide small colleges. It includes clear discussions of many of the concepts embedded in the process while providing practical guidance for those undergoing review.

THE PHILOSOPHY OF ACCREDITATION

Voluntary accreditation is a procedure developed specifically to meet the needs of American colleges and universities. It is a system of quality assurance, based on the premise that the diverse institutions of higher education in the United States can best be evaluated through a process combining self-evaluation and peer review. According to Kenneth F. Young (1979), it is based on these assumptions:

1. As a general rule, self-regulation of institutions is preferable and in the long run more effective than external regulation.

2. Any system of external regulation can be effective only to the extent that it recognizes and builds upon a community's willingness to engage in self-regulation.

3. A substantial number of individuals and institutions will regulate themselves if they know what behavior is expected and why.

4. An overwhelming majority of individuals and institutions will regulate themselves if they believe that they might otherwise be identified by their peers as doing something wrong.

5. Only a small number of individuals or institutions deliberately engage in behavior that they know is not in the public interest. (144)

THE PROCESS OF ACCREDITATION

Accreditation uses a two-step process of evaluation, combining institutional self-study based on published standards or criteria and a visit from a team of experts. While every accrediting agency uses this model, each has its own procedures. For further information about the specific procedures used by any agency, the reader should consult the guides published by that agency. Librarians might also wish to consult the book by Sacks and Whildin (1993) cited above.

But that being said, some general comments can be made. Dudley Yates (1976) found that most librarians serving on visiting teams believe that the self-study is by far the most important part of the process. This study is generally conducted by faculty committees using the published guidelines. Consultants may be used, but, in general, the study is broadly based with wide participation from a variety of campus constituencies. A report is produced and forwarded to the accrediting agency, which then makes a determination as to whether a campus visit is warranted. If it is, a team of experts is assembled and sent to campus for three to five days to validate the study and to make independent recommendations as to the readiness of the institution for accreditation. Institutions are given an opportunity to respond to the recommendations of the visitors, and then the accrediting agency makes its decision as to whether the institution should be accredited.

HISTORICAL BACKGROUND

Accreditation is relatively new to American higher education. Until this century, almost anyone could start a college in the United States and operate it with little outside interference. But in the last quarter of the nineteenth century, some of the leading institutions of higher education became concerned about the uneven quality of American education. Representatives began meeting to discuss these concerns and to find appropriate solutions to the problem. As a result of these meetings, six regional associations were formed: the New England Association of Colleges and Secondary Schools (1885), the Middle States Association of Colleges and Secondary Schools (1889), the North Central Association of Colleges and Secondary Schools (1895), the Southern Association of Colleges and Schools (1899), the Northwest Association of Secondary and Higher Schools (1917), and the Western Association of Schools and Colleges (1924).

These groups first assumed the task of identifying high schools that provided adequate preparation for college work. However, the associations soon began to evaluate colleges as well and to publish lists of those meeting their standards. The first list of this kind was published by the North Central Association in 1913. Other regional associations followed the North Central's lead. The first list of colleges accredited by the Southern Association was published in 1919 (Selden 1960).

Over the past seventy years, voluntary accreditation has become a fixture in the governance of higher education. According to a Delphi study completed by Jerry W. Miller in 1972, accreditation is generally seen to serve two functions. First, it identifies for public purposes educational programs that meet established standards. In so doing, accreditation protects both the public and the community of higher education from inferior institutions. Second, the accreditation process serves to stimulate improvement in institutions through the application of standards and through a process by which faculty and staff of the institution are included in an ongoing process of self-evaluation, institutional research, and planning.

In recent years, the thrust of accreditation has changed. In an effort to "help ensure that Federal money devoted to education is spent wisely," the Reagan administration's secretary of education, William Bennett, proposed in 1987 that accrediting agencies put more emphasis on the assessment of documentable student achievement (Evans-Layng 1989). This served notice on these organizations that a new emphasis should be placed on the development of assessment models that emphasize institutional effectiveness and educational outcomes. Currently developing programs emphasize continuous program evaluation that addresses the need for an integration of accreditation and other evaluation tools into an ongoing planning process.

ACCREDITATION AND THE LIBRARY

The library is given considerable attention by accreditors. William E. Troutt (1978) notes that the standards of virtually all of the associations reflect an appreciation of the need for a good library. The Southern Association includes a librarian on each visiting team, and even though others do not, all of the regional accrediting groups pay close attention to the adequacy of library collections and services when developing their standards and criteria and when making evaluations. In fact, Herbert V. Ferster (1971) found in his content analysis of accreditation reports from the Middle States Association that the library was one of six areas most often cited in recommendations of visiting teams. Despite this attention, questions have been raised as to the impact accreditation has on library programs and collections.

THE UTILITY OF ACCREDITATION

At the heart of the matter is the question of the continuing validity of the accreditation process as an evaluation tool. There is general agreement that accreditation has served a useful purpose, but not everyone is convinced of its continuing utility (Elliott 1970). More recently, Ralph Wolff summarizes the debate in an article in the *Chronicle of Higher Education* (1993) called "Restoring the Credibility of Accreditation." He contends that while accreditation can be useful in serving the public interest, in developing a new definition of accountability for higher education, for providing a voice for quality in the higher education community, and for making accountability public, its place as a mechanism for self-regulation is not assured.

One of the problems encountered when defending the viability of accreditation as a tool for assessment is that little research has been produced to support accreditation's claims of effectiveness. Even less is available on accreditation's impact on individual components of academic institutions. Most of the information that has been published on the relationship of accreditation to the library relates to changes in the standards and criteria of the various associations and of the Association of College and Research Libraries (ACRL). ACRL standards (1988) are not viewed as proof of the adequacy of the library by accrediting agencies, but they are frequently used to supplement those of the regional associations in the evaluation of academic libraries. Their application is sometimes believed to have a greater impact than accreditation itself.

But the ACRL standards are not without their critics. K. L. Stubbs began developing a model for defining and evaluating research models through statistical comparisons in *Quantitative Criteria for Academic Research Libraries* (1984), and John Minter and others published *Statistical Norms for College & University Libraries* (1990) to help libraries see what they are doing in comparison with their peers. Van House, Weil, and McClure have taken another track in looking at how well libraries are doing. They developed a manual for the application of output measures to academic libraries in the *Measuring Academic Library Performance* (1990). While most accrediting associations have developed their own standards for accreditation, and do not recognize these tools as measures of library effectiveness as they define it, the techniques provided can contribute much to the self-study.

ACCREDITATION STANDARDS AND CRITERIA

The standards and criteria by which institutions are judged have changed radically over the years as higher education in this country has matured and as evaluation has become more refined. The original standards used for accreditation were quantitative in nature and focused on determining whether the university under study had enough of what it needed to do its job, and some professional accreditors (most notably the Association of Colleges and Schools of Business) still have this kind of standards. But regional accreditors and most other groups engaged in this process have moved to more qualitative assessments of institutions over the years.

Some research is available on the kinds of standards that are most effective in assessing the quality of colleges and universities. Alan D. Covey (1959) analyzes the standards of the Western Association, those of the National Commission for the Accreditation of Teacher Education, the ACRL standards, and a new set of standards that were being considered by the California State Commission on Accreditation. He concludes that the most useful standards are those that combine quantitative and qualitative criteria; that seek to evaluate the quality and appropriateness of the book collection; that concern themselves with the quality of the library building; and that assess the role and status of the librarian in the academic community. He recommends that the schedules used for the evaluation appear in a questionnaire format. The schedules should serve the institution by providing guidelines for the self-study; the accrediting agency, by providing information to facilitate informed judgments; and the state, by encouraging diversity within higher education. According to Covey, schedules should be explicit and should provide information that is germane to the evaluation process. The standards should be unbiased, and the studies that arise from them should be economical to conduct. Standards should also reflect attitudes that correlate positively with other measures of institutional excellence. Above all, the evaluation of the library should be made within the context of the institution as a whole. Covey concludes that the primary standard against which the library should be judged is its capacity to support the university's academic programs.

Antoinette M. Kania took a different approach to the development of library standards. In an article drawn from her dissertation (1988), she outlines a set of model standards drawn from those of the various regional agencies and emphasizing performance measures. At about the same time, she published a bibliography of articles relating to the application of performance measures to academic libraries (1988b).

Beck and Nolf (1992) report that their attempt to apply standards at California University of Pennsylvania was successful. They feel that the combination of a set of standards that make use of existing standards and a good climate for change and staff involvement can provide an environment that can be used to encourage change in organizations.

But at the debate on the effectiveness of accreditation has intensified in the last decade, a question has been raised as to whether the idea of a standard is the best benchmark to use in program evaluation (Evans-Layng 1989). As accreditation has begun to focus on outcome-based institutional effectiveness measures and on assessment as a part of the evaluative process, regional accreditors have begun to replace their standards with criteria that are more specific and that relate directly to institutional outcomes (Mather 1991). The issues relating to this debate are laid out in articles by Ralph Wolff (who speaks for qualitative standards) and Myron Marty (who prefers specific, measurable criteria) in 1989. Assessment requires that universities develop sets of performance indicators against which they can be judged and then find ways to measure their success against those indicators. Developing a coherent philosophy to support this activity has generated much discussion in the last decade (e.g., Hudgins 1991; Kells 1990, 1992; Linke 1992; Lucier 1992; Mentkowski and Loacker 1985; Simmons 1988), and this material should be consulted as institutions try to come to grips with this process.

For many, this change to outcomes assessment is difficult to comprehend. For those who need a practical explanation of the "nuts and bolts" of outcomes assessment, the College of Education at the University of Minnesota has produced *Educational Outcomes and Indicators for Students Completing School* (1993). The focus of the book is on student outcomes in secondary education, but the clear, graphic description of the application of outcomes assessment will be useful to anyone who finds this concept confusing.

One of the difficulties that libraries have with outcomes assessment is that they do not have experience relating their work to the educational outcomes produced in the university (Troutt 1979). Van House, Weil, and McClure (1990) address the idea of library outputs, but their work does not tell the evaluator what accreditation adds to a student's education or a researcher's work within the context of the larger university. And this problem of determining what it is that libraries contribute to the educational process will intensify with the introduction of new technology and with the development of more sophisticated tools for accreditation.

Institutional effectiveness is, after all, a compromise position that was reached in the accrediting community when it was determined that the stricter measure of "value-added" assessment was too amorphous for practical application (Evans-Layng 1989). Value-added evaluation requires an elaborate system of pretests and posttests for students coming through higher education to see what they actually learned while in these institutions (Hutchings and Marchese 1990). Fully implementing this kind of program will be difficult, but it is clear that we are moving in this direction and will continue to do so. Counting books on hand, circulating books, floor space, and staff clearly does not address the questions that will be asked as this process becomes more refined.

THE QUESTION OF EFFECTIVENESS

Measuring the effectiveness of accreditation is a particularly difficult task, especially when one considers the two basic functions of accreditation. On one hand, accreditation establishes the reputation of the university for quality. It is understood to signify that the university has clearly stated goals; that these goals occupy a legitimate place in the context of higher education; and that university programs are effective in meeting these goals. On the other hand, the process is expected to provide an evaluation that is critical enough to help schools make needed changes in their programs. To do that, it must clearly specify areas in which these goals are not met. These two functions are often in conflict. For accreditation to serve as a change agent, the self-study prepared by the institution must be a critical analysis, and the university must present itself for close scrutiny by both internal and external study teams. The self-study must be designed to identify areas of the program that are less strong so that it can help the institution develop strategies for improving those areas. But the first objective of an institution is survival, and caution dictates a less than candid approach when the results of the evaluation are to be presented to an outside audience (J. W. Miller 1972).

And, as Kenneth Ashworth (1979) noted, the problem is compounded by the rewards that are attached to accreditation. A failure to gain reaccreditation can lead to the loss of governmental support, students, and faculty. Losses of this kind can force even reasonably strong institutions to close. Because of the risk involved, questions must be raised about the willingness of marginal institutions to disclose their weaknesses to the accrediting bodies. In some cases, the internal objective (self-improvement) can conflict directly with the external objective of the accrediting association (quality assurance).

Ashworth (1979) notes that the problem is complicated by the fact that more prestigious universities are becoming less willing to provide leadership for the regional associations. These institutions know that they are in little danger of losing their accreditation, and their interest in the regional associations has declined. He is concerned that soon many of these institutions will not be willing to spend the time and energy required to make accreditation a profitable exercise when there is no possibility of their being disaccredited.

ACCREDITATION AND QUALITY ASSURANCE IN HIGHER EDUCATION

The most reasonable approach to questions relating to the effectiveness of the accreditation process is to separate the quality assurance function of accreditation from its use as a mechanism for fostering change. Quality assurance was the first reason given for the development of the accreditation process, and regulation remains a major concern of the various associations. Still, several questions have been raised about how well the process serves this function. The first question relates to the kind of standards that should be used to evaluate institutions. Accreditation has been designed to facilitate the assessment of diverse groups of institutions and to allow as much flexibility as possible in the development of institutional programs. As a result, the standards of criteria that have been developed by accreditors have become increasingly qualitative and open to local interpretation. Each institution is expected to establish its own goals, and once those goals have been accepted as valid, they become the primary benchmark against which the institution is judged. While the peer review portion of the process ensures that the academic program fits within the broad framework of higher education, the standards and criteria themselves are very general. All of the judgments that result are, therefore, highly subjective.

Visiting teams have tended to interpret the standards conservatively, and the values that are used are likely to be those of older, more established institutions. Lloyd H. Elliott (1970) contends that this procedure has not been useful in the rapidly changing world of higher education. While he admits that accreditation has accomplished much in the past, he holds that it has outlived its usefulness, at least as it has traditionally been applied to institutions. Elliott writes that accreditation has not protected society from third-rate programs and that its conservatism has bred inflexibility into the educational system over the years.

Alan Pfinster (1973) is less negative in his appraisal of traditional accreditation. While he agrees that examining boards have not always been willing or able to deal with radical departures from tradition, he contends that the fault for their seeming rigidity has not lain entirely with the accrediting agencies. Pfinster notes that accreditation visits to more innovative campuses often entail situations in which "the examiners are unwilling to accept something as being good just because it is new and exciting, and the college can't understand why the questions all seem to be based on a non-sympathetic and traditional approach" (20). While the results of this confrontation in values are often frustrating to the innovator, Pfinster sees this kind of conservatism as an exercise of healthy skepticism that requires organizations to think about how they might justify change. He contends that this kind of skepticism is a major function of any process that is designed to ensure that innovation in higher education is undertaken responsibility.

A second question relating to the effectiveness of accreditation deals with the qualifications of the people performing the evaluation. As Pfinster notes, the premise is that "any person from any reasonably good institution can evaluate any other program" (20). Discussions of the capacity of self-study committees to do their work have centered on the sort of qualifications that should be expected in members of the visiting team. Gerald Baysore (1971) concluded that examiners selected for visiting teams have already been identified as professionals in the areas that they are being asked to evaluate; therefore, it can be assumed that their work experience and professional competence have prepared them for the task that they are being asked to perform. When Baysore was writing, most associations did not have formal programs to train evaluators, but he concluded that members of visiting teams generally understood their duties and were competent to make the required judgments.

Dudley Yates's study (1976) of library evaluators on visiting teams in the Southern Association also noted that little training was given to team members prior to their visits. However, he was less willing to accept professional competence as adequate preparation for an accreditation visit. Yates felt that the "fluctuation in quality in evaluation which is caused by the individual evaluator's inability to translate a nebulous, ill-defined standard into specific needs and recommendations" (12) was the major cause for the continuing calls for consumer protection in higher education. He called for additional training for visiting team members of one solution to this problem.

The problem of evaluator competence was exaggerated by the shift in emphasis from traditional standards-based evaluations to outcomes assessment. Institutional effectiveness has proved to be a difficult concept for many to understand and has caused considerable discomfort among the community of higher education. As a result, many of the accrediting associations have revamped their material for the orientation of members of visiting teams and have begun to invest more in training. Some accreditors, like the Middle States Association and the American Library Association, have instituted training programs, while all have spent more time making their materials more "user-friendly.'' For instance, the Southern Association has recently produced a new guide for accreditors designed to walk the evaluator through the process. At the same time, they have produced a series of videotapes to acquaint potential visitors with ''best practice'' and are developing similar materials for those preparing self-studies. As these materials develop, they should encourage consistency in evaluation. Anyone required to work with the process should immediately contact the accrediting association and acquire these materials.

This is not to say that there is anything like universal dissatisfaction with the accreditation process, at least for libraries. In fact, George Calvin Grant (1982) found that most librarians in the Middle States Association were not overwhelmingly dissatisfied with either the processes or criteria used by that group for the evaluation of libraries. But this might well be because they see the potential of using accreditation and its reports as a tool for justifying requests for additional resources. And Ralph Wolff (1992) reaffirmed the importance of the role librarians must play on accrediting teams and the importance of properly assessing the condition of the library in this process.

ACCREDITATION AND CHANGE

Accreditation is also expected to serve as an agent of change. As Cyril Houle (1972) explained it, this expectation is based on the premise that ''anyone who asks and keeps on asking 'how well are we doing?'...is likely to arouse an uneasiness among his colleagues which leads eventually to a broader awareness for the need for fundamental change in the program'' (1982–83). Members of the Southern Association and most other supporters of accreditation see this awareness as the primary function of the process. In fact, the association's *Manual for the Institutional Self-Study Program* (1977) begins with the assertion, ''The essential purpose of the *Institutional Self-study Program* is the improvement of educational effectiveness in institutions of higher learning'' (1). Paul Dressel (1971) is even more emphatic. He contends: ''Self-study is wasted effort unless it serves as an agent of change'' (288).

But the results of research relating to accreditation's capacity to meet this objective are not conclusive. This is not to say that there is no comment in the literature attesting to the capacity of the process to facilitate change. John Dale Russell (1950) contends that ''the accrediting associations have been responsible for enormous improvement in the quality of the service in higher education in this country'' (84). And, while Lloyd Elliott (1970) questions the continuing utility of regional accreditation, he concludes that in his experience in using the process ''every visitation and every self-study has resulted in improvements'' (13).

Further evidence of the role of accreditation in the change process was found in a survey of the presidents of members of the Council for the Advancement of Small Colleges conducted in 1977 by Brent Poppenhagen. Poppenhagen found that 90 percent of his respondents felt that accreditation visits had been helpful in bringing about change in their institutions. He noted that they were perceived as particularly helpful in matters relating to general administration and decision-making processes. On questions relating to the impact of accreditation on innovation, more than half of the respondents said that the process had a positive impact on their capacity to make changes in eight of the fourteen categories listed. One should note, however, that only a quarter of the presidents felt that the process helped institutions look beyond traditional criteria for quality assurance. Almost 11 percent said that the process retarded the development of newer criteria for measures of excellence. This 11 percent represented the highest negative response to any question in Poppenhagen's study. In a later study, Anna Waggener and colleagues (1991) surveyed 582 college presidents of accredited and unaccredited two- and four-year institutions in the region covered by the Southern Association and found that 76 percent of them felt that accreditation was either important or very important to the future of their institutions, indicating that confidence in the process remains high.

But Poppenhagen's study also indicates that accreditation is a process that emphasizes conservative value structure in higher education. It also shows that the majority of his respondents felt that accreditation fostered change in all of the categories that related to the library (to include the rate of library acquisitions, the distribution of library holdings across disciplinary lines, and the size of the budget for instructional materials). In related research, Morris Gelfand (1960) found that librarians viewed accreditation as a stimulus to change. His study examined libraries that had recently been visited by the Middle States Association. He found that the process was generally perceived to have been helpful in making needed changes.

THE CHANGE PROCESS IN ORGANIZATIONS

Before looking further at the claims made for the role of accreditation in the change process, one needs to understand how organizations foster innovation. Studies of the change process have identified elements within organizations and the processes acting on them that enhance or retard their capacity to adjust to changing situations. In general, such studies relate to what J. Victor Baldridge (1972) calls "the human relations school of management." Advocates of the human relations approach contend that there are two separate structures within any organization. The first, based on a formal, bureaucratic model, is designed to facilitate the use of the authority of the organization's managers. The second structure is based on informal, interpersonal relationships established among members of the organization. This informal structure allows individuals on each level of the organization's hierarchy to protect their own interests. People who stress the importance of this dual structure contend that while change can be brought about by using the power built into the bureaucracy (the first or "formal" structure), it is more effective to take into account the values represented in the informal structure when making modifications. As a result, most change studies have attempted to analyze how innovation affects this informal structure and how changes can be introduced without placing undue stress on interpersonal relationships within the organizations.

THE DILL-FRIEDMAN FRAMEWORKS

As a matter of convenience, David D. Dill and Charles P. Friedman (1972) have suggested four models around which change literature can be organized. These are the complex organization model, the diffusion model, the conflict model, and the planned change model. One should understand that components of the change process do not break neatly into discrete packages. All of the elements identified in each model are related and have an impact on the entire process. Thus, any breakdown is artificial. But even so, the models offered provide a useful framework to be used when examining the factors relating to the capacity of organizations to change.

These four paradigms approach the change process from different directions. The complex organization model and diffusion models attempt to define those characteristics in the organization that either enhance or discourage change. The difference between them is their point of focus. The complex organization model focuses on structural characteristics like the centralization of authority, the formalization of decision making, and the size of the organization as predictors of the organization's capacity to change (Hage and Aiken 1970). The diffusion model, on the other hand, relates change to the cultivation of appropriate communications channels within the informal structure of the organization. E. M. Rogers (1962) and others feel that "the capacity to adapt depends on the degree to which managers understand who in the organization can be used to spearhead reform and how those people can be influenced to assist in tailoring change to fit the values of the organization." In both the complex organizational model and the diffusion model, the idea is to assess the receptivity of the organization to change prior to the introduction of specific innovations through the use of surveys. Casserly (1987) attests to the success of this kind of study by identifying eleven of these factors that can influence the success of accreditation in the library.

The Conflict Model of Change

The third model presents a different view of organizations. The conflict or political model looks primarily at the values operating in the process through which organizations innovate as opposed to examining preexisting conditions. This approach is based on the premise that organizational decision making is a result of interaction among a variety of interest groups operating informally within the organization and among the users of its services. It contends that people within these interest groups join together in a variety of coalitions based on specific issues to ensure that their interests are protected and to influence the policies of the organization so that they might better reflect the values of the interest group. The conflict model suggests that conflict will be generated each time a change in policy is suggested, but it suggests that this kind of conflict is healthy in that it unfreezes the coalitions in the organizations and allows for the introduction of new ideas. In the view of J. Victor Baldridge (1971), Ernest House (1979), and Jack Lindquist (1968), the major obligation of the change agent is to determine the nature and composition of the interest groups operating in the organization, to identify the values of each group, and to determine how each of them influences the decision-making process. In this way, changes can be phrased in ways that are more acceptable to those constituencies of the organization who will be affected by any change that occurs. The primary contribution of the conflict model is to introduce into the literature of evaluation a consideration of interpersonal relationships and the individual values that affect decision making.

The Planned Change Model

The last of the Dill and Friedman paradigms, and the one that most closely relates to most descriptions of the accreditation process, is the planned change model. This model focuses primarily on the process through which change can be effectively introduced into an organization. It assumes that those who use the planned change will have an understanding of the elements of the other three paradigms and builds on these paradigms a set of procedures that can help change agents working in organizations. The planned change model then outlines techniques for introducing innovations into the organization. Planned change is based on the work of David Clark and Egon Guba (1966), Harry Levinson (1972), and others and is often referred to as *Organizational Development (OD)*. One of the clearest statements of planned change was developed by Ronald Havelock (1972). Havelock outlined a process based on the premise that change takes place as part of a rational process that is continually going on in organizations. Change follows an orderly progression from research to development to dissemination to implementation. As a result, any appropriate change will be accepted in an organization if the need for it can be established, if the change itself is an appropriate response to the problem at hand, and if the solution to that problem is presented to the organization in a reasonable way. OD proponents contend that the organization can best handle its problems through the use of a person or group of persons acting as a change agent. This agent can come from within or from outside the organization and may serve a number of roles. The agent may be the catalyst for change if that person creates the disturbance that begins the change process, or that person may serve as the solution giver—the person who brings the appropriate solution to the problem at hand to the organization. The change agent may also be a process helper if the role taken is one of helping the organization work its way through a problem-solving process. That person may also take the role of resource linker by connecting the organization to people and resources in its environment that are needed for problem solving.

The change agent in the organization is expected to accomplish a number of things. First, the agent must develop a positive relationship with members of the organization. Then the change agent must help find a clear definition of the problems to be treated. It is at this point that some sort of intervention begins. Usually, this takes the format of a group-centered, problem-solving process designed to find solutions to existing problems and to determine where changes in the organization might be helpful. Once the immediate cause of the intervention is dealt with, efforts are made to establish a continuing capacity for self-study and problem-solving in the organization. After accomplishing this, the change agent withdraws from the organization or assumes another role within it, and the intervention is done.

The planned change model describes a process in which a free exchange of ideas is encouraged within organizations, and an atmosphere of trust is created between superiors and subordinates and among peers. The process is expected to enhance the organization's ability to diagnose its problems, to find solutions for them, and to facilitate the implementation of those solutions. However, the most important result of this process is to develop, in the course of a problem-solving exercise, a mechanism through which the organization can continue to study itself and to implant that process into both the organizational structure and the organizational consciousness. In this way, it is expected that planned change will improve the capacity of the organization to adapt to emerging situations.

Planned change adds the idea to evaluation literature that the success of change is at least as dependent on the way it is introduced to the library as it is on other factors within the organization. When this sense of process is added to a consideration of preexisting conditions in the library and a consideration of the values of those who help make decisions for it, an effective process for introducing innovation into the organization will result.

ACCREDITATION AND THE CHANGE MODELS

The process described in the Southern Association's *Manual for the Institutional Self-Study Program* (1977) closely parallels Havelock's planned change model (1972), and Mary Casserly's 1987 article "Accreditation-Related Self-Study as a Planned Change Process" clearly indicates that the accreditation process fits within the planned change model. By requiring a self-study every ten years, accreditors fulfill the role of "catalyst" by providing the rationale for a broadly based examination of the institution's operations. The accrediting agency is less successful as a "process helper," although it does provide standards, useful manuals, a set of procedures for guidance, and in some cases, training for evaluators. While there may be an outside consultant to assist with the self-study, the bulk of the work done in the evaluation is done internally. As a result, the importance of the outside change agent is minimal at best. At the same time, potential internal change agents can be constrained by the conservative nature of accreditation. Periodic contacts with the Southern Association staff and the intervention of a visiting team can be helpful, but the absence of an impartial facilitator with a full understanding of the process limits the capacity of accreditation to influence change.

The level of participation envisioned in the planned change model is ensured in the accreditation process through the use of the committees. By delegating the study to a variety of faculty committees, an institution ensures that any opinions are heard and that the sentiment of various elements on important issues can be expressed. This, in turn, serves to acquaint committee members and campus leaders with areas in which improvement is needed. This group can then help make the changes that are recommended more palatable to the larger university.

Broad participation can be particularly helpful in a service area like the library that is primarily designed to provide assistance outside the classroom. The library is enough unlike what most of the faculty are doing as they pursue their research and teaching that it is useful to reacquaint their representatives with its procedures and to draw out their reactions to library services. During the accreditation process, the internal operations of the library tend to be examined by the library staff, while faculty and students look at library services. Often the library subcommittee consists of librarians, other library staff members, faculty, students, and administrators. In some cases, two separate subcommittees are formed, one with members from the library staff and the other with faculty and student representatives. In any case, the library staff and others combine to form what Havelock called an inside-outside change-agent team. Administrators in the library may act as consultants in the process, and experts from outside the institution may be called on for specific expertise. But the bulk of the work is done by the library subcommittee(s).

Once the self-study report is produced, the official duties of the library committee are finished. But if the study has been done well, this team can be used to help sell its findings in the university community. At best, the work of the self-study committee should produce a group of people who have reached a consensus as to what the problems of the library are and what solutions might be proposed to solve them. These people, in turn, can then be of assistance in convincing their colleagues in the library and in the larger university community of the need to make those changes.

When the self-study ends, the report of the committee is forwarded to the accrediting agency for validation. But the expectation is that the fact-finding and discussions that have gone on during the study will provide the kind of perspective that can carry through into planning for the development of the library in the years that follow.

EVALUATION IN A UNIVERSITY SETTING

The self-study process has been designed to facilitate change, and the basic process takes into account many of the elements of the planned change model that have the potential to enhance its capacity to do so. But there is little research to support the contention that change has been influenced by the process, either in the university as a whole or in components of the institution like the library. To fully understand the potential impact of the process, it is necessary to go beyond the literature of accreditation to determine what researchers have found about the operation of related evaluation procedures. The examination of evaluation procedures in higher education and in other not-for-profit enterprises provides information about how evaluation influences change that can then be considered in light of the special character of the accreditation process.

Information about a variety of evaluation techniques has found its way into the literature of higher education. Most of the work builds on experiences of administrators in the application of various forms of self-study. Generally, self-studies are evaluations of the institutions or portions of its program by committees made up of its faculty and staff. While the planned change model emphasizes group dynamics and group problem solving by those who will be asked to implement change, self-studies tend to be more traditional studies using a variety of research techniques and culminating in a report.

The use of self-studies in higher education is not limited to accreditation. In fact, it is the method most often used to assess activities on campus. Paul Dressel (1976) and others have gone to great lengths to detail a variant called "institutional research," and he and his associates have done much to explain how this process can be used to help institutions adapt to meet changing times. In another treatment of self-studies outside of the accreditation process, the State University of New York (SUNY) (1979) has developed a handbook of self-assessment procedures outlining methodologies that have been used to examine various portions of university programs. Using a series of cases relating to self-studies conducted on SUNY campuses, this monograph shows how effective self-assessment can be. While many of the studies were based on work in progress at the time the book was prepared, there is clear evidence of the effectiveness of self-assessment as a change agent.

However, Dwight Ladd's 1970 Carnegie Commission study of self-studies adds a sobering note. Ladd examines studies not related to the accreditation process conducted on eleven campuses during the 1960s. While he found that change did result in some instances, he concluded that such change is unlikely unless a significant proportion of the faculty has accepted the fact that change is necessary prior to the start of the study or unless significant pressure for change is exerted by agencies outside the institution. He holds that the main function of the self-study process is to package innovations that have wide support on campus in such a way that they can be accepted by those in authority, a concept that is closely akin to Dill and Friedman's (1979) conflict model.

KELLS AND THE SELF-STUDY PROCESS

H. R. Kells has produced what is perhaps the best single guide to the application of the self-study process to higher education. His book *Self-Study Processes: A Guide for Post-Secondary Education and Similar Service-Oriented Organizations* (1988) is designed to assist in all kinds of self-assessments. While Kells focuses on accreditation, his aim is to develop a plan of action for integrating a variety of self-studies into an ongoing planning process.

Kells believes that the success of the self-study depends on the support given to it by the chief administrative officer and other senior administrators of the institution. He also contends that the most effective studies are those that are conducted with institutional goals in mind. Kells holds that if a good analysis of the institution is done, the report that is forwarded to the outside agency will be a mere formality at the end of the study. An earlier Kells and Kirkwood (1978) study supports this contention. That study found that required responses to outside agencies tended to take care of themselves if the self-study committee believed that the prosecution of the study was important to the internal workings of the university. Contrast this to Ashworth's (1979) position discussed above.

Kells contends that, to be effective, the self-study effort must be well planned and must have a clear sense of what it is expected to produce. He supports the kind of broad participation in the process outlined by Havelock in the planned change model and encouraged by the regional accrediting agencies. His book is a step-by-step analysis of the process that Havelock contends is required to "unfreeze" the organization so that it might look objectively at its problems and develop a consensus about solutions to those problems.

Kell stresses the importance of the readiness of the staff to participate in a self-study. Are staff members in the organization up to the intellectual and emotional rigors of this kind of process? If institutional morale is low or if the study comes at the end of a period of emotional upset, there can be an impact on the self-study process.

SELF-EVALUATION AND THE LIBRARY: MANAGEMENT REVIEW AND ANALYSIS PROGRAM

Self-evaluation has also become a fixture in academic libraries. For instance, consider the development of the Management Review and Analysis Program (MRAP) by the Office of Management Studies of the Association of Research Libraries. According to Michael Buckland (1976), this program was designed to help individual libraries examine their management programs through a highly structured self-evaluation. MRAP was expected to increase the degree to which members of the library staff participate in the decision-making processes of the library and to increase the degree to which employees relate to library goals. Grady Morein (1979) says that the self-evaluation process was chosen for this project because it was assumed that the library staff is in the best position to identify needed changes in the program and that the inclusion of staff in the self-study will allow them to learn to use group decision-making processes. Duane Webster (1974) noted that the likelihood that changes will occur as a result of this process is dependent on the readiness of the library staff to change, the support given to the implementation of MRAP by the library administration, and the degree to which staff members are encouraged to involve themselves in the evaluation process.

Edward Johnson, Stuart Mann, and Carol Whiting (1977) found in their evaluation of the MRAP program that the results of the process are mixed. On the average, 60 percent of the recommendations generated by MRAP were implemented, but the range of percentages of implementation went from a high of 90 percent to a low of 10 percent. The study found that staff members in institutions that participated in the program generally had a positive impression of MRAP's capacity to encourage change. The authors thought that the staffs of participating libraries were more accepting of innovation after the evaluation than they were before. However, the researchers also found that the overall perception of the value of the program varied widely within individual libraries and between libraries. In general, they concluded that the success of the program rested on the same issues identified by Webster, Morein, and others. The authors also noted that much of the difficulty with the application of MRAP stemmed from differences in perception among library staff members as to what the library's goals were, what role they were expected to play in the organization in which they worked, and the purpose of the evaluation. This lack of agreement led to much dissatisfaction.

Johnson, Mann, and Whiting emphasized the need for increased preparation before using a process of this kind and the need for increased involvement of library directors and middle managers in future MRAP studies. In short, these researchers found that the limited success of MRAP resulted from a failure to consider the elements identified by the Dill and Friedman (1972) models and to a failure to build within the organization the support for the evaluation that Kells (1988) contends is critical to the process.

SURVEYS

One other major study has been conducted relating evaluation to the process of change in academic libraries. In 1958, Ernst Erickson studied the results of twenty library surveys conducted with the help of outside consultants between 1930 and 1952. These surveys consisted of thorough appraisals of library programs that produced a series of recommendations just as do accreditation or MRAP self-studies. Erickson found that over 72 percent of the recommendations generated in the course of these studies were implemented and that many of the changes that resulted were related directly to the recommendations included in the survey report. Failure to implement recommendations generally related to a lack of funds, personality problems, institutional restrictions, or a failure on the part of the library director or the library staff to accept the validity of the recommendation.

Both the MRAP program and the library surveys differ in technique and mission from accreditation studies. But both of these evaluative tools have been used to access the quality of library programs and to effect change, and both offer insights into how the evaluative process affects academic libraries. It is significant that the findings of impact studies relating to these other techniques are in general agreement with the studies of the impact of accreditation and reinforce their conclusions as to which elements are required to ensure that the process produces an atmosphere more conducive to change.

EVALUATION IN HUMAN SERVICES DELIVERY

Before ending consideration of evaluation processes, it is important to look at evaluation procedures in human service delivery organizations. Because of requirements placed on them by federal and state agencies, social service organizations have developed sophisticated program evaluation techniques. Since the 1960s, substantial literature has emerged in this area. But even here, few impact studies have been completed, and the bulk of the evidence presented has been in the form of case studies. Howard R. Davis and Susan E. Salasin (1975) did conclude, however, that those evaluations that most often brought about change were the ones that took into account the political realities of the organization. Peter Rossi, Howard Freeman, and S. R. Wright (1993) contend that the primary use of evaluation is as a political lever. As they put it, "[I]n any political system that is sensitive to weighing, assessing and balancing the conflicting claims and interests of a number of constituencies, one can expect that evaluation will play the role of an expert witness to the degree of effectiveness of the program" (302). They concluded that evaluation can be particularly useful in cases where there is a clearly demonstrated need for change and where recommendations conform to the goals and values of the audience to whom the report is addressed. They also contend that those issues most effectively addressed are the ones where technical advice provides specific information on clearly defined problems or those for which a clear alternative is offered to something that has clearly failed.

PREEVALUATION: WHOLEY'S CONCEPT

The literature relating to program evaluation has many of the same characteristics as that relating to the self-study process in higher education. However, this literature treats one area that is almost entirely missing from articles about higher education. The concept of "evaluability" has grown out of a concern that organizations do not always make the best use of evaluations. Students of the field have begun to look closely at this failure. Howard Davis and Susan

Salasin (1975), Joseph Wholey (1979, 1987), and others have come to the conclusion that not all organizations are equally able to benefit from such programs. Wholey contends that the organization must be willing to accept the concept of evaluation for it to be helpful. Therefore, he proposes that a preevaluation should be conducted as part of the preparation for an evaluation. He feels that this is the only way that organizations can identify and deal with factors that might make the evaluation less effective. During this preevaluation, he suggests that the evaluator should determine how amenable the organization is to the process, how well defined its goals and objectives are, how plausible those objectives are in relation to the actual program, and how well management has considered the potential usefulness of the study results. To get this information, Wholey suggests the following program:

1. Define the program to be evaluated.
2. Collect information on the intended project.
3. Develop a concise description of the program.
4. Determine the extent to which the library program is documented in measurable terms.
5. Collect information on program reality.
6. Synthesize all of the information that is acquired about the organization into a more inclusive description of its operation.
7. Identify options for evaluation.
8. Present the results to the administrator who must authorize the evaluation.

This kind of preevaluation can determine what kind of obstacles the organization presents to the evaluator. Wholey contends that if one is willing to use this procedure prior to an evaluation, many of these obstacles either can be eliminated before the evaluation begins or can be addressed early in the self-study process. Preevaluation speaks precisely to the needs expressed by Johnson, Mann, and Whiting (1977) for better preparation for MRAP studies and for support from all levels of administration for the process. It also indicates other preconditions for success for all self-studies.

There is one problem for librarians in the application of Wholey's concept. This methodology has a strong prejudice for programs in which there is a paper trail of activities and discounts the value of any program evaluation that does not have clear goals and whose progress cannot be quantified. Its reliance on statistical information is helpful in technical services, but it is less applicable in public service areas. Even so, it does offer one option for the administrator who is trying to prepare the organization for evaluation.

AVICTORY

Another approach to the idea of evaluability has been developed by Howard Davis and Susan Salasin (1975). They dubbed their technique AVICTORY, using an acronym derived from the eight basic characteristics they believe to be necessary for a successful evaluation. These are the *Ability* of the organization to carry out an evaluation; the *Values* of the organization as they related to change; the *Information* available to support an evaluation process; the *Circumstances* surrounding the organization that might relate to its capacity to accept criticism; the *Timing* of the proposed evaluation; the *Obligation* felt by members of the organization to find out how they are doing; the *Resistance* to evaluation in the organization; and the anticipated *Yield* of the process. Based on these factors, Davis and Salasin developed a questionnaire to test the readiness of an organization for evaluation. Their technique has some advantages over Wholey's in that it relies less heavily on statistical data, but the questionnaire provides only a general overview of the situation in the organization. Still, AVICTORY provides a solid alternative for determining evaluability.

SHARON STUDER AND PREEVALUATION

Sharon Studer (1980) asks managers to consider several other factors before deciding whether an evaluation will be of use to the organization. First, she stresses the personal factor in evaluation. Evaluations are most successful when there is a commitment on the part of management to the process being used to make the assessment. Success also requires an agreement prior to the beginning of the process as to how the results are to be reported and how they are expected to be used. Studer also contends that there should be a clear understanding of the kind of results that should be expected from the process. Finally, the author argues that the organization must expect that the evaluation will be worth the cost of conducting it before it commits to the process for an evaluation to induce change.

The preevaluation tools offer another component in the development of an effective evaluation process. They give the evaluator a tool to determine, at the beginning of the process, which of the elements of the diffusion and complex organization models might impact on the process and which values operating in the library might affect the capacity of the organization to accept change. This kind of analysis gives that person the information needed to develop an appropriate evaluation tool for use in the organization.

ACCREDITATION, EVALUATION, AND CHANGE

The difficulty in studying the impact of any evaluation process is that applications of the process should be tailored to meet the specific needs of the organization under study. As a result, evaluation studies tend to be highly personalized processes that are difficult to view in general terms. The literature of accreditation reflects this problem. By broadening the literature review, it is possible to identify some of the characteristics of the evaluation process and of the organization and communications patterns in the library. These characteristics are likely to influence the capacity of the evaluation process to encourage change. To go further, it is necessary to assimilate this information into a paradigm against which specific applications of the accreditation process can be viewed. Even so, one must understand that consideration must be given to the special conditions accreditation encounters in individual institutions.

Several important elements emerge from this survey of the literature. The first is that accreditation is a tool to be used to ensure funding and to promote change. Change can occur as a result of accreditation, but there is no assurance that it necessarily will. Second, the personal relationships represented in the informal structure affect the capacity of the organization to accept and use suggestions for change. In particular, the support of managers is required for the process to have an effect. An appropriate preplanning process is required to determine how this informal structure will eventually affect the use or the results of accreditation. Third, the process used to study the institution is likely to determine the impact it will have. The more open the process is and the broader the participation in it, the more likely it is to enhance the capacity of the library to change. Fourth, accreditation or any other evaluation process will accomplish more if the issues it treats reflect the values of the university and expectations of those within the library organization. Fifth, and finally, accreditation should be viewed as both a process for gathering information and a mechanism for persuading both managers and others in the academic community of the need for a proposed change. It is a political process that should be used to see how well a change might be accepted and to build a constituency for a specific proposal.

The literature provides much information about what the accreditation process is supposed to accomplish and how this is to be done. But much has not been said. Librarians must eventually begin to assimilate and use the theory of evaluation and develop assessment models that fit their unique circumstances. Until this is done, there is little prospect that academic libraries will answer the question, "How well are we doing?" to the satisfaction of those they serve and those who provide them with the resources they need.

REFERENCES

Adams, M. 1992. "The Role of Academic Libraries in Teaching and Learning: An Interview with Howard Simmons." *C&RL News* 53: 442–45.

Ashworth, K. 1979. *American Higher Education in Decline.* College Station: Texas A&M University Press.

Association of College and Research Libraries. 1988. *ACRL Guidelines and Standards, 1974–1988.* Chicago: American Library Association.

Baldridge, J. V. 1971. *Power and Conflict in the University.* New York: Wiley.

———. 1972. "Organizational Change: The Human Systems Perspective vs. the Political Systems Perspective." *Educational Researcher* 1: 4–10.

Baysore, G. C. 1971. "The Selection, Training and Evaluation of Examiners in Selected Accrediting Associations." Ph.D., University of Denver.

Beck, W. L., and Nolf, M. L. 1992. "The Process and Value of Self-study in a Medium-Sized University Library. *College and Research Libraries*, 53: 150–62.

Bibliography on Postsecondary Accreditation. 1984. Washington, D.C.: Council on Postsecondary Accreditation.

Buckland, M. K. 1976. "The Management Review and Analysis Program: A Symposium." *Journal of Academic Librarianship* 1: 4–14.

Casserly, M. F. 1986. "Academic Library Regional Accreditation." *College and Research Libraries* 47: 38–47.

———. 1987. "Accreditation-Related Self-Study as a Planned Change Process: Factors Relating to Its Success in Academic Libraries." *Journal of Library Administration* 8: 85–105.

Clark, D., and E. G. Guba. 1966. *Effecting Change in Institutions of Higher Education.* Bloomington, Ind.: National Institute for the Study of Educational Change. (ERIC Document Reproduction Service no. 028 685)

Covey, A. D. 1959. "Evaluating College Libraries for Accreditation." Ph.D. diss., University of Southern California.

Davis, H. R. and S. Salasin. 1975. "The Utilization of Evaluation." In *Handbook of Evaluation Research*, vol. 2, edited by E. L. Struening and M. Guttentag. Beverly Hills, Calif.: Sage.

Dill, D. D. and C. P. Friedman. 1972. "An Analysis of Frameworks for Research on Innovation and Change in Higher Education." *Review of Educational Research* 49: 411–18.

Dressel, P. 1971. *Institutional Research in the University.* San Francisco: Jossey-Bass.

———. 1976. *Handbook of Academic Evaluation.* San Francisco: Jossey-Bass.

Elliott, L. H. 1970. *Accreditation or Accountability: Must We Choose?* New York: Middle States Association of Collegiate Registrars and Officers of Admissions. (ERIC Document Reproduction Service no. 047 603)

Erickson, E. W. 1958. "College and University Surveys, 1938–1952." Ph.D. diss., University of Illinois.

Evans-Layng, M. 1989. *Here Come the Judges: The Assessment Movement and its Potential Impact on UCSD.* Washington, D.C.: ERIC (ERIC Document Reproduction Service no. 311 764).

Ewell, P. T., and R. P. Lisensky. 1988. *Assessing Institutional Effectiveness.* Boulder, Colo.: Consortium for the Advancement of Private Higher Education.

Ferster, H. V. 1971. "Criteria for Excellence: A Content Analysis of Evaluation Reports by a Regional Accrediting Association." Ph.D., State University of New York at Buffalo.

Franke-Wikberg, S. 1990. "Evaluating Education Quality on the Institutional Level." *Higher Education Management* 2: 271–91.

Gelfand, M. A. 1960. "A Historical Study of the Evaluation of Libraries in Higher Education Institutions by the Middle States Association of Colleges and Secondary Schools." Ph.D. diss., New York University.

Grant, G. C. 1982. "Attitudes of Higher Education Library Administrators Toward Adequacy of Middle States Association Library Evaluation Criteria and Processes." Ph.D. diss., University of Pittsburgh.

Hage, J., and M. Aiken. 1970. *Social Change in Complex Organizations.* New York: Random House.

Havelock R. G. 1972. *The Change Agent's Guide to Innovation in Education.* Englewood Cliffs, N.J.: Educational Technology Publications.

Houle, C. O. 1972. *The Design of Education.* San Francisco: Jossey-Bass.

House, E. R. 1979. "Technology versus Craft: A Ten Year Perspective on Innovation." *Journal of Curriculum Studies* 11: 1–15.

Hudgins, J. 1991. *Institutional Effectiveness: A Strategy for Institutional Renewal.* Washington, D.C.: ERIC. (ERIC Document Reproduction Service no. JC 9101 377)

Hutchings, P., and T. Marchese. 1990. "Watching Assessment: Questions, Stories, Prospects." *Change* 22: 12–38.

Johnson, E. R., S. H. Mann, and C. Whiting. 1977. *An Assessment of the Management Review and Analysis Program (MRAP).* University Park: Pennsylvania State University.

Kania, A. M. 1988a. "Academic Standards and Performance Measures." *College and Research Libraries* 49: 16–24.

———. 1988b. *Performance Measures for Academic Libraries: A Twenty Year Retrospective.* Washington, D.C.: ERIC. (ERIC Document Reproduction Service no. 293 540)

Kells, H. R. 1988. *Self-Study Processes: A Guide for Post-Secondary Education and Similar Service-Oriented Organizations.* Washington, D.C.: American Council on Education/Macmillan.

———. 1990. "The Inadequacy of Performance Indicators for Higher Education: The Need for a More Comprehensive and Developmental Construct." *Higher Education Management* 2: 258–70.

———. 1992. "An Analysis of the Nature and Recent Development of Performance Indicators in Higher Education." *Higher Education Management* 4: 131–38.

Kells, H. R., and Robert Kirkwood. 1978. *Analysis of a Major Body of Institutional Studies Conducted in the Northeast, 1972–1977.* State College, Pa.: Association of Institutional Research (ERIC Document Reproduction Service no. 010 540).

Kells, H. R., and R. M. Parrish. 1986. *Trends in the Accreditation Relationships of U.S. Postsecondary Institutions, 1978–1985.* Washington, D.C.: Council of Postsecondary Accreditation.

Ladd, D. R. 1970. *Change in Educational Policy: Self-Studies in Selected Colleges and Universities.* New York: McGraw-Hill.

Levinson, H. 1972. *Organizational Diagnosis.* Cambridge, Mass.: Harvard University Press.

Lewin, K. 1947. "Frontiers inn Group Dynamics: Concept, Method and Reality in Social Science; Social Equilibria and Social Change." *Human Relations* 1: 5–41.

Lindquist, J. 1968. *Strategies for Change.* Berkeley, Calif.: Pacific Soundings Press.

Linke, R. D. 1992. "Some Factors for Application of Performance Indicators in Higher Education." *Higher Education Management* 4: 194–208.

Lucier, P. 1992. "Performance Indicators in Higher Education: Lowering the Tension of the Debate." *Higher Education Management* 4: 204–14.

Marty, M. 1989. "Standards vs. Criteria: The Case for Criteria." *North Central Association Quarterly,* 64: 395–400.

Mather, J. 1991. "Accreditation and Assessment: A Staff Perspective." *North Central Association Quarterly* 66: 397–405.

Mayhew, P. H., and H. L. Simmons. 1990. "Assessment in the Middle States Region." *North Central Association Quarterly* 65: 375–80.

Mentkowski, M., and G. Loacker. 1985. "Assessing and Validating the Outcomes of College." In *Assessing Educational Outcomes*, edited by P. T. Ewell. San Francisco: Jossey-Bass.

Miller, J. W. 1972. "Organizational Structure of Nongovernmental Postsecondary Accreditation." Ph.D. diss., Catholic University of America.,

Miller, R. I. 1979. *The Assessment of College Performance: A Handbook of Techniques and Measures for Institutional Self-evaluation*. San Francisco: Jossey-Bass.

Morein, P. G. 1979. "Assisted Self-Study: A Tool for Improving Library Effectiveness." *Catholic Library World* 50: 422–23.

National Professional Accrediting Associations: How They Function. 1973. Washington, D.C.: American Education Association.

Peterson, J. C. 1990. "Assessment in the Western Accrediting Commission for Community and Junior Colleges." *North Central Association Quarterly* 65: 401–5.

Pfinster, A. O. 1973. *The Future of Voluntary Accreditation*. San Francisco: Annual Meeting of the American Association of Colleges (ERIC Document Reproduction Service no. 071 559).

Poppenhagen, B. W. 1977. *Institutional Accreditation and the Private Liberal Arts College*. Washington, D.C.: ERIC Clearinghouse (ERIC Document Reproduction Service no. 138 217).

Rogers, E. M. 1962. *Diffusion of Innovation*. Glencoe, Ill.: Free Press.

Rogers, J. T. 1990. "Assessment in the Southern Commission on Colleges." *North Central Association Quarterly* 65: 397–400.

Rossi, P. H., H. E. Freeman, and S. R. Wright. 1993. *Evaluation: A Systematic Approach*. Beverly Hills, Calif.: Sage.

Russell, J. D. 1950. "The Accrediting of institutions of Higher Education." *Journal of Teacher Education* 1: 83–93.

Sacks, P. A., and S. L. Whildin. 1993. *Preparing for Accreditation: A Handbook for Academic Librarians*. Chicago: American Library Association.

Selden, W. K. 1960. *Accreditation: A Struggle over Standards in Higher Education*. New York: Harper.

Simons, H. L. 1988. "Institutional Effectiveness in the Community College: Assessing Institutional Effectiveness Through the Accreditation Process." Paper presented at the League for Innovation in the Community College Conference, Charlotte, N.C., July 17–20, 1988. Washington, D.C.: ERIC (ERIC Document Reproduction Service no. JC 880 375).

Southern Association of Colleges and Schools. Commission on Colleges. 1977. *Manual for the Institutional Self-Study Program*. Atlanta: Southern Association of Colleges and Schools.

State University of New York. Office of Self-Assessment. 1979. *A Handbook of Self-Assessment*. Albany: Office of Self-Assessment.

Statistical Norms for College & University Libraries. 1990. Boulder, Colo.: John Minter Associates.

Stubbs, K. L. 1984. *Quantitative Criteria for Academic Research Libraries*. Chicago: Association of College and Research Libraries.

Studer, S. 1980. "Evaluative Needs Assessment: Can They Make Evaluation Work?" *Bureaucrat* 9: 15–22.

Thrash, P. A., ed. 1979. "Accreditation." *Journal of Higher Education* 50 (March/April): 115–232.

———. 1990. "Assessment in the North Central Region." *North Central Association Quarterly* 65: 358–62.

———. 1991. "Evaluation and Accreditation of Institutions of Postsecondary Education." *North Central Association Quarterly* 65: 487–98.

Troutt, W. E. 1978. "The Quality Function of Regional Accreditation." Ph.D. diss., George Peabody College for Teachers.

———. 1979. "Regional Accreditation Evaluative Criteria and Quality Assurance." *Journal of Higher Education* 50: 199–210.

University of Minnesota. College of Education. 1993. *Educational Outcomes and Indicators for Students Completing School.* Minneapolis: National Center on Educational Outcomes.

Van House, N. A., Beth T. Weil, and C. R. McClure. 1990. *Measuring Academic Library Performance: A Practical Approach.* Chicago: American Library Association.

Virgo, J. C., and D. A. Yuro. eds. 1981. *Librarians and Accreditation in Institutions of Higher Education: Proceedings of a Conference Held in New York City, June 26–27, 1980.* Chicago: Association of College and Research Libraries.

Waggener, A. T., A. Southerland, and R. Leonard. 1991. "College Presidents' Attitudes Toward the Importance of Regional Accreditation. "Paper presented at the annual meeting of the Mid-South Educational Research Association, Lexington, Ky., November 13–15, 1991. Washington, D.C.: ERIC (ERIC Document Reproduction Service no. HEO 25 173).

Webster, D. 1974. "The Management Review and Analysis Program: An Assisted Self-Study to Secure Constructive Change in the Management of Research Libraries." *College and Research Libraries* 35: 114–25.

Wholey, J. 1979. *Evaluation: Promise and Performance.* Washington, D.C.: Urban Institute.

———. 1987. "Evaluability Assessment: Developing Program Theory. In *Using Program Theory in Evaluation,* edited by L. Bickman. San Francisco: Jossey-Bass.

Williams, D. E. 1988. "Accreditation and the Process of Change in Academic Libraries." *Advances in Library Administration and Organization 7: 161–207.*

———. 1993. *"Accreditation and the Academic Library." Library Administration and Management* 7: 31–37.

Wolff, R. 1989. "Assessment in the Western Accrediting Commission for Senior Colleges and Universities." *North Central Association Quarterly* 65: 403–14.

———. 1990. "Standards vs. Criteria: The Case for Standards." *North Central Association Quarterly* 64: 387–94.

———. 1992. "Rethinking the Librarian's Role on Accrediting Teams." *C&RL News* 53: 450–51.

———. 1993. "Restoring the Credibility of Accreditation." *Chronicle of Higher Education* 39: B1–B2.

Yates, D. 1976. *The Impact of Regional Accrediting Agencies upon Libraries in Post Secondary Education.* Knoxville, Tenn.: Biennial Conference of the Southeastern Library Association, 1976 (ERIC Document Reproduction Service no. 135 337).

Young, K. F. 1979. "New Pressures on Accreditation." *Journal of Higher Education* 50: 132–44.

Young, K. F., C. M. Chambers, and H. R. Kells. 1983. *Understanding Accreditation.* San Francisco: Jossey-Bass.

Glossary of Commonly Used Terms in Accreditation

Compiled by Edward D. Garten

This glossary lists the most commonly encountered words and phrases in accreditation along with what are widely used operational definitions. It is compiled with the needs of information professionals engaged in various aspects of accreditation in mind.

accreditation. The process whereby a private nongovernmental agency or association grants public recognition to an institution or specialized program of study that meets certain established qualifications and periodic evaluations. The primary purpose of the accreditation process is to provide a professional judgment as to the quality of the educational institution or program and to encourage its continued improvement, thereby protecting the public against professional or occupational incompetence of its graduates.

accreditation, continuing. The status of accreditation based on reevaluation of an accredited program.

accreditation, manual. A publication summarizing key policy documents and describing the structure, purpose, and responsibilities of the constituents of an accrediting agency.

accreditation, specialized. A status of recognition accorded a unit or program of specialized study by an accrediting agency. The unit accredited may be a school, division, department, program, or curriculum. It may be a part of an educational institution, part of an independent specialized institution, part of an educational unit within a primarily noneducational institution, or a stand-alone facility.

accreditation status. A formal categorical designation of recognition given an institution or specialized program for meeting established standards of educational quality as determined by an institutional or specialized accrediting agency.

advanced standing. Placement on the basis of transferable credit, equivalency examination, or developmental experiences, where appropriate.

application for accreditation. Formal documentation submitted by a sponsoring institution wishing to initiate the accreditation review process for a program.

assessment. The gathering of data to be used for subsequent evaluations and decision making. In general, the term is used in most standards to mean the use of an instrument or process to gather data so that faculty, students, and administrators can make specific decisions about people or processes.

candidate status. Accreditation status awarded, following approval, by accrediting agencies to institutions or programs that meet the published prerequisites for such status and appear likely to qualify for accreditation within a specific period. Candidate status does not ensure eventual accreditation.

certification. The process by which a nongovernmental agency or association grants recognition to an individual who has met certain predetermined qualifications specified by that agency or association.

competency. The level of skill; displaying special skill or knowledge derived from training and experience.

competency objective. The specific level or nature of ability to be achieved by the learner/performer. Such objectives ordinarily are stated in written form and provided to faculty and students and are available to site visitors during a visit to the program.

complaint. A written, signed allegation that an academic program has engaged in actions that represent a possible violation of accreditation standards.

concerns. Areas of educational program identified during the accreditation review process that need attention or further development by the program.

conditional accreditation. A status granted by some accrediting bodies, both regional and professional, when a program, although possessing deficiencies that place it out of compliance, nonetheless demonstrates to the accrediting body that it has the ability to correct the deficiencies in a short period.

confidentiality. Assurance that certain information, such as self-study reports and site visit reports, will not be made public by site visitors or the review committee.

conflict of interest. An incompatibility between the personal interests and the official responsibilities of a person, or between the competing interests of a person holding responsible positions with more than one entity. Persons in the accreditation process who find themselves in such a position must identify and excuse themselves from engaging in decisions regarding those activities where a conflict is or may be present.

consortium. Two or more institutions that have agreed to formally share sponsorship of an educational program by forming an entity structured to perform the responsibilities and functions of a sponsoring institution.

Council on Postsecondary Accreditation (COPA). A national, nonprofit private sector organization whose major purpose was to support, coordinate, and improve all nongovernmental accrediting activities conducted a postsecondary educational levels in the United States. COPA ceased operation in 1993.

credentialing. The formal recognition of professional or technical competence as by certification or licensure.

criterion. A predetermined element or specified expectation forming the basis for testing or judging whether a standard has been met.

curriculum. The body of courses and formally established learning experiences presenting the knowledge, principles, values, and skills that are the intended consequences of the formal education offered by a program.

educational objectives. Statements developed by academic programs that describe the purposes of their teaching and learning processes. Such objectives, if they are to be useful for accreditation purposes, must lend themselves to evaluation.

educational outcomes. Anticipated or achieved results of academic programs are formulated in statements of outcome. Indicators of achievement of educational outcomes may include, but are not limited to, student attitudes, knowledge, and performance in courses; the performance of students at the time of graduation; and the performance of graduates in practice and in subsequent educational programs. Educational outcomes are developed and tested in relation to their consistency with the educational objectives of the program.

eligibility. The set requirements that an academic program must meet to be considered for accreditation by a regional or disciplinary accreditation body.

evaluate. To determine the quality of an educational program by careful appraisal and study. When applied to a site visit, evaluation includes the team's assessment of the program's compliance with criteria or standards.

evidence. Written documentation supportive of the self-study and often made available to the visiting team.

exit conference. The oral presentation of the findings of a site visit team regarding relative compliance with the standards of a regional or professional accreditation agency. Also referred to as an *exit interview*.

experimental/innovation program. Courses of study containing approaches or methodologies that vary substantially from traditional pedagogical or laboratory methods.

external degree. An academic award earned through prior learning, credit by examination, specially devised sponsored experimental learning program, self-directed study, or satisfactory completion of campus or off-campus courses.

goals and objectives for academic programs. Written targets for achievement that are measurable and provide a baseline against which to measure program effectiveness.

governance. Governance addresses responsibility for policy development, program initiation, ongoing evaluation, leadership and coordination with other campus units, the maintenance and support of all professional programs, selection and evaluation of faculty, and fiscal matters. Governance establishes ultimate accountability for the quality of programs in professional education and the quality of students who are graduated from professional programs. Visiting teams are concerned with the forms governance takes.

guidelines. Explanatory statement accompanying standards or criteria.

institutional accreditation. Applies to the *total* institution and signifies that the institution as a whole is achieving satisfactory education objectives.

internship. A highly structured field-centered and professionally supervised field experience that generally occurs during the junior or senior year of the academic program and requires extensive full-time involvement, receives academic credit, and is a shared responsibility between the academic unit and the selected field agency.

licensure. The process by which an agency or government grants permission to an individual to engage in a given occupation upon finding the applicant has attained the minimal degree of competency necessary to ensure that the public health, safety, and welfare are reasonably well protected.

measurement. The act of identifying the amount or dimension of an attribute or distinguishing characteristics and an estimation of how much of a trait an individual displays or possesses.

mission. The duty, however prescribed or imposed, that an academic program is to carry out, the needs it is to meet, and the problems it is to solve.

multiple sites. Various geographic locations in which the curriculum for the academic program being accredited is taught. All sites covered by the accreditation action will typically be specified in the final accreditation report.

observer. An individual accompanying the site visit team who represents a legitimate interest of another agency or serves as a trainee for future on-site evaluation purposes. With regional teams, the observer may be a staff member of the particular regional commission.

oral report. A report of findings provided by the site visit team to appropriate academic program and institutional representatives at the conclusion of a site visit.

peer review. A characteristic of the program review process conducted by site visit teams and review committees. All participants in the process should be qualified as professional peers.

performance measure. Actual accomplishments relative to a standard.

performance objectives. The interim competencies achievable by students within the course of their educational experience and the terminal competencies to be achieved by students by the end of the program. Assessment frequently includes verification of written performance objectives and their application within the curriculum and the supervised clinical phase of training.

practicum. An extended period of full-time experience (weeks or months) in professional practice during which students reconstruct and apply the theory they have learned and during which clinical proficiency is developed.

process evaluation. The practice of evaluating educational programs by examining the process through which the learner passes.

professional competencies. Those knowledges, understandings, and abilities that a professional in a particular discipline or profession should have.

professional program. The curriculum and associated activities and services offered by the academic unit; the curricular aspect is composed of foundation understandings and professional competencies; also referred to as a *program.*

program integrity. The dedication of an educational program to preparing students for professional activity and the identification of the program as such, distinct from other programs or courses of instruction.

program outcome. The end toward which effort is directed, the overall student, competence as a practitioner, or the end product.

public interest. The primary purpose served by the accreditation process, even though it is conducted by independent, nongovernmental bodies.

reader. A system used by many accrediting bodies as an audit of the reported work of the site visit team as well as an aid to the review process and final decision. Among the objectives of the reader system are to improve the accuracy, consistency, and value of the visiting team reports.

recognition. Status granted by the U.S. Department of Education to accrediting agencies that meet established criteria or provisions.

recommendation. A recommendation made by the site visit team for correcting a deficiency based on findings during the visit.

self-study. A comprehensive analysis of the educational resources and effectiveness of an academic program in relation to its objectives. The immediate product of this process is the self-study report.

self-study report. A documented written account of the self-study/self-assessment/self-evaluation outcomes necessary to indicate substantial compliance with the criteria or standards. Such reports usually reflect an organized effort involving program officials, faculty, administrators, directors of support services, students, graduates, and a self-study steering committee.

site evaluation. A site visit during which the accreditation team observes academic program components or the entire institution in order to verify information obtained from the self-study report and other sources and also makes evaluative judgments regarding the degree to which the program complies with standards or criteria.

standards. The criteria by which programs or institutions are reviewed for accreditation purposes.

strengths. If the unit exhibits features or characteristics that add to its overall quality or cause it to excel at meeting a standard, these characteristics or features are considered strengths.

substantive change. An alteration in a program's mission, status within the larger academic setting, or curriculum that may be significant enough to alter compliance with standards or affect the ability of the program to maintain compliance.

suggestion for improvement. A recommendation regarding possible or potential improvements treated by the site visit team and the program as a suggestion. It is not mandatory that an institution implement a suggestion for improvement.

United States Department of Education. The federal agency authorized by federal statute to publish a list of accrediting agencies and associations recognized by the secretary of education as reliable authorities concerning educational quality.

weaknesses. If an academic program or the whole institution fails to meet a standard, or does not address a compliance criterion, or exhibits features or characteristics that detract from the effectiveness of the unit, the lack or ineffectiveness of these areas may be considered weaknesses.

Index

About the Editor and Contributors

EDWARD D. GARTEN is dean of Libraries and Information Technologies at the University of Dayton. He is a consultant-evaluator with the North Central Association of Colleges and Schools, Commission on Institutions of Higher Education, where he currently serves on the commission's Accreditation Review Council. His academic specialties include accreditation, program evaluation, and organizational development. He writes in the areas of higher education administration, library and information science, and personnel administration. With Delmus E. Williams he is coeditor of *Advances in Library Administration and Organization*. His previous works include *Using Consultants in Libraries and Information Centers*, which was published in the Greenwood Library Management Collection.

THOMAS E. ABBOTT is dean of Learning Resources and University Development at the University of Maine at Augusta. Most recently he has chaired that University's self-study process. He serves as an evaluator for the New England Association of Schools and Colleges. He was recently elected as a member-at-large for the American Library Association's Association of College and Research Libraries (ACRL) Extended Campus Library Services Section. He is also a lecturer in business administration at the University of Maine at Augusta.

SUSANNE O. FRANKIE has been dean of the Library at Oakland University since 1982. She has over thirty years of professional experience, including administrative positions with the American Society for Information Science and the Association of Research Libraries. She has served on the American Library Association (ALA) Committee on Accreditation and the ALA Subcommittee that revised the standards for accrediting library and information studies programs. She is an experienced ALA site visitor.

CYNTHIA HARTWELL is executive director of Learning Resources at the University of Phoenix, a private postsecondary institution for working adults that offers bachelor's degrees in business and management and nursing and master's degrees in business and management, nursing, computer and information science, education, and counseling. She has extensive experience in the development and implementation of applied research programs as well as experience in program evaluation. She has published works in the areas of higher education, special education, and alternative mechanisms for the delivery of information services.

PHYLLIS O'CONNOR is associate dean of University Libraries at the University of Akron where she has worked for the last fifteen years. She is the chair of the OhioLINK Inter-campus Services Committee and represents OhioLINK on the Association of Research Libraries' North American Interlibrary Loan/ Document Delivery Project. She is a member of the University of Akron's Assessment Steering Committee.

KENNETH L. PERRIN is senior vice president of the University of Hawaii System and chancellor of the University of Hawaii at Hilo and West Oahu. He formerly was president of the Council on Postsecondary Accreditation (COPA) in Washington, D.C. He has also served as president of West Chester University of Pennsylvania.

HOWARD L. SIMMONS is currently executive director of the Commission on Higher Education, Middle States Association of Colleges and Schools. He has been with that association since 1974. He speaks and writes frequently on the topics of bibliographic instruction and information literacy. His most recent publication in that area was *Information Literacy: Developing Students as Independent Learners*, appearing in the Jossey-Bass New Directions in Higher Education Series.

MIMI HARRIS STEADMAN is a doctoral student in higher education administration at the University of California at Berkeley. She completed a graduate internship with the Western Association of Schools and Colleges. Her research interests focus on improving undergraduate teaching and learning.

ROBERT W. TUCKER is senior vice president for Research and Information Services at the University of Phoenix; Senior Research Fellow for the Center for Higher Education and Economic Development; and founder and editor of *Adult Assessment Forum: Journal of Quality Management in Adult-Centered Education*. A measurement scientist and philosopher of scientific measurement, he developed the Academic Quality Management System, a decision-support system for managing academic quality under multiple educational delivery methods and locations.

DELMUS E. WILLIAMS is dean of University Libraries at the University of Akron. He was formerly the director of Libraries at the University of Alabama at Huntsville and has worked in libraries at Western Illinois University and Washington & Lee University. Williams previously has written about the accreditation process and change in academic libraries. As a member of the consultant-evaluator corps for the Southern Association of Colleges and Schools, he has participated in accreditation reviews at numerous institutions of higher education in that region.

RALPH A. WOLFF has served since 1981 as the associate executive director of the Senior College Commission of the Western Association of Schools and Colleges (WASC). He coordinated the comprehensive rewriting of the commission's accreditation standards from 1986 to 1988, which included significant revisions to standards dealing with libraries, academic freedom, general education, assessment, and diversity. Since adoption of these new standards, he has been responsible for developing WASC policies on assessment. He has published and spoken extensively on improving accreditation to make it more responsive to public concerns.

JOAN H. WORLEY is director of the Lamar Memorial Library at Maryville College, Maryville, Tennessee, where she has served since 1984. Previously she served as a reference librarian with the John C. Hodges Undergraduate Library at the University of Tennessee, Knoxville. She has published essays and reviews on a variety of topics, notably college librarianship and collection development; edited *Tennessee Librarian*, the official journal of the Tennessee Library Association; and has held a variety of offices in state and national library organizations. Since 1984 she has served on numerous visiting teams for the Southern Association of Colleges and Schools.